FIGHTING TO SERVE

★ ★ ★ ★ ★

BEHIND THE SCENES IN THE WAR TO REPEAL "DON'T ASK, DON'T TELL"

★ ★ ★ ★ ★

ALEXANDER NICHOLSON

CHICAGO REVIEW PRESS

Published by Chicago Review Press, Incorporated
814 North Franklin Street
Chicago, Illinois 60610
ISBN 978-1-61374-372-0

Library of Congress Cataloging-in-Publication Data
Nicholson, Alexander.
  Fighting to serve : behind the scenes in the war to repeal "don't ask, don't tell" /
Alexander Nicholson.
     p. cm.
  Includes index.
  ISBN 978-1-61374-372-0
  1. Nicholson, Alexander. 2. Servicemembers United (United States) 3. Gay
military personnel—Government policy—United States. 4. Gay rights—United
States—History—21st century. 5. United States. Army—Gays—Biography.
6. Gay military personnel—United States—Biography. 7. Homosexuality—
Political aspects—United States—History—21st century. I. Title.
  UB418.G38N53 2012
  355.0086'640973—dc23

                              2012021821

Interior design: Jonathan Hahn

Printed in the United States of America
5 4 3 2 1

★ ★ ★ ★ ★

To all those who served under the cloud of
"Don't Ask, Don't Tell" and its predecessor policies,
and to those in generations to come who will never have
to bear any such burden as a result of our hard-fought but
narrowly won victory in this dirty political war.

★ ★ ★ ★ ★

CONTENTS

* * * * *

ACKNOWLEDGMENTS

I never intended to write a book about this truly unique experience, and I actively resisted efforts aimed at recruiting me to do so for over a year. However, the patience and persistence of my exceptionally wise agent, Jon Sternfeld, ultimately led me to put this brutally honest testimonial down on paper, and I am eternally grateful for his confidence and guidance throughout the process. Similarly, I could not have withstood the intellectual, emotional, and technical rigors of such a project without my talented editor, Jerry Pohlen, to whom I also owe an enormous debt of gratitude for his enthusiasm and mentorship along the way. I would also like to thank all of those who fought honorably alongside us over the years. You know who you are, and the impact of your collective contributions is substantial. And last, there are countless others out there whom I would like to thank for the many bruises and scars inflicted throughout this saga, for I am exponentially stronger and wiser now as a result of those gifts.

1

★ ★ ★ ★ ★

"I AM NOT AN ACTIVIST"

"This is done." With those three simple words, the president of the United States signed into law the "Don't Ask, Don't Tell" Repeal Act of 2010 on the morning of December 22, 2010. As I sat in the front row of the packed room, directly in front of the desk at which President Barack Obama signed our hard-won repeal bill into law and spoke those memorable words, I did not feel the sense of elation or fruition I thought I would feel after all those years of work. Perhaps it was because, as the five hundred politicians and progressive advocates seated behind me cheered, deep down I knew that the work was far from done. It would be up to us to continue the exhausting and draining fight to actually finish the job that had already bruised and bloodied us enough over the preceding years.

Instead of experiencing one "on top of the world" moment as hundreds did that morning, I had the privilege of being able to experience firsthand the dozens of small triumphs along the path leading up to that day. As the founder and executive director of Servicemembers United (SU), the nation's largest organization of gay and lesbian troops and veterans during the "Don't Ask, Don't Tell" (DADT) repeal fight, and as the sole named veteran plaintiff on the only contemporary lawsuit to successfully challenge the constitutionality of the DADT law, I have the unique distinction of being the only person in the country to have been at the fore of each and every front in the war against DADT—the grassroots, the media, Congress, the administration, the Pentagon, and the courts. Several others were substantively involved in several of those fronts, but no one else helped lead the charge in *all* of those categories except for me, a distinction of which I am quite proud.

It is that body of experience that allowed me to recognize and truly live the small victories along the way, primarily because I was involved in or witnessed most of them personally. But all those experiences diminished the cumulative moment for me on that chilly December morning in 2010. I had not only seen firsthand the sausage making that was the DADT repeal fight; I had actively participated in the grinding. I'd helped change the course of the fight, but the course of the fight had also significantly changed me.

I used to tell myself that if I ever wrote a book, it would be called *I Am Not an Activist: One Activist's Journey*. That's because when I first started doing DADT repeal advocacy work, I would always say to reporters and others who tried to label us veterans with that "a" word: "We're not activists. We're not professionals. We're just ordinary people who are leaving our lives behind for a little while to do our part." But within six months, I had stopped saying that.

In the spring of 2006 a documentary filmmaker named Johnny Symons, who had been chronicling the DADT repeal movement for PBS, reminded me of how I used to say "I am not an activist" all the time when he first met me. He then asked me on camera if I still thought of myself as a nonactivist. I wish I could see the look I must have had on my face when I first realized that maybe this new lifestyle of politics and advocacy wasn't just temporary. Although that scene didn't make it into the groundbreaking documentary, a film aptly named *Ask Not*, PBS managed to capture the moment when I truly felt like I had become the unlikely activist.

★ ★ ★ ★ ★

I always found it funny when people would tell me that they came from a small town too, and that their small town had only about forty or fifty thousand people in it. To me growing up, a town of forty or fifty thousand was the "big city." I would almost always win that "Whose small town is smaller?" contest, because as I always used to say at speaking events to give me some "down home" creds, I grew up in a small town in rural South Carolina with two thousand people and two stoplights. We had to drive an hour to get to the nearest mall or airport, we had no Walmart or real grocery store—we had to drive over to North Carolina for those—and we had one high school for the whole county, because even the county only had about twenty-seven thousand people in it.

I consider myself to have grown up in a military family, although we weren't really a traditional military family. We never lived on post and we didn't have to move around a lot, but my father spent a career in the US Army, which carried over into the first decade of my life. But by the time I was born, his military time was spent primarily in the Army Reserves, although I certainly remember the frequent drills and tours of duty that would send him away—for far too long, as far as I was concerned. I remember holding onto his leg as he tried to leave for one reserve tour and not letting go until my mother repeatedly reassured me that she would make a special trip up to Virginia with me so that I could go visit him this time around.

Then in 1992, my father deployed to the Persian Gulf for Operation Desert Storm. I was one of only two kids in my school with a parent deployed for the Gulf War, but our little elementary school rallied around us like the whole school had been deployed. They held marches and tied yellow ribbons, and my whole fourth-grade class wrote frequently to my dad. Somehow he found the time in Saudi Arabia to write back to everyone, in between dodging Saddam's Scuds and running supply convoys up to the front lines in Kuwait. He kept all of those letters from my classmates too, and I read some of them after he got back. I remember being shocked and appalled that some of the other kids in my class had asked him to send them some of the delicious chocolate "Desert Bars" that he had sent me and that I had taken to school to show off. Didn't they know that all candy procurements he could make were to go directly to me?

My father was a strict disciplinarian while I was growing up; my mother was the sensitive and compassionate parent, as mothers usually are. My dad's drill sergeant ways finally made perfect sense after I joined the army at age nineteen and got randomly assigned to do boot camp at Fort Benning, Georgia—the only all-male boot camp left in the army and the one at which the infantry is trained. For the first time ever, my dad revealed to me that early in his army career he had been a drill sergeant at Fort Benning. I distinctly remember him remarking on my assignment, "Benning's the toughest one, but you'll be better off for having gone there."

Those who knew me before I joined the army probably never thought I'd actually go and do something like that. (Of course, there are plenty of others I've thought that about myself who are doing quite well on active duty.) I was always a nice little geeky kid who preferred the almanac, encyclopedias, and *National Geographic* to video games and recess. I was quite entrepreneurial too, coming up with a new business idea every other day. My first childhood foray into business was a small table I set up in my front yard out by the road to sell the only thing I could find to sell: sticks. And I actually made money. My aunt said she would give me a dollar if I would stop selling sticks and get away from the road. I took the dollar, closed up shop, and declared my first endeavor a success.

On another occasion I painted a variety of world flags on some rocks from my driveway, saving the largest one for the American flag. I then set up shop with my cousin in her front yard and actually sold two of my flag rocks to two different neighborhood kids. In the end, though, I only netted one sale, because one of my customers came back and said he had to return his previous purchase. He assured me that he liked my wares, but his mom had yelled at him for buying a rock and told him to go get his money back.

Thus was my childhood growing up in Small Town, USA. With a rather isolated existence and a conservative Southern Baptist upbringing, I never really even knew about the concept of homosexuality until my sexual orientation began naturally manifesting itself in my psyche during my early teens. The same characteristics of that small rural town that had given me such a wholesome and happy childhood began to bring torment to my life during adolescence as I began to realize that I was different from the other guys I had grown up with. As we grew older, they were more and more interested in girls, yet I remained solely interested in burying myself in my own private world of travel, languages, history, and anything else that helped me mentally escape. As a result, I know the capital of virtually every country in the world and I'm still the person you want on your team for trivia night. But being isolated in a small town while trying to come to terms with my sexual orientation nearly killed me, as the weekly fire and brimstone condemnation of this evil "lifestyle" from the pulpit and the rising social pressures to be "normal" had me, like many others before and after, well on the way to becoming another gay teen suicide statistic. Luckily, I got out of that small town at just the right time.

My family moved around a little, and I ended up finishing high school in Greensboro, North Carolina, which is where I also went to my freshman year of college. After that one expensive but enlightening year of university, the money ran out and I was feeling quite restless. So in the summer of 2000 I decided to move to Miami (I ended up in suburban Kendall) and get a job without ever having even visited there before. By that time I spoke Spanish fluently, and I thought the hub of Latin life in the United States would provide a good adventure during my hiatus from college—and that it did.

Soon, suburban life in Kendall gave way to the more glamorous life of South Beach. You can get away with just about anything when you're young and attractive in South Beach, and I was fortunate enough that few knew that I was only nineteen at the time. The food, the shopping, the beaches, the people, the clubs—it was an amazing experience that I am also fortunate to have survived, probably because I never touched drugs, then or ever. Nevertheless, I burned out of that lifestyle after one year and longed for some familiar structure, stability, and purpose, and the pendulum swung all the way back to the gates of Fort Benning, Georgia.

I enlisted in the army on June 20, 2001, and quietly celebrated my twentieth birthday five days later in the 30th AG Reception Battalion at Fort Benning. I certainly knew I was gay before I went into the army and was comfortable with myself and open to at least my friends. I vaguely recall knowing that one had to hide being gay in the military, but I didn't think it would be a problem at all. "Don't Ask, Don't Tell" seemed so simple, reasonable, and manageable at the time. No one would ask me about my sexual orientation, and as long as I kept my private life private, everything would be OK. But I would soon find out that the misleading sound bite of "Don't Ask, Don't Tell" was more like "Don't Ask, Don't Tell, Don't Happen to Get Found Out, Any Time, Any Place, in Any Way." But of course that more accurate title was too much for the headlines.

Boot camp at Fort Benning was a challenge, but I don't think that my training experience was significantly different from that of anyone else who went through Benning. Just as it should, Basic Combat Training made me a better person, and I was still young enough to get the full transformation experience that the training regimen is intended to facilitate. I think there was at least one other gay guy in my platoon at Benning, but I had no interest whatsoever in finding out. Much later on, I always found it rather hilarious when DADT repeal opponents would talk about those allegedly intimate scenarios, like boot camp, in which known gay people would surely cause all sorts of problems with their pernicious gay ways. It was always people who had never actually been in one of those scenarios, or who hadn't been there for many decades, who made that argument. Anyone with a fresh memory of boot camp would know how utterly impossible normal social dynamics of any kind are during Basic Combat Training. It's just too busy, too stressful, and too focused a time for any of their crazy predictions to happen, even if the premises were true.

In fact, we were so busy at Basic Combat Training at Benning that I actually became Mormon for a few weeks just to get a reprieve. Well, sort of. The only break we got each week from that boot camp atmosphere was for Sunday religious services. If you went to the "regular" services, you got an hour-long break. However, if you went to the Mormon or Muslim services, you got a three-hour break. Needless to say, many of us learned about either Mormonism or Islam for no other reason than to get two extra hours of reprieve from the drill sergeants. After the first four Mormon "discussions," however, I decided I needed something a bit more animated, even if I had to endure two more hours of hell, so I opted for the mainline Protestant service for the remaining five weeks.

I finished up at Benning on Friday, September 7, 2001. My parents could not have been prouder, but I couldn't have been more relieved. I absolutely loved the army, but I was ready to get on with training as a human intelligence collector, better known as an interrogator. That same afternoon, I flew out to a little intelligence base in southern Arizona called Fort Huachuca to begin the next phase of my army career and the next chapter of my life.

Many people hate Fort Huachuca because it's isolated and desolate and because there isn't much to do in the tiny adjoining town of Sierra Vista. The nearest city is an hour away, and even that city, Tucson, is relatively sleepy. I, however, instantly fell in love with Huachuca. The beautiful, serene southern Arizona landscapes made me feel instantly at ease, and the mile-high elevation made for a much cooler late summer than the intense heat of southern Georgia. Little did I know how this tiny piece of desert paradise would change my life.

Upon arriving at my new unit late on a Friday afternoon, the first thing that took me by surprise was the presence of females. Benning was all male, and after my first two and a half months there I had just grown accustomed to not having women around—and not even noticing it. So it was quite strange for me and my fellow newbies to walk up to the end-of-week company formation to see not only the much more relaxed environment of the intelligence training brigade at Huachuca but also the very different social dynamic with females in the mix. As the formation concluded, the first sergeant sounded off with his characteristic reminder, "No glove, no love," deepening my amusement. And on top of that, that afternoon marked the beginning of the weekend, meaning that I suddenly had two free days to relax and enjoy my new home. This was just all so strange and surreal to me at the time, but it only made me love the army, and Fort Huachuca, even more.

After that much-needed weekend break, and a day of in-processing into the new unit on Monday, came my first morning of duty at Fort Huachuca: the morning of Tuesday, September 11, 2001. The day began with a dawn formation followed by a brisk and rejuvenating morning run during which I struggled to catch my breath at a much higher elevation than I was used to, but it was nevertheless refreshing. Afterward, we all returned to the barracks area for another formation before showers and breakfast, and yet another morning formation to kick off the day. As most of the company milled about outside, one of the platoon sergeants yelled out across the staging area and asked if anyone was from New York. A few soldiers raised their hands or shouted in the affirmative, and we all then got our first jolt of the day: "A plane just crashed into the World Trade Center in Manhattan. You all go call home and make sure your loved ones are OK."

Like many across America that day, we all naturally just assumed that the first crash was a tragic accident. After everyone else was dismissed, many of us filtered into the various barracks common rooms to watch news footage of the first tower burning and to tune in to the evolving analysis of what was going on. Then, right in front of our eyes on live television, the second plane hit. Gasps and expletives filled the room as some of us tried to work out whether this could still be an accident. Was New York's air traffic control system going haywire and sending planes way off course? Was the weather there bad or something? None of the explanations made any sense, but neither did two planes flying into the World Trade Center. Within minutes, reality set in, and everyone standing there knew that none of our lives would ever be the same again. Indeed, some of the friends standing there that morning would later lose their lives as a result of the ensuing conflicts.

I thoroughly enjoyed interrogation school, and I actually learned a lot of useful and fundamental information there that I still use to this day. The major problem with the army's interrogation and human intelligence collection training at the time, however, was that it was all geared toward Cold War–era threats and conflicts. Even after 9/11, the training regimen continued in Cold War style, which would surely handicap military intelligence collection efforts in at least the first few years of the conflicts in Afghanistan and Iraq.

Despite being around a lot of like-minded people at the US Army Intelligence Center and Schools at Fort Huachuca, I maintained a relatively guarded social demeanor. The introduction of the female dynamic, however, inevitably meant that personal, social, and sexual interest from members of the opposite sex would arise—and it did—and that accompanying expectations to return that interest at some point would also arise—and they did. When you have beautiful women flirting with you over the course of weeks and months, and the interaction never progresses to another level, suspicions naturally develop. I managed to make a few friends and acquaintances at Huachuca who perhaps knew better than to probe too deeply into those dynamics, and I appreciated the respectful discretion. There were one or two others in our unit whom I suspected might be gay too, but I was too scared to even consider trying to figure that out. I wasn't interested in either of them sexually or romantically anyway, so that made it easy to just keep my head down and enjoy what I was there to do—become a US Army interrogator.

Within a few months the winter holidays were upon us and I was finally able to take a real break from army life and fly back to the East Coast for two weeks. Once again, my parents could not have been prouder of me, and I could not have been more relieved to finally be able to get away for a while. After Christmas, I headed up to New York City for New Year's to meet up with some friends.

Going back home to South Carolina for Christmas had given me enough of a taste of my old home life and family, but getting to New York reminded me once again of my real life immediately prior to joining the army, a life in which I was comfortable being gay and relatively open about it to those around me. It also gave me another taste of the thrill of being young and attractive and gay and free in a big city, and of going out and having fun and being a typical twenty-year-old again.

That trip gave me one of the most enjoyable New Year's Eve nights I've ever had. My friends and I had an absolute blast going out to several big clubs in Manhattan and taking in some great New Year's Eve performances by some pretty big divas of the year. I met a lot of great new people, and the fact that I was in the army seemed foreign to them. I was settling into the role, though, so it wasn't so foreign to me anymore. When we finally left the last huge warehouse dance club of the night, it shocked me to realize that it was daylight outside. It shocked me even more to look at my watch and see that it was almost noon.

When I got back to Fort Huachuca in Arizona, I began to feel like I could reasonably bridge and manage the two different aspects of my life that I loved so much—one side as a soldier in an army that was gearing up for war, and the other side as a young gay guy still growing and maturing and loving all of the things in life that young guys in their twenties do. The past seven months of experiences and growth had changed me dramatically, and I finally felt like I could put my wild pre-army life in Miami behind me and move forward. And one of the things I felt I had to do in order to do that was make amends with the last guy I had dated, whether he was ready to or not.

Andre, a male model and recent transplant from Brazil, had been one of my few really good friends in Miami. He was four years older than I was, but the experience of living independently in South Beach was a learning experience for both of us, which for a while we went through together. We became good friends and then dated for a time, but everything ended, as relationships often do, with a huge fight, after which we didn't speak to each other again.

Nearly a year later, after the transformative experience of joining the army and starting to get comfortable in my new skin, I decided to write Andre a long letter expressing regret that we had ended things in such a way and saying that I hoped we could someday be friends again. I wrote the letter entirely in Portuguese, assuming that even if someone else saw it, he or she wouldn't be able to read or understand what I was writing about.

That assumption turned out to be a grave mistake. Military intelligence units often contain a lot of very smart and talented people, and all human intelligence collectors in the army have to be at least bilingual before they're ready to work as interrogators. That's why most of them leave Huachuca and go on to the Defense Language Institute in Monterey, California, to acquire a second language. Some, however, come into the army already bilingual or multilingual, like I had, and evidently at least one other person in my unit came in knowing Portuguese. Who would have thought?

An acquaintance came over one day in the dining facility while I was working on a draft of this coded letter to Andre. I really didn't think much of it at the time, but within a week or two I started seeing evidence that others suddenly knew my secret. One fellow soldier later came up, called that acquaintance by name, and mentioned something about her saying she had lost respect for me after seeing some letter I had written. She cautioned me about safeguarding personal information and warned me that my secret was getting out. At that moment, panic began to set in. In a perhaps foolish but desperate attempt to quell the spread of information about my orientation, I cautiously spoke with my supervisor about the situation with the hope that he could help put the fires out. However, in what I know now to be a classic outcome, he reported the information up the chain of command and my fate was sealed.

Many gay, lesbian, and bisexual youth have gone into the military over the years with the same misunderstanding of the DADT policy as I had. It just sounded so reasonable and manageable, and for many it was. Hundreds of thousands of gay, lesbian, and bisexual servicemembers did navigate DADT over the course of their careers, but at a tremendous personal cost. But tens of thousands more could not. Some were abruptly fired after their secret was discovered and the information spread out to their peers and then up through their chain of command, as in my case, while others were maliciously outed by jilted lovers, jealous fellow servicemembers, or bigoted acquaintances who discovered their secret.

People have often asked me over the years if I harbor any ill will toward the person who let out the secret I had tried so hard to keep. The truth is that I really don't. As I see it, it wasn't an overtly malicious act on her part. Was she judgmental and two-faced? Probably. But when you're nineteen or twenty years old, information like one's sexual orientation is often treated as careless gossip. And that's what I think it was—gossip. I don't think she, or anyone else who spread it around the unit, really knew or understood the ramifications of gossiping about that particular piece of information, just as many of us who served under and whose continued service became victim to DADT never really understood just how easy it would be for this historic policy mistake to manifest itself in our lives.

I still remember the precise moment on March 22, 2002, that I abruptly became a civilian again. It was a Friday, and a friend of mine from Phoenix drove down to meet me at the front gate to the post. When he got there, I walked through the gate with a few bags containing all of my possessions, we loaded them into his SUV, and we drove off. While I was lucky enough to have a very compassionate friend who offered to let me live with him rent-free up in Phoenix until I could get back on my feet and figure out what I wanted to do next, others who have been discharged have found themselves abruptly out on the street with no income. When you had planned to spend at least the next five years of your life in the military, with a steady stream of income, a place to live, a job you liked, and a good circle of friends around you, and then all of a sudden your life turns upside down and all of that gets taken away, it can be quite traumatic, especially for someone so young.

Toward the end of my time in the army, I had started dating an air force ROTC cadet at the University of Arizona up in Tucson. Things were going well with David at the time, which provided relief from the downer of being discharged, but on the day I was actually discharged I completely shut down and isolated myself from just about everyone and everything for the next three days. I told David earlier that day that I would call him when I got to Phoenix to let him know that I had arrived OK, but I didn't call him until the following Monday. It wasn't that I didn't want to talk to him or see him but rather that I didn't want to talk to or see *anyone*. I just shut myself up in my friend's home in Phoenix and began walling off the previous nine months of my life.

Not knowing then what I certainly know now about the political history of the DADT issue and about the moral failings of DADT as law and policy, I went through what thousands of others have experienced after an untimely—although fully honorable on paper—discharge. I was ashamed and embarrassed, and I placed the blame for everything that had happened so fast squarely on myself. I second-guessed my actions and reactions and wondered how differently things would have turned out had I written that letter in Italian or Spanish instead of Portuguese. I wondered if the spread of my "secret" would have died out had I left it alone and ignored it instead of acting to try to stop it. I wondered if I should have gone to someone else for help with the matter instead of the person I chose to confide in. And I wondered if I should have tried to fight my discharge instead of being intimidated into signing away my right to fight.

One afternoon a few weeks after I moved up to Phoenix, I got a call on my cell phone from my mom. After exchanging a few pleasantries, she surprised me by asking me if I was still in the army. Once again, that gut-wrenching panic set in. Only a few close friends knew at that point that I had been kicked out of the military for being gay, and none of them even knew who my parents were or where they lived. When I told her that I thought that was a strange question and asked why she was inquiring, she explained that an envelope from the army had just arrived at their home and that my father, thinking anything coming from the army to their home must be for him, had opened it up. My father and I have the same name—I'm the third and he's a junior—and my parents' address had been listed on my military records as my "home of record" address, as is the case with most young recruits. When he opened it up, my father, who didn't know at the time I was gay, realized that the discharge paperwork he was looking at was clearly not for him, but for his gay son. At that moment, I hit rock bottom.

2

* * * * *

REVIVAL

In the wake of the US Supreme Court's *Lawrence v. Texas* ruling in 2003, which struck down state laws criminalizing same sex sexual relations, a significant opportunity presented itself to attack the DADT law on constitutional grounds through the courts. The following year, a young gay lawyer named Marty Meekins at the Los Angeles office of the international law firm White & Case approached his office's pro bono committee about mounting a challenge to DADT on behalf of a political organization with which Marty was involved—the Log Cabin Republicans (LCR), a gay Republican group founded in California but based in Washington, DC. Despite the long odds, White & Case took on the challenge, and firm partner Dan Woods agreed to spearhead the legal team for the case.

LCR asserted standing as an association whose members were being harmed by the DADT law. Organizations suing the government by claiming associational standing are normally required to name at least one member who has a claim in his or her own right, so LCR found a gay, active duty army officer within its membership to serve as the lead plaintiff on whose claim of harm LCR could build a case against the constitutionality of the DADT law. Given that this officer could be discharged under DADT if his identity were revealed, LCR opted to proceed with him as a "John Doe" plaintiff to protect both his identity and his military career while the merits of his case made their way through the legal process. LCR even offered to provide details of John Doe's identity, activity with the organization, and military service in a sealed affidavit, if necessary.

As the lengthy process of laying the groundwork to sue the US government to overturn an entrenched law got under way in 2004, another Washington, DC–based organization also decided to file a lawsuit challenging DADT. The Servicemembers Legal Defense Network (SLDN) provided free counsel and representation to those who found themselves caught up in the web of DADT while on active duty. Staffed primarily by civilian lawyers and professional activists, SLDN had been founded in 1993 out of the remnants of the Campaign for Military Service, the unsuccessful effort to lift the ban on gays in the military in the early 1990s.

For a decade, SLDN had been the only organization that continued to serve and advocate for lesbian, gay, bisexual, and transgender (LGBT) servicemembers as other gay rights organizations largely abandoned the gay military community after the DADT law was enacted. As a legal services organization, it did its best to protect those whose careers could be salvaged and do damage control for those whose careers were destroyed as a result of the DADT law. But, in the words of one of SLDN's prominent board members, the one thing none of those lawyers had done in that decade was that which lawyers are usually known for: suing.

With strong precedent set in the courts in the 1990s on the DADT issue (after the noble but unsuccessful legal challenges mounted by Paul Thomasson, Tracy Thorne, Rich Richenberg, Mark Philips, Andrew Holmes, Jane Able, and others) and the heavily fortified tradition of judicial deference to the military on defense policy matters, it is certainly understandable that no one wanted to expend the time, effort, and resources to challenge DADT in the courts again, even in light of changing public opinion in favor of open and honest service by gays and lesbians in the military. But the landmark ruling in *Lawrence v. Texas* changed the legal landscape for a lot of issues, and DADT was once again prime for a fresh legal assault.

With LCR's case ready to go, attorney Dan Woods and his legal team at White & Case filed their lawsuit, *Log Cabin Republicans v. United States of America*, in a Los Angeles federal court in October 2004. This launched another useful assault against DADT and opened a new legal front for the repeal movement, but based on the reaction you would have thought the assault had been launched against gay and lesbian servicemembers themselves. SLDN, whose attorney-activists thought that they were going to be able to enjoy the distinction of having the preeminent post-*Lawrence* legal challenge to DADT, reacted harshly to the news of LCR's filing. According to LCR staff members at the time, attorneys from SLDN marched down to LCR's Washington, DC, offices to scold them for daring to file a lawsuit challenging DADT. SLDN had its own comprehensive legal strategy, they said, and LCR's lawsuit was going to screw it all up.

Both of these cases were originally filed against the Bush administration, and the government immediately filed a motion asking the court to dismiss each suit. In these types of cases, in which the government is being sued and in which military policy is implicated, courts often quickly dismiss such actions under the long-standing rationale that experienced military leaders are in a better position to make defense policy and should not be second-guessed by civilian judges. Courts also recognize the unique circumstances and requirements of military life, especially the requirement to maintain cohesive units that are always ready for combat, and they are often willing to lower the constitutional bar in cases that involve such issues.

Therefore, such cases are typically dismissed quickly. In both of these cases, however, the presiding judge took an unusually long time to rule on the government's motions to dismiss them. The SLDN case ultimately failed at the district court level—the motion to dismiss was eventually granted—and that loss was affirmed by the Court of Appeals for the First Circuit. However, the LCR case, which many people affiliated with SLDN criticized as poorly conceived, poorly argued, and poorly timed, later proved to be one of the most significant driving forces behind the DADT repeal effort, although not before the case took many strange and surprising twists and turns along the way.

Not long after these bicoastal lawsuits challenging the constitutionality of DADT were filed in the courts, a feisty Democratic congressman, Marty Meehan, from Lowell, Massachusetts, known for championing term limits and campaign finance reform, agreed to take the lead on a bill in the US House of Representatives to repeal the DADT law. When it was finally introduced in the House on March 2, 2005, the Military Readiness Enhancement Act (MREA, or "Maria," as some called it) was an ideal full repeal bill. At its core, MREA immediately struck the DADT law from the US code, but it also mandated an affirmative nondiscrimination policy based on sexual orientation throughout the armed forces, a significant distinction from later versions of the legislation.

Before DADT, the US military had a regulatory policy prohibiting gays and lesbians from serving. The Department of Defense was able to formally put in place such a policy shortly after World War II not only because it was fashionable then to abhor gays and lesbians and to find any way possible to discriminate against them, but also because no law or executive order existed that prohibited such discrimination. Simply deleting Title 10 Section 654 from the United States Code would likely have just returned us to the days when there was no law from Congress mandating that the Department of Defense (DOD) fire gays and lesbians and DOD could just do so on its own.

Keep in mind that in 2005, senior defense leaders in the Pentagon were still in no mood for backing major changes to such long-standing personnel policies. Two full years later we still had the chairman of the Joint Chiefs of Staff, Marine Corps General Peter Pace, saying publicly that homosexuality was immoral and that allowing gays and lesbians to serve openly would amount to condoning that alleged immorality. Even though civilian society had progressed remarkably since the early 1990s, the policy-making circles at the Pentagon offered no guarantees that simply wiping the DADT law off the books would be a step forward for gays, lesbians, and bisexuals in the military. A realistic possibility existed at the time that it could actually have been a step backward.

This is why the affirmative nondiscrimination component to MREA was so critical at the time. With General Pace at the helm across the Potomac, who knew how gays and lesbians might be treated if the issue were left entirely up to the Pentagon, even in 2005. The nondiscrimination clause, however, prohibited discrimination within the armed forces on the basis of sexual orientation, much the same way that discrimination on the basis of race and religion are banned outright in military personnel policy.

MREA represented the reasonably ideal position of the pro-repeal community in 2005. It eliminated the DADT language that required the Pentagon to fire anyone found to be gay, lesbian, or bisexual; it took effect almost immediately; and it prohibited further discrimination based on sexual orientation. But one's ideal position—even one's "reasonably" ideal position—isn't usually what one ends up with after the sausage making of the Washington political bazaar. In the future, this bill would go through quite a bit of evolution, and that nondiscrimination mandate would prove to be a particularly controversial provision, but not for the obvious reasons.

Congressman Meehan maintained a dedicated page about MREA on his website, including stories from a few servicemembers who had been adversely impacted by DADT. By then I had heard of a few others who had been outed or found out and discharged pursuant to DADT, but I had never read or heard the details of these people's lives and experiences with this law. A few news stories existed at the time, largely thanks to the advocacy of New York University professor and DADT repeal advocate Dr. Nathaniel Frank, about servicemembers who had been discharged under DADT who also had been in critical occupational specialties, but these few blips on my radar screen seemed to focus narrowly on the bad policy of discharging linguists. The servicemember entries on Congressman Meehan's website, on the other hand, were the first testimonials I had seen about the personal side of getting discharged.

After years of suppressing my own experience of being discharged under DADT, I began to realize for the first time that perhaps the way I had framed and dealt with that experience was wrong. The DADT/ MREA page on Congressman Meehan's site invited others who had been discharged under DADT to e-mail the congressman's office with their own stories. Despite having put my discharge far behind me with no intent to ever really bring it up again, I felt inexplicably compelled to put a summary of my own experience in words in the site's online contact form and nervously hit SUBMIT. It was only a few short paragraphs and I don't even really remember what I talked about, other than having been a US Army human intelligence collector trainee who spoke several languages and who had also been discharged under DADT, but something about what I wrote evidently caught the attention of the congressman's staff.

Within a few days, some quotations from my e-mail appeared on the congressman's website, constituting the first time I ever spoke publicly and willingly about what had happened to me and how being discharged affected me. I realized that seeing others speak out about being discharged under DADT had not only empowered and inspired me to do so but also completely changed my frame of reference for the issue. I no longer thought of my discharge as just a failure on my part; instead I started gaining the perspective to put it into a larger political and policy context. I finally started to understand the issue, and I immediately thought that this was the kind of thing that others, especially conservative and mainstream Americans, needed to start seeing too, so that they could also see the light on this issue. All it would take, it seemed, would be for people like me to get in front of them and start talking, but on a massive scale.

3

★ ★ ★ ★ ★

A CALL TO DUTY

Just as it would be bizarre to see mostly men running the National Organization for Women or white people running the National Association for the Advancement of Colored People, it was also strange to me to see those who had never been impacted by DADT—often those who had never even served in the military—advocating, negotiating, lobbying, and making decisions on the DADT issue. It also struck me as odd to see those with no direct connection to this issue or to the gay military community representing our community, our voice, and our experiences in the public sphere, particularly in the media. While we were, are, and always will be grateful to those allies who worked hard to help push our cause forward, it just didn't seem right to me at the time that those actually affected by DADT were not at the forefront of the debate and truly driving the conversation on DADT in Washington.

The cause of DADT repeal had broad appeal to liberal and progressive activists and lawyers of all stripes, but it made little sense that their participation in the movement should be at the expense of those who really ought to have been at the head of the negotiating table—those who had firsthand experience serving under and being impacted by DADT. There had always been individuals affected by DADT involved in the repeal movement—from Michelle Benecke, who cofounded SLDN, to Alastair Gamble and Ian Finkenbinder, who did the media rounds on behalf of the Arabic linguists discharged from the Defense Language Institute. But Benecke, an air force veteran, had been elbowed out of SLDN (so the story went) by a lawyer-activist who had never served in the military, and the discharged servicemembers who appeared in random media spots from time to time were almost always there as a result of civilian activists who arranged their appearances and offered such opportunities up as long as their rules were followed. Many prominent gay servicemembers, I later learned, got so fed up with being stage-managed that they gave up on the advocacy after one or two media appearances. This just wasn't a community in control of its own destiny.

The level of prominence of the DADT issue on the national political and policy stage also seemed to be lagging at the time. While the *New York Times* or National Public Radio or the *San Francisco Chronicle* doing a story from time to time on the DADT issue was certainly appreciated, these weren't the types of reports that were going to seriously reach out to and strike at the heart of "Betty and Bob on the couch in Nebraska," as I called my hypothetical targets. We had the support of Joe Q. San Francisco and the votes of his senators, but we did not have the support of Betty and Bob Q. Omaha, and we certainly didn't have the support of or any interest from their senators—yet.

One weekend afternoon in the late summer of 2005, I was lying on my living room floor with my laptop in Arlington, Virginia, just outside Washington, DC, when all of these random thoughts, complaints, and frustrations came together in my mind. I soon came across and began reading an Internet article about yet another group of people who had never been in the military and didn't know a thing about real life under DADT, yet who were going out and preaching to the military community and mainstream America about how gays and lesbians should be allowed to serve openly. Little did they know, although they should have known or should have at least sought advice from someone who would have known, that there were three primary problems with their particular approach.

First, the military and veteran communities don't want to listen to someone who has never been in the military talk about appropriate internal military personnel policies. Second, talking about being "openly gay" in the military conjures up images of open (i.e., public) gay *behavior* rather than open or known gay *orientation*, and the careless handling of this delicate distinction can turn off even moderate supporters. And third, you just don't put skinny kids with blue highlights and nose rings in front of crusty old Vietnam War veterans in Iowa—or younger Iraq War veterans, for that matter—and make them think that these are what "gays in the military" would look like. That's not what we look like, and activists should know better than to put forward someone who does not in the least resemble the talked-about population as a representative of that community.

I wondered why someone couldn't just take ordinary young veterans with compelling skill sets and stories, like myself, who actually looked like they just stepped out of the military and stick them in front of audiences in Nebraska and Georgia and Iowa and Nevada and Texas. Not only should these be the people in front of mainstream American audiences, but these people—real gays in the military—should also be the ones in the media and in Washington talking about this issue. But more important, these people, the ones actually impacted by the policy, should be the ones calling the shots on the issue. With tens of thousands of us out there, there was no need for a few of us to act as media puppets for the civilian activist handlers or just sit in honorary board positions or on speakers bureau lists to only be called up when a safe opportunity arose. Our community was perfectly capable of representing and speaking for itself, thank you very much, just as women were capable of running NOW and African Americans were capable of running the NAACP.

On my living room floor that afternoon was born a project that would not only remedy these obvious problems with the DADT repeal movement at that time; it would also lead to the formation of the largest gay military organization in the country and ensure that when the DADT issue finally exploded on the political agenda years later, those actually affected by the issue would have a prominent seat at the table on Capitol Hill, in the White House, and at the Pentagon.

Without knowing anything about grassroots organizing or political activism, I first reached out to SLDN to pitch the idea of helping to proactively put more recent gay and lesbian veterans out in front of mainstream audiences and place them more squarely at the center of the political process. Now, in retrospect, I certainly understand how I must have been viewed. At Servicemembers United, people would approach us all the time saying that we should be doing this or that, or that they would be willing to help us do this or that. But about 90 percent of the time, these people are either "cocktail party activists" or "armchair activists," two distinct breeds, or they are just nuts. About 5 percent tend to be smart people with really good ideas, but they just don't have the desire, resources, or skill to put those ideas into action. And the remaining 5 percent—maybe even fewer—are the ones that organizations should sit up and take notice of, listen to, and try to find a way to work with because they have good ideas and the will and skill to put those ideas into action.

When SLDN staffers brushed me off, I knew that either I could continue to watch the gay military community be controlled and represented by those who were largely not a part of it, or I could try to change that. SLDN board members have since tried to convince me that the organization's board and advisory board constituted the "face" of the SLDN and, therefore, the gay military community. However, this argument rang quite naïve at best. While board members do serve an important function for organizations that use strong-board models of governance and administration, one would be foolish to believe that attending a few organizational board meetings per year, doing one lobby day per year, attending a few receptions and fund-raisers per year, and following the issue out of personal interest even remotely compares to being the true face of an issue on the cable talk shows, sitting in the room with congressional committee leaders and high-level administration officials when negotiation takes place, and frequenting the Pentagon to help shape the direction of developments. The latter set of roles is what organizational staffers engage in, while the former set of roles is what board and honorary advisers engage in. And even back in 2005, I knew that if those of us actually impacted by DADT didn't step forward to get involved, when the caca hit the fan it would be those who had never even served under DADT who would be doing most of the substantive representation and negotiation on our behalf.

Even though I knew something had to be done, I had absolutely no clue at the time where to start. So I began where billions of previous blind endeavors have begun before and since—an Internet search. The terms "discharged," "gay," and "veterans" brought up a list of news articles, and at the top of that list was an article about a recently discharged army bomb technician named Brian Muller. With a little cross-referencing and research, skills actually well honed in the army's interrogation school, I was able to dig up this random guy's e-mail addresses. I reached out to him cold to explain the various problems I saw in the DADT repeal movement and the partial solution I had dreamed up to begin to help remedy it. And to my utter amazement, Brian, who remains a friend to this day, quickly responded.

While he expressed sympathy with what I wrote to him, Brian was living in Atlanta then and was bogged down in personal and professional pursuits that didn't afford him the luxury to just up and leave and become a radical homosexual activist. But Brian did refer me to someone else he thought could refer me to others who could help and get involved. Brian kindly e-mailed Dr. Aaron Belkin, then a political science professor at the University of California at Santa Barbara, who had taken an academic interest in the DADT issue, and connected us.

Belkin, a quirky and sometimes downright eccentric academic who founded and ran the largely one-man, oddly named operation called the Center for the Study of Sexual Minorities in the Military, was a little more open-minded and nimble than the DADT activists at SLDN on the other side of the country had been. After a quick phone conversation, he agreed to connect me with some individuals who might agree with my vision and be willing to help me realize it. Two of those individuals turned out to be crucial to the movement revitalization effort: Patrick English and Al Steinman.

English was a US Army Korean linguist who was deployed to Iraq to do everything except Korean linguistics. Way to utilize our resources! While he was over there, he received the above-referenced e-mail from Belkin introducing him to me and telling him about my idea to get more Iraq- and Afghanistan-era veterans involved in the DADT repeal movement.

English had started the first-ever organization for active duty gay and lesbian troops, called Gay and Lesbian Service Members for Equality (GLSME). The group grew out of a prior group called the Gay Luck Club that had been half-joke, half–gay linguist social circle at the Defense Language Institute in Monterey. While still in Iraq, English e-mailed another former Gay Luck Club member and fellow underutilized Korean linguist, Jarrod Chlapowski, who was stationed at Fort Lewis, Washington, at the time, and told him about the new effort he had heard about to reinvigorate debate on the DADT issue. English insisted that Chlapowski had to be involved in the initiative and promised him that he would tell him more about it in two weeks when he finished his deployment to Iraq and returned to Fort Lewis. Both men had only a few weeks left in the army, and both were looking for something worthwhile to get involved in over the next six months or so before going back to college on the GI Bill. The perfect storm of opportunity, availability, and enthusiasm to effect change was brewing.

The other individual who stepped forward from Belkin's introductions to offer help was Al Steinman of Dupont, Washington. Al was an MIT- and Stanford-educated medical doctor in the Public Health Service and the US Coast Guard who rose through the ranks to eventually become his branch's director of health and safety, equivalent to the surgeon general of the other military branches. In 1997 he retired as a two-star admiral, and, perhaps most notably for this narrative, he came out on the front page of the *New York Times* in 2003 to become the nation's highest-ranking military officer to ever publicly self-identify as gay after retirement from the armed forces. Unlike thousands of others whom I've met over the years who considered themselves to be "involved" in the DADT repeal movement, Al, whom I call by his first name at his insistence, is one of the 1 percent who actually has been realistically and substantively involved in the DADT repeal movement in an advisory capacity—and often more—as opposed to just cocktail party, board (including "advisory" board), or armchair activism.

While Patrick English was still in Iraq preparing to return home to Fort Lewis, I proposed to these new acquaintances my idea of getting together a cadre of recent, young, gay and lesbian veterans to tour the country together and do public appearances, press conferences, town halls, panel presentations, speaking engagements, and media appearances, all with the intent to raise the profile of the DADT repeal issue nationally. This idea also fit within the broader vision to put those actually impacted by DADT at the center of the public discourse on the issue and to show America what actual gay and lesbian servicemembers looked, sounded, and acted like: just like them. I asked for feedback from the others on what we should call the tour because my favorite name, Tour of Duty, had already been put to use by the antiwar activist Cindy Sheehan. After nearly a week of radio silence from Patrick in Iraq, causing several of us to become concerned, he finally shot me an e-mail back to say that he would be back in Seattle in a week and that he had a name suggestion for my revolutionary new project: Call to Duty.

It was quite a fitting name, I had to admit, and it succinctly encapsulated another theme that we grew to embody, namely the effort to snatch younger servicemembers and veterans away from the clubs and bars for a little while and get them interested in and involved in the DADT repeal movement, even if only for a short stint. We knew that such a bold initiative like a large-scale national publicity tour for a controversial political issue needed more than just us in order to sustain itself, but we also were not in any position to start an organization and actually pay anyone to be involved. If we were going to do this, we really did need to tap into young gay veterans' sense of duty, not just to their country but also to their (LGBT) community.

After Patrick returned from Iraq and settled back into Fort Lewis, I flew out to Seattle to meet up with Jarrod, Al, and him for a long weekend of maniacal planning, scheming, brainstorming, and beer. We managed to recruit a few others to get involved as well, some of whom were able to join us in Seattle over Halloween weekend of 2005. Also joining us was a documentary film producer named Johnny Symons who was just beginning to work on a new film for PBS about the DADT issue. I was rather skeptical of putting this nascent initiative on film when we really didn't even know where it would go yet, but Johnny was quite a nice guy who had already produced a film, *Daddy & Papa*, that had been nominated for an Emmy, so I reluctantly agreed to allow him to come up from California and interview and film us for his new documentary. Little did any of us know that so much would come out of that weekend—friendships, work partnerships, a national tour, a national organization, a full-length documentary, and the forced restructuring of the balance of power within the movement.

Another seed planted that weekend involved a former chairman of the Joint Chiefs of Staff. Admiral Steinman managed to score our group a unique opportunity to meet privately with retired general John Shalikashvili, who lived just south of Seattle outside of Fort Lewis. Al had cultivated a relationship with "Shali" and over time had invited several other prominent repeal activists to meet with him too, including SLDN's Dixon Osburn and Aaron Belkin from the Center for the Study of Sexual Minorities in the Military, which by this point had been renamed the Palm Center. But it seemed to be General Shali's meeting with our group of young gay servicemembers and veterans that had the biggest impact on the influential former Joint Chiefs chairman.

For most retirees of General Shali's seniority, the pace of generational change within the military and its accelerated impact on social issues had largely escaped them. They were often still held captive by outdated stereotypes of what they thought "gays in the military" meant and how our contemporary peers would react to knowing that we were gay. But once we youngsters began opening up to him about what it was like these days, especially among the more junior guys, he was quite perplexed. It surprised him to hear that the "rednecks" weren't quite as sheltered as they used to be in his day. He was especially astounded that one of our guys was a submariner who had been openly gay to his submarine crew without issue.

Just over a year later, General Shalikashvili announced in an op-ed in the *New York Times* that he had changed his mind on the DADT issue and had come to believe that gays and lesbians could serve openly without undermining the force. Referring to his meetings with our Call to Duty Tour members, he wrote: "Last year I held a number of meetings with gay soldiers and marines, including some with combat experience in Iraq, and an openly gay senior sailor who was serving effectively as a member of a nuclear submarine crew. These conversations showed me just how much the military has changed, and that gays and lesbians can be accepted by their peers." The op-ed was actually ghostwritten for him, but he certainly signed off on every word of it and even went on to support us in other ways behind the scenes over the ensuing years.

The historic impact on the momentum of the repeal movement of a former chairman of the Joint Chiefs of Staff coming out in favor of repeal cannot be understated. The development so incensed Elaine

Donnelly—head of the Center for Military Readiness and the most rabid of anti-repeal activists—that she immediately and shamefully accused the former chairman of literally being out of his mind and accused us radical homosexual activists of having co-opted him and turned him into our puppet.

Nothing could have been further from the truth. Shali did have health problems, but they weren't mental. And if we had co-opted him, we would have surely wanted him to be much more publicly active on the issue than he ever was. He wasn't interested in testifying at a congressional hearing, and he wasn't interested in signing onto a joint letter of flag officers (generals and admirals) calling for repeal. He was, however, genuinely convinced that times had changed and that public policy needed to keep up with those changes.

While Patrick and Al stayed in the Seattle area, Jarrod joined me in Washington, DC, and jumped headfirst into working full-time on developing the Call to Duty Tour with me. Rather than relying on the same old networks of DADT donors who already rallied around SLDN, we worked for the next few months to expand the pool of donors interested in repealing DADT in order to help finance this ambitious new project.

We got a significant early boost from an angel donor named Bryan Hodges, who ran a successful information technology company in the Midwest and whom I had met a few months before in DC. When I happened to mention in passing that I was working on an outside-the-box project to raise awareness on the gays in the military issue and rebrand and restructure the issue to more accurately reflect those affected by the law, he eagerly asked to hear more. Ever since, Bryan has been a major donor to and personal supporter of our work. Without him and his early investment in our project, none of our subsequent accomplishments would ever have come to pass.

In addition to several seed donors, the first organization to step forward and offer to help us out was the Log Cabin Republicans. LCR immediately offered us ten grand for the tour with no strings attached. The Human Rights Campaign (HRC), a large gay rights organization based in Washington, DC, soon followed suit, offering equal support with only a few strings attached. Neither HRC nor LCR staff were involved in creating or implementing the Call to Duty Tour except for equal help from both organizations with pitching media about our upcoming events, although we later found out that HRC had led many on their various boards to believe that the Call to Duty Tour was "their" tour entirely. To this day, we still occasionally run across HRC board members who are shocked to find out that the Call to Duty Tour was not an HRC-led project, or an HRC project at all. Equally amusing is the fact that we still run across people who think that Servicemembers United is "an arm of Log Cabin" or "controlled by HRC" because we have at various points worked with each of these organizations and others. The ease with which people jump to these types of conclusions just goes to show how rare true independence and bipartisanship are in Washington.

One organization that wanted to offer a fraction of the support but with not just strings but hefty bands of solid rope attached to what we were doing was SLDN. That organization, which originally brushed us off as an annoyance, now came back to offer a whopping one grand to help finance a major national publicity tour that would end up costing nearly fifty times that amount. And the best part was that it demanded that the entire thing be publicly labeled as "presented by SLDN." Needless to say, we turned down its oh-so-generous offer.

Fundraising, logistical planning, and event scheduling for the tour proceeded through the fall of 2005, although we were still not sure at this point that we could actually pull off what we had promised. We arranged for a big kick-off event in Boston with Congressman Meehan, followed by a sprint down the East Coast into God's Country, the Southeast. We then intended to go into the conservative areas of the Midwest, then down into Texas and the Southwest before heading up to Utah and on up to the Northwest. Then we aimed to head down the Pacific coast, with heavily militarized San Diego designated as the end point of the tour.

Nothing on this scale had been done before on any gay rights issue, or if it had then no one stepped forward to volunteer what it was and how they pulled it off. The scale and ambition of the Call to Duty Tour was unprecedented, and we still weren't quite sure that we wouldn't crash and burn at the very beginning. We wondered if anyone would show up to the events we carefully planned across the country, or if any media would cover our presence in these mostly conservative areas in which DADT repeal and "gays in the military" rarely got any news coverage, especially not positive coverage.

On February 14, 2006, we were given a big publicity boost in the gay community when the *Advocate*, the nation's premier gay news magazine, ran a cover story about the upcoming Call to Duty Tour. Jarrod and I had both done a photo shoot for the magazine in Washington, DC, just four days into the new year. It was freezing cold outside and we did the shoot outdoors at the Korean War Memorial in a version—just pants, boots, and undershirts—of the brand-new Army Combat Uniform.

Respecting regulation and custom, we refused to wear the full uniform as the photographers had wanted but opted for a respectable variation of it instead. In just that thin army undershirt, it was so cold that morning on the National Mall that we had to don heavy jackets between shots. The photos turned out quite nice, though, especially the cover photo. Jarrod was disappointed that he didn't make the cover along with me, but, as he says, at least he had the centerfold.

The story made quite a splash when it came out: "Marching on Washington. The End of the Ban: Congress may soon dump it. The public opposes it. Can a group of gay veterans with a new battle plan finally kill it?" SLDN was furious; the next issue of the magazine included a letter to the editor from SLDN's executive director, Dixon Osburn, chastising the article's author for not making more of the article about SLDN. Osburn did at least include a kind nod to us and the nobility of our work in his angry letter, but only after SLDN staff attorney Sharon Alexander pressured him to do so.

We finally kicked off the Call to Duty Tour in Boston in late February 2006 with a big event planned at Harvard's Kennedy School of Government. Except for Admiral Steinman, and of course Congressman Meehan, none of us had ever done any public speaking before. Thinking back, it was really quite naïve of us to do our first-ever public speaking gig at Harvard, but, as I would say many times later, the only reason we were able to pull off so much of what we did on that first tour was because we were genuinely unaware of what we were doing and of how impossible so much of it really was. That first event was a trial by fire for all of us, but we not only packed the room but filled an overflow room as well. The lengthy standing ovation at the end of our remarks also served as confirmation for us that maybe we had done something right and that the gamble of going big or going home had paid off.

Our big Harvard launch was an extraordinarily successful event, but we knew that we had set the bar quite high for ourselves—and we were only at the beginning of the journey. As crazy as it was to think of Harvard as the easy part, the whole point of the initiative was to head into unfriendly territory with the message, the image, and the tour. That came next, as we headed not only down South but also into real enemy territory along the way, visiting various American Legion halls throughout many conservative areas.

Before leaving the largely supportive New England area, however, we did head up for a quick two-day detour north into the great state of Maine. Not a lot of people understood why we wanted to linger in the Northeast, which was usually thought of as a bastion of liberal support, but we knew quite well even back then that Maine's two Republican senators could likely be won over if we played a good ground game in that state to build chatter about and demonstrate support for repeal there over the long term. So when a last-minute invitation came to put together an event in Maine, we eagerly accepted. And not only did we pack our second event on the tour and begin to lay the groundwork for grassroots work in what would become a crucial target state on the issue, but we also began some local outreach to the famously hostile American Legion.

Nearly every year at its national convention, the American Legion had automatically and unanimously passed a resolution calling on Congress to put stronger prohibitions on gay military service back in place. It was a truly nasty and mean-spirited effort that passed with overwhelming support each and every year. We had been told many a time by older DADT repeal activists that reaching out to the American Legion was a lost cause, but we bucked the conventional wisdom about this behemoth legacy veterans organization and decided to test the waters. So while in Maine, we looked up the nearest local American Legion post and asked if we could send someone over to talk to the post commander about the DADT issue. We made clear that we were veterans and that we were pro-repeal, and we were surprisingly invited to come on down and talk with the local post's leadership.

Since he had just returned from Iraq a few months earlier, we sent Patrick alone on what everyone thought would be a suicide mission to talk to them about gays in the military, while the rest of us carried out the event we had been invited to Maine to do. When we finished the event and returned to the hotel, we were all eager to find Patrick and see how the American Legion meeting went. To our surprise, and somewhat to our concern, Patrick had not yet returned to the hotel. When he finally did return later that night, we all gathered around nervously to find out just what had gone down at the meeting.

To our surprise, Patrick reported back that these Legionnaires were not only supportive but relatively welcoming of him as an out gay combat veteran. The reason he had come back to the hotel so late was that the post had a karaoke machine at its bar, and the older Legionnaires had invited Patrick to stay and do karaoke with them that night. Patrick happily stayed to belt out a few songs with the guys, including his signature karaoke tune, "Zoot Suit Riot." If only we had a picture of this hilarious scene, the hardened walls of discrimination throughout the ranks would have surely crumbled right then and there.

After leaving the Northeast, the tour headed straight down the East Coast into Dixie, with public events, media, and more veterans organization meetings in Virginia, South Carolina, and Georgia. The American Legion meetings in Virginia and South Carolina went shockingly well. The Virginia post commander ended up donating $100 to the tour, and the hardened Vietnam-era commander of the post we visited in South Carolina invited us back to try to change the minds of the rest of his post members on the issue, as we had evidently done with him.

As we would soon find, freethinkers at the individual level within the American Legion found themselves in agreement with us after a sit-down conversation. This was true at every local post we visited across the country on that tour except for one. This ratio of agreement to disagreement shocked us nearly as much as it shocked those who had warned us that we would find virtually no agreement with our views on repeal throughout the entire organization.

While we didn't expend anywhere near as much energy on the big legacy veterans service organizations over the next few years as we would on our other education and advocacy targets, we did make some efforts to reach out to the Legion and VFW leadership on their organizations' archaic positions on DADT. While it was never our goal to actually win over these behemoth legacy organizations, we thought it was within our reach to at least neutralize them—in other words, to get them to tone down their rhetoric and perhaps stay out of the DADT fight. And while they certainly did not become champions of personal freedom and equality, these powerful organizations indeed did substantially moderate their opposition when the issue heated up in the end. The following year, that nasty resolution that the American Legion had passed without question year after year was suddenly nowhere to be found.

South Carolina also provided a colorful example of anonymous opposition over the airwaves. At each stop along the tour, we held meetings with local editorial boards, visited with politicians, and appeared on local morning and afternoon television news shows. We also tried to get on as much local right-wing radio as possible. This was, after all, our target audience on this tour, and the in-person events along the way provided a hook for local television and radio affiliates to cover the DADT issue and to have us on to talk, answer questions, and debate. So it was no surprise that in a place like South Carolina, we got some "interesting" callers when we went on drive-time talk radio in Columbia.

My favorite radio caller remark, which luckily made it into a clip of the PBS documentary, *Ask Not*, came from a call at the local Clear Channel talk radio station in Columbia. The guy, clearly an opponent, ended his diatribe by asking, "Would you rather be in a foxhole with John Wayne or Liberace?" While the response I gave to this caller certainly put him in his place, a better response perhaps would have been simply, "I'd rather be in a foxhole with whoever has the best marksmanship." But the longer answer I did give about bullets flying and not worrying about who's looking at your backside when you're going for your bulletproof gear made the same point.

Another southeastern stop on the tour, at North Georgia College, provided us with a golden opportunity to reach another important target of our work, namely the up and coming junior military officer corps. North Georgia is one of six congressionally designated Senior Military Colleges around the country (the others are the Citadel, Virginia Military Institute, Norwich, Texas A&M, and Virginia Tech) that train future military officers in much the same way that West Point and other service academies do. The Senior Military Colleges lie somewhere between the service academies and regular college ROTC programs in terms of officer training immersion, and their strategic focus on recruiting and training military officers means that these institutions turn out hundreds upon hundreds of new officers each year. Needless to say, exposing these future leaders to real gay and lesbian servicemembers and breaking down the stereotypes that DADT perpetuates through forced silence was an important systematic goal of ours, and North Georgia provided a unique opportunity to begin doing just that.

We actually spent several days at North Georgia on that first tour and got to know a number of key influencers at the institution who wanted to see more of our type of work done on the ultraconservative campus. By complete coincidence, Jarrod and I would both end up moving to the metro Atlanta area after the Call to Duty Tour wrapped up, attending North Georgia College (Jarrod to finish his undergraduate degree, since he was from Georgia, and me to complete a master's in public administration), and continuing to highlight the DADT issue over and over again on a campus that continuously ranked among the highest producers of new army officers.

Despite our very public advocacy work on a controversial political issue throughout the ultraconservative Deep South, we never really felt unsafe until we reached Knoxville, Tennessee. Following what some perceived to be threatening remarks from a caller on a local right-wing radio show the morning of our event there, as well as perceived incitement from the host, we actually had to request police protection at our public event that evening. Our appearance on that radio show went quite well otherwise, and the host even asked if he could take a photo of Jarrod and me and put it up on the show's website because he was so shocked that we didn't "look gay" but rather "looked like we belonged in the military." During a break the producer even came in the studio and told us they had more callers waiting in queue to comment or ask a question than they had ever had for any previous show. But as soon as we were done with that hour-long interview, an uneasiness settled over us, and for the first and only time I felt quite nervous about exiting the building and walking to our vehicle.

While we didn't end up having an incident at our guarded event in Knoxville that evening, we did succeed in getting quite a few rabid opponents to show up, in addition to a good mix of supporters and neutral folks, including straight local veterans. In fact, one straight veteran stood up at the beginning of the Q&A at the end of the event that night and told us that he had been a Special Forces operator in the army for eighteen years. As Admiral Steinman later told us, this was the moment he always feared at each event, when someone with solid "grunt" credentials would stand up and declare that known homosexuality in "real" military units would never fly. This guy, however, remarkably and memorably declared that he would be "honored, honored, honored" to serve with any one of us, openly gay or not. That declaration surely muted what might have been an otherwise hostile ganging up on us by a number of other audience members who had clearly turned out to debate.

But the testimonial from the eighteen-year Special Forces veteran, who surely had more than twenty years of total army service, didn't stop the hating from the young religious fundamentalists who turned up. Evidently some students from a local Christian college had heard the morning right-wing radio broadcast about gays in the military and the event coming up that evening. We knew the debate was about to get good when one of them introduced their trio by announcing, "You have been saying that you encourage those with opposing views to speak up. We are now here to provide you with those opposing views."

The resulting twenty-minute set of exchanges, although polite, was unsurprisingly typical of the arguments from the religious right that we would constantly battle over the next five years, including the blatant suggestion that church and state should be joined and that modern civil laws should be based on the reactionary interpretations of biblical law favored by the individual doing the pontificating. To me, this line of thought is not only unwise but downright un-American, and it should be unequivocally treated as such. As I once blurted out on one of those right-wing talk radio shows, if someone wants to live in a theocracy, then he should move to Saudi Arabia or Iran.

The rest of the Call to Duty Tour carried on in much the same manner, albeit with a little less drama than in the first few weeks. As we settled into a rhythm, we learned how to turn out bigger crowds, how to score more local media for the issue, and how to blow out the entire electrical system of an SUV by overloading it with multiple plugged-in laptops on the road. Twice. Over the next several weeks, the snow of Nebraska—where we got stuck for three days in North Platte—gave way to a gorgeous early spring as we rolled through Texas, Arizona, and Utah, up to Seattle, and down the Pacific coast in the final leg, and seventh straight week, of the tour.

Two days before a scheduled event at Stanford, DC–based lobbyist Mark Glaze called my cell to ask if we had time to squeeze in a side trip to Sacramento. Several weeks before, Jarrod and I had run into his boss, Robert Raben, with Daniel Zingale, then chief of staff to California first lady Maria Shriver, on the street in DC. After introducing us by name briefly, Zingale asked Raben who we were, to which Raben jokingly responded, "Oh, I'll explain later." Although we didn't think much of it at the time, evidently he did explain later, and Zingale wanted to arrange a meeting for us with Governor Arnold Schwarzenegger while we were in California. Glaze called that week just in time to catch us while we were in the state and only an hour away from Sacramento. Naturally, we jumped at the opportunity to meet with and lobby a moderate and highly influential Republican governor about possibly endorsing repeal.

Jarrod was particularly excited to meet Arnold Schwarzenegger because he had become rather dedicated to fitness and bodybuilding during his last year in the army. Jarrod was in the best shape of his life at the time, and he confessed that it had always been a dream of his to get workout tips from Schwarzenegger. But when we finally did meet the governor, I could nearly see the fumes coming out of Jarrod's ears when Schwarzenegger entered the room, shook my hand before his, and remarked in his deep Austrian accent while shaking my hand, "Wow. Big arms." I rarely worked out then, and Jarrod even teased me for being a slacker about going to the gym. But in my prime I always just appeared somewhat built because of my frame, and the fitted polo with muscled sleeves evidently gave the Governor the impression that I worked out more than I did. When he got to Jarrod, he just shook his hand and said, "Nice to meet you." The look on Jarrod's face told me that he was pissed and that I was in trouble for stealing his moment.

We spoke with Schwarzenegger for a good twenty minutes or so about DADT, on which he was largely uninformed. When Admiral Steinman routinely mentioned that, among other things, the law meant that gay and lesbian servicemembers had to remain celibate, Schwarzenegger exclaimed, "What? You mean you can't have sex?" It was another one of those "duh" moments when we all realized that the "Don't Ask, Don't Tell" concept, which seemed so reasonable and rational to most people but was much more far-reaching and intrusive, was just as misunderstood in the political class as in the general population.

At the end of the meeting, Schwarzenegger again went around the room and shook hands with each of us vets. When he got to me, he memorably poked me again by saying, "Keep pumping." We all laughed, then he shook Jarrod's hand next and said nothing. As soon as we left the state capitol building, Jarrod let out a rousing, "That was complete horses—t!" I had to hear it all the way back to Palo Alto, but I just took it. We all got a good laugh out of the whole thing in the end.

After a predictably friendly event the next day before a packed house at Stanford Law School, a staff member at the Naval Postgraduate School (NPS) arranged for us to come talk to a large auditorium of senior military officers there before heading down to our final tour stop in San Diego. In order to squeeze in the NPS event, we had to give up about five hours of travel time in an already tight schedule that final week. We had to be in San Diego bright and early at nine the following morning for the first of four two-hundred-plus-person events, but of course we couldn't pass up the opportunity to do an event at the prestigious military graduate school in Monterey. So we just threw caution to the wind in those last two days of the tour, did the NPS event that evening, drove seven hours to San Diego, got two hours of sleep, and dragged our corpses over to the University of California at San Diego campus the next morning. In that final day alone, we talked DADT to more than a thousand people in person and to hundreds of thousands in the San Diego area through the various local and regional television interviews we did between events throughout the day.

That evening, some local vets threw us a big end-of-tour party in Hillcrest, for which we were very appreciative. But after seven weeks on the road, thirty events in twenty cities, more than three thousand people engaged in person, over three hundred media pieces on television and in print, seven hours of driving the night before, and only two hours of sleep before a full day of events and interviews, all I wanted to do that last night was sleep. So after just one more hour of obligatory socializing, the Call to Duty Tour ended and I could finally wrap up my involvement in this crazy world of political advocacy and go back to my normal life as planned.

But considering how successful the Call to Duty Tour had been across the country, and how much sheer enthusiasm we'd found for something, anything, that could get more people inspired and involved in the movement, we were forced to reconsider whether we could just let things return to the status quo. Even though they were doing good work in their respective areas, a handful of DC lawyers, professional activists, and academics simply couldn't organize a true movement of those actually impacted by DADT and generate mass participation on the scale that would be needed to move us out of the doldrums.

Thus, out of the momentum of this initial project was born Servicemembers United, an ongoing national organization whose purpose was to recruit and organize those actually impacted by the issue and place them front and center in the movement to educate politicians, thought leaders, and the general public on the realities of DADT as law and policy. Servicemembers United, however, would not just seek to have us serve as case studies, stories, and spokespeople but also fight to finally give us a seat at the table in Washington, a true voice in the debate and the negotiations to end DADT. Much later, when the political fight was at its peak, I would often look around the room in a critical White House or Capitol Hill meeting only to realize that if I were not there, not a single person impacted by this policy would have been in the room to directly influence the direction of the issue with the nation's most powerful political leaders.

4

★ ★ ★ ★ ★

NEW PARTNERSHIPS

Back in March 2003, the full might of the US military rolled across the border from Kuwait into Iraq to begin the land invasion to topple Saddam Hussein's regime. Three hours into that invasion, a marine vehicle convoy stopped just inside Iraq for what should have been just a brief period. As the marines waited for the convoy to start up again, Staff Sergeant Eric Alva dismounted his vehicle and opened an MRE, the US military's prepackaged meal, to grab a bite to eat during the respite. Alva quickly realized that he had forgotten something in his vehicle, and he walked back around the vehicle to retrieve it—but along a slightly different path. To this day he does not remember what forgotten item prompted him to walk back. Before Alva reached his Humvee, his footsteps triggered a land mine buried in the Iraqi desert. In the massive explosion that followed, Staff Sergeant Eric Fidelis Alva of San Antonio, Texas, became the first US servicemember injured in the Iraq War.

Although a number of his fellow marines knew that he was gay, none of the marines in Alva's unit hesitated to come to his aid that day in Iraq. Along with several fellow marines who were injured by subsequent land mine detonations, Alva was rushed back to a military hospital in Kuwait, where one of his legs had to be amputated above the knee to keep him alive. After his condition stabilized, Alva was transferred to a military hospital in Germany and then on to Walter Reed Army Medical Center outside of Washington, DC, to recover. Everyone from President and Mrs. Bush to Donald Rumsfeld to the Marine Corps commandant visited Staff Sergeant Alva in his hospital bed at Walter Reed. *People* magazine profiled him and Oprah Winfrey covered his recovery on her show.

After moving back home to San Antonio and trying to resume his life as a medical retiree, Eric met and began dating a man named Darrell Parsons. Darrell had been a member of the Human Rights Campaign, and he suggested to Eric that he should consider getting in touch with HRC because of the notoriety he had obtained as the first injured US servicemember in the Iraq War. Eric had made the national media rounds once already, but he had naturally remained publicly closeted. Eric eventually relented and decided to send an e-mail to someone at HRC to introduce himself.

He chose to contact HRC's communications director at the time, Brad Luna, with what came across as an oddly formal e-mail from a polite former marine from Texas. "Dear Mr. Luna," the e-mail began, as Eric and Brad would both jokingly mock later. Immediately realizing the value of the e-mail he had just received, Luna went to David Smith, vice president of programs (i.e., policy and strategy) at HRC, and told him that he would never believe the message he had just received.

Smith, who effectively controlled HRC, had never been fond of Dixon Osburn, who ran the show down the street at SLDN. SLDN would normally have been the obvious place for Eric to go to get publicly involved in advocacy work, but, as luck would have it for HRC, Eric's partner, Darrell, had only been familiar with HRC. Smith, surely recognizing the coup that it would be to have such a star DADT repeal advocate all to themselves, agreed to fly Eric out to Washington to meet with senior HRC staff. From that point on, Eric and HRC cemented a partnership that would carry both of them through repeal.

Nearly four years after his injury in Iraq ended his career as an active marine, Eric publicly came out as a gay man via a round of national print and television media. By doing so, he showed America that the first person injured in the Iraq War was not only gay but was out to many of his peers who rushed to his aid when that land mine went off in the Iraqi desert on the first day of the war back in 2003.

Eric became a strong and valuable—and largely exclusive—HRC advocacy and fundraising asset in the years to follow. HRC would fly Eric around the country to appear at ritzy gala dinner after ritzy gala dinner, and Eric would regale enthralled HRC audiences with his compelling war story and his testimonial for equality. The primary thought I had about the whole deal at the time was "Go, Eric!" As far as I was concerned, HRC should have just given him the whole damn organization. He deserved every bit of what he was getting from HRC and more, and HRC had it to give. Eric seemed to genuinely enjoy becoming a public advocate for LGBT equality at the time, and HRC provided him with a great platform to further a cause that had clearly become very important to him.

While Eric's intentions were certainly good, you would be hard-pressed to find a soul who would argue that HRC's intentions with Eric were entirely altruistic. Eric was doing what he was doing for the right reasons, but HRC was clearly using Eric as a major fundraising tool for the organization and as a way to make HRC relevant in the growing national debate on the DADT issue. A number of SLDN staff and board members were quite livid over the fact that HRC had "landed" Eric and SLDN had not. I once asked Eric why he never went to SLDN to do his advocacy work, and he innocently responded at the time that no one from SLDN had ever asked him to do anything for them.

Given that HRC so clearly and boldly had proclaimed Eric to be an excusive HRC asset, it is not surprising that SLDN didn't dare try to "steal" him away, as it surely would have been seen by HRC. In the months that followed, SLDN tried desperately to find stars of its own. When a US Navy Hebrew linguist, Jason Knight, wrote a piece for the overseas military newspaper *Stars and Stripes* saying that he had been discharged under DADT but accepted back into the navy and deployed to Kuwait as an openly gay sailor, clearly an administrative oversight on the navy's part in calling him back to duty, SLDN seized on the opportunity to try to "land" Knight and hold on to him tight.

SLDN expended quite a bit of effort promoting Knight and his curious story, and its communications director even put out an e-mail blast to SLDN's supporters pronouncing that Knight and his story were "exclusive" to SLDN, prompting several board members to remark to me that they had never seen SLDN use such possessive language in reference to one of its clients before. Indeed, the whole situation was quite strange and desperate on SLDN's part, but the organization's leadership certainly felt a great deal of pressure given the mainstream celebrity that Eric Alva was generating—all while standing in front of an HRC logo.

Shortly before Eric Alva came onto the scene, another marine named Tony Agnone was deployed to Iraq as a combat engineer platoon leader. First Lieutenant Agnone's job was to find, dig up, and destroy enemy munitions that could be used to make improvised explosive devices (IEDs). While Tony was in Iraq, his partner, Brandon, saw the cover of the *Advocate* magazine on which I had appeared and sent it over to Tony to read. When he returned from deployment, Tony and Brandon looked me up on the Internet and reached out to me via e-mail. Tony wanted to vent and seek advice about a problem he was having with a first sergeant in his unit, and through subsequent conversations about the issue Jarrod and I became friends with him and his partner. Tony was especially interested in getting more involved in DADT advocacy work after he got out of the Marine Corps, so Jarrod and I stopped over in Wilmington, North Carolina, one weekend while Tony was still stationed at Camp Lejeune to get to know the two better.

While staying with Tony and Brandon that weekend, I asked Tony one night where the bathroom soap was and he yelled from another room to look under the sink. When I opened the cabinet door, I suddenly caught a vision of a gay man's dream—a view of what looked like an Aveda outlet store underneath his bathroom sink. I was more than a little baffled as to why he had dozens of bottles of Aveda soap and body wash and shampoo and conditioner and lotions and more underneath a sink in his apartment, so I just had to ask. The explanation, as it would turn out, was even more amusing.

When Tony was stationed in Iraq, family members of the marines in his combat engineering unit would send over care packages for the unit, as was the case with most units. Tony said he walked into a room one day at their compound and saw rows upon rows of Aveda products laid out on a table. Being a gay man, Tony naturally had the same reaction to the sight that I did. As it turned out, the mother of one of his marines was an executive with Aveda and regularly sent over boxes of skincare and bath products to his unit. None of the marines wanted any of the "foo foo" Aveda products, so Tony surreptitiously scooped them all up and stockpiled them to take back home. For who knows how many months or years after he returned from Iraq, Tony's guests never had a pore problem while they stayed with him and Brandon.

After Tony finished up his obligation to the marines, he and Brandon moved to Washington, DC, and Tony began interning as a policy advocate for the Human Rights Campaign around the same time that Eric Alva went public. Meanwhile, the presidential primary season was also beginning to heat up. Although we had no delusions about getting all presidential primary candidates to come out in favor of repealing DADT, we did have a realistic hope of getting all of the Democratic candidates to declare support for repeal. So Tony (who began going by his full first name of Antonio once he got out of the marines and started working at HRC), Jarrod, and I began working on a plan to get HRC to pay for us to do another nationwide publicity tour for the DADT issue in advance of the presidential primary fights.

With Eric now helping to raise interest in the DADT issue within HRC's ultraliberal membership base, HRC's David Smith naturally saw this as a good way to continue to utilize Eric and to also further cement HRC's ties to that outside group of young servicemembers and veterans that had done so much high-profile, public DADT advocacy work around the country the year before. Smith readily agreed to have HRC pay for us to do another DADT tour largely identical to the one we had done the year before. However, with HRC footing the bill for our entire tour this time, they insisted that it be branded exclusively with HRC's logo.

Even though we would be doing the majority of the planning and using our people to carry out the work, it didn't really bother us at the time that HRC wanted to make this second tour look like an HRC-only initiative. The important thing to us was that the work that we thought needed desperately to get done was actually going to get done. Thus began a partnership between Servicemembers United and HRC that would have its highs and lows, its share of successes and betrayals, and a thorough education in the realities of organizational politics.

The Legacy of Service Tour, our second major national publicity tour for the DADT issue, launched in early June 2007 in Des Moines, Iowa. Shortly before the start of our first event, which was held at the Iowa Historical Society in downtown Des Moines, an Associated Press news photographer wanted to get a casual-looking photo of a few of us vets sitting around the building getting ready for the kick-off. As Jarrod, Antonio, and I sat down together side by side on a wide staircase in the building lobby so that the photographer could snap his photo, an HRC communications staffer ran over and hurriedly handed each of us a folder containing the event's press release and our speaker bios. I found the move rather strange, but we just held onto the folders while the photographer started snapping. I didn't realize the underhanded brilliance of the move until later when I saw the AP photo all over the web. There we were, the three of us casually sitting there with the HRC logo on the front of those folders prominently visible in the picture.

This first event was very well attended; guests included the state senate's majority leader, Mike Gronstal, former Iowa governor Tom Vilsack and his wife, and representatives from the Iowa operations of every major Democratic presidential campaign. But the audience wasn't really the mix we wanted to target. Whereas we had always tried to draw out a typical demographic slice of the local area in which we were doing an event, this event, like many to come in which HRC was involved, was attended almost entirely by staunch supporters of repeal. While we certainly appreciated their support, I'm not sure that HRC needed to spend tens of thousands of dollars to solidify that support. It was more of an upscale pep rally than a true town hall event, but given that our overarching goal was to make some noise in the state ahead of the Democratic presidential primary debates and caucuses, we were satisfied with the event's outcome.

As turned out to be the case with much of the work we did with HRC, where we went on this tour ended up being dictating by the wishes and whims of its donors more than the needs of the issue. So while we still made it to three of the top four early presidential primary states—Iowa, New Hampshire, and Nevada—we also had to add in additional trips to the states in which local HRC fundraising clubs griped the most about not being included on the tour schedule, as if we were doing this as entertainment. I begged to add a South Carolina stop too, since it's an incredibly influential early primary state and I know the state well, being from there and all, but HRC didn't have a strong fundraising base in the state; it being a smart place to do an event alone just wasn't enough. We soon found out that the smart thing or the right thing to do was rarely the primary driving force behind what HRC's senior staff wanted to do.

As the Legacy of Service Tour continued, it became less and less of an effective advocacy tool for DADT repeal and more and more of an HRC throw-our-members-a-bone type of show. I remember at one point finally coming to terms with the fact that the whole event series had gotten away from its original intent—to educate audiences about the facets of DADT and to raise awareness about the issue for the purpose of bringing it back onto the national policy stage—and had devolved almost entirely into an HRC self-promotional campaign. The events had become extremely costly—unnecessarily so—and, more important, they had become extremely cost ineffective. Whereas the Call to Duty Tour had been a highly effective, strategic, and targeted national initiative on a shoestring budget, the Legacy of Service Tour was little more than an expensive series of vacations with occasional military-themed meet-and-greets with HRC members thrown in.

Even though we were putting on the show every time, with HRC in control of the purse and logistical strings I was powerless to renegotiate the terms midway through the tour. So I finally gave up trying to do battle with the HRC side of the house and decided just to treat the remainder of the summer like one big vacation. I decided to stop stressing about doing the right thing and simply enjoy the cocktail parties and the dinners and the free travel. The worst of it, from a moral standpoint, was a post-event dinner that HRC staff asked us go to at one stop for which the bill just for the tour participants alone totaled more than $600, all on HRC's dime.

The financial waste was beyond belief, but I had no sway left over that. Even back then, the little fighting of this waste and abuse that I did try to do left me exhausted and bruised. So I thought, if this is what HRC members want, if this is what they condone by their choice to feed this organization more and more money every year, then who am I to fight it? That thick steak was damn good that night, after all, so thank you very much.

Despite the difficulties with HRC, the group was nevertheless the gay community's primary repository of organizational money. In other words, if you wanted anything done without a fundraising base of your own, that's where you had to go. The staff of SLDN, which had a few dollars but not nearly as much as HRC, had been hostile from the beginning of our existence anyway, so when I got the idea one day to do a big commemorative event on the National Mall in Washington, DC, for those who had been discharged under DADT, naturally I approached HRC again to help me finance the idea.

In Dahlonega, Georgia, where I was living at the time while attending North Georgia College and pursuing a master's degree in public administration, the town lined its main roads with American flags for about a week on either side of each Memorial Day and Veterans Day. It was quite a beautiful sight twice each year. One day during this display I noticed that the town also affixed small nameplates to each flagpole, one for each resident of the town who had served in the military. From this, the idea occurred to me to find some way to erect one American flag for each servicemember who had been discharged under the DADT law. When I thought about where to do this, the grassy expanse of the National Mall was the only place I could picture that many flags both fitting and fitting in. I ran the idea by Jarrod, who was hesitant about the logistical nightmare that such an idea would inevitably entail, but the aura of impossibility or a lack of precedent had never deterred me before, and I decided to move forward with the scheme.

Over the summer of 2007, I negotiated financing of the project with HRC and LCR, and with a little arm-twisting by HRC, I even got SLDN to play along and pitch in. I was later told by another senior HRC staff member that HRC wasn't keen on doing another big DADT project, but when David Smith realized that I was moving forward on it with or without HRC, the organization wanted to be on board and agreed to pitch in a share of money. Of course, HRC being involved in a partnership, we had learned the hard way by this point, meant that it wanted to be the dominant and most visible partner, regardless of its share of the budget or the effort. And as far as its membership was concerned, it wanted to be seen as the only partner. To this day, I still run across ill-informed individuals who try to tell me all about "HRC's 12,000-flags event on the National Mall." I still cringe every time I hear such misinformation about our community's history, but I also know that sometimes it's just simply not their fault that they don't know these things. HRC went quite far out of its way to give everyone who would listen the impression that this was an HRC event—violating explicit co-branding agreements in the process.

Of course, what I eventually named the "12,000 Flags for 12,000 Patriots" event on the National Mall was conceived, designed, implemented, and led by Servicemembers United. I oversaw the logistics, I called the shots, I led the press conference with the unprecedented display—a rolling field of red, white, and blue—in the background, but once again HRC tried to do everything it could to brand it an HRC event, both overtly and covertly. But it certainly wasn't just HRC, and it wasn't even just Servicemembers United and HRC. SLDN, realizing that this was going to be an impressive event right on their doorstep, atypically agreed to come on board, play along, and pay up to help put the show on. For the Call to Duty Tour, SLDN had wanted to pay one-tenth of what the other organizations had paid to help finance it, yet it wanted exclusive and sole branding of the entire event as a condition. But by the time the "12,000 Flags" event came around in late 2007, SLDN had a new leader and less baggage than before.

The SLDN cofounder and executive director who had been so hostile to us in the beginning had recently and suddenly been sacked by the organization's board of directors, and fellow South Carolina native Aubrey Sarvis, a former Senate staffer and telecommunications lobbyist, had been hired to replace him. Aubrey was significantly older than virtually everyone else working on DADT, and he did not exude the militaristic look or bearing that many assumed SLDN's board would look for in a spokesperson for their organization moving forward. Rather, Aubrey came across as quite "old school." Nevertheless, he was the new face of SLDN, and they were now ever so slightly nicer to us, so we rolled with it.

SLDN agreed to help sponsor our event on the National Mall, and so I agreed to let Aubrey join me, as Servicemembers United's executive director, along with HRC's president, Joe Solmonese, and LCR's executive director, Patrick Sammon, for the press conference on the DADT issue in front of the display of flags on November 30, 2007—the fourteenth anniversary of the signing of the DADT law by President Clinton. We were also flanked by several other gay and lesbian veterans I had asked to join us, as well as two straight retired flag officers, Major General Dennis Laich and Major General Alexander Burgin. While the "12,000 Flags for 12,000 Patriots" display was impressive enough, intended to be one flag for every servicemember discharged under DADT at that point in time, the real news hook for the press conference was the generals.

Aaron Belkin of the Palm Center had identified twenty-eight flag officers by then who agreed to publicly call for the repeal of DADT. Before that point, there had really only been three flag officers who had publicly and prominently called for the repeal of the DADT law, and they were all gay. The twenty-eight that Belkin had in reserve for a great PR moment like this was quite a coup, and I was delighted that he approached me about using our event to go public with the names. Naturally, I agreed, and the result was an event and press conference for the DADT issue unlike any that had been seen before. "Twelve Thousand Flags for 12,000 Patriots" was unprecedented, and the visual impact of all of those flags firmly planted in the ground and waving on the National Mall has provided great patriotic stock photography ever since.

But one thing many people don't know is that most of the photos you see of the "twelve thousand flags" aren't actually of all twelve thousand. We ordered that many flags, and we put all of them up in an even grid across the Mall between Seventh and Fourteenth Streets the day before the press conference. Jarrod and I started setting out the string grid and putting up the first flags by ourselves at about 8 AM on November 29, and more and more scheduled volunteers joined us to help put up flags throughout the day. We personally oversaw the installation of the first five thousand beginning on Fourteenth Street and working eastward toward Seventh Street, but after that first batch was erected I had to go attend to other logistical matters related to the three-day series of events, leaving others in charge of installing the remaining seven thousand flags.

When I returned late that evening to check on progress, I was stunned to see that hundreds of American flags had fallen over throughout the grid because of shoddy and shallow installation. The first five thousand were still perfect, but the rest were substandard. And what was worse, the volunteers who were still there installing the last few hundreds flags, all interns who had been "voluntold" by HRC to come help set up flags, were continuing to just lightly plop flags down into the dirt, severely underutilizing the metal ground-insertion attachments that accompanied each flag and that had kept the first five thousand so sturdy and erect. The new flags fell over almost as fast as these lax interns put them in the ground.

I was beyond embarrassed. I was actually quite mortified. By now it was about 11 PM and we had a major press conference the following morning in front of this pitiful display. All I could think about was someone tipping off Fox News and the network sending one of its cameras down there to create the headline "Gay Activists Disrespect American Flag All Over National Mall." I immediately called the HRC staffer in charge of the volunteers and asked him to return to the Mall. When he got there, all I got was, "Well, it's done now. There's nothing we can we do about it except straighten up as many as we can." So for a few minutes, we tried righting them, but with the wind picking up late that night, the hundreds of overturned flags turned into thousands. Those first five thousand, however, stayed firmly put.

I had had enough at this point. I felt angry and frustrated at what these slack volunteers had let happen. I had trusted them to do a decent job and had trusted their supervisors to ensure that they did. Not all of the volunteers that day did sloppy work. In fact, you could see patches of flags that were installed correctly and held up to the wind as planned. But too many were sloppily installed for us to risk a devastating visual behind the press conference the following day, so I made the call about midnight that all seven thousand flags in the second grouping had to come up. With all of the volunteers gone already, however, it ended up being me, Jarrod, the HRC staffer, and a good friend of mine from New York City who had come down for our event the following day who together de-installed those seven thousand flags. A good number of random passersby came over and volunteered to help us take up flags too, and from midnight until about 3 AM we gathered up seven thousand American flags and packaged them back up.

The following morning, there were so many flags still left out on the National Mall in a perfect grid—five thousand is still quite a large number—that few noticed that the full twelve thousand weren't there. Adding to our fortune was the fact that the National Mall sloped upward slightly heading east from Fourteenth Street and then back downward at about the exact point that our first grouping of five thousand flags ended, so from the beginning of the display where the press conference was held you couldn't really even tell if there were zero flags beyond that hill or a million flags. All you could see was just a sea of red, white, and blue behind us as I launched into one of the most significant, successful, and well-staged major press events the DADT issue had seen thus far.

5

* * * * *

HEARINGS AND ELECTIONS

The DADT issue was indeed gaining momentum, but slowly, over the course of years. In 2004, two lawsuits had been filed in federal court challenging the constitutionality of the DADT law. In 2005, Congressman Marty Meehan had introduced a repeal bill, the Military Readiness Enhancement Act; it was, of course, going nowhere in the Republican-led Congress, but it was at least a step in the right direction. In 2006, we'd revitalized the grassroots movement with the unprecedented Call to Duty Tour, following that up in 2007 with the Legacy of Service Tour and the "12,000 Flags for 12,000 Patriots" event. But that pace would soon accelerate.

After the "12,000 Flags" event in November 2007, Servicemembers United made the strategic decision to lay low throughout the highly charged general presidential election of 2008. Our forte had become going into moderate and conservative areas of the country and challenging the locals to face the realities of DADT head on, but we were advised that if we kept it up, it could potentially make gays in the military into a wedge issue in the general election. In addition, the money to work on DADT from our past organizational funders was running dry as everyone diverted most of their giving to the historic presidential contest. During this period of downtime, Jarrod and I both finished up our degrees at North Georgia College and enrolled at my alma mater, the University of South Carolina; he pursued a master's in international relations and I a doctorate in political science with a focus on interest groups and social movements.

But one significant DADT-related event did occur in 2008. Susan Davis, a Democratic congresswoman from San Diego and chair of the Military Personnel Subcommittee of the House Armed Services Committee (after it changed to Democratic control following the 2006 elections), agreed to hold the first congressional hearing on DADT in the law's then-fifteen-year history. Since SLDN and HRC were the only two major players on this issue in Washington at the time, Congresswoman Davis's office naturally went to those organizations, primarily SLDN, for help with putting together a witness panel for the hearing.

Since at the time Servicemembers United was still almost exclusively a grassroots organization, I wasn't yet in the inner Washington political loop. I wasn't even aware that a hearing was in the works until I got a call one afternoon from a highly ticked-off Aaron Belkin. Belkin gave me a heads-up that he had heard about this hearing, although he was clearly frustrated that he had been effectively elbowed out of the subcommittee's witness selection process by SLDN.

Witness selection for a Capitol Hill hearing is a big deal. Being a witness can make someone into an instant mini-celebrity within an issue community, and if a witness is affiliated with an organization, then the entire process can serve as a major publicity boost for that organization. The major national newspapers and cable television shows all want to land star congressional witnesses following a big hearing, and that can serve as another opportunity for self-promotion by the organizations that are stage-managing or handling those who wind up testifying.

Belkin was continuing to expand his list of straight generals and admirals who supported the repeal of DADT, so he had some great potential witnesses in his pocket. Among them was a retired Marine Corps general whose credentials alone, without him saying one word, would have made for a revolutionary appearance before the Military Personnel Subcommittee. Belkin also had several other great potential witnesses within his grasp who would have fit in very well with what we, through our work on the ground across the country, had found to be the most effective messages and messengers. Belkin's colleague at the Palm Center, Dr. Nathaniel Frank, had done some truly amazing work for the DADT repeal effort over the years that really had gone a long way to putting the Palm Center on the map. In the course of doing research for his groundbreaking book *Unfriendly Fire*, Frank had tracked down, met, and interviewed hundreds of servicemembers who had been impacted by DADT, and one category of discharged servicemembers that he kept running across over and over again was linguists.

The Defense Language Institute in Monterey, California, is where most military linguists train in languages critical to US security interests. For anyone who's been through there, it's often remembered as a little slice of heaven that they look back on fondly. But there was something about Monterey that seemed to make it excessively gay, or so the jokes went. No one knows if it's the beautiful weather, the relaxed campus-like atmosphere of the duty station, its proximity to San Francisco, or, as the joke always continued, "something in the water," but the Defense Language Institute always seemed to be a place that attracted a lot of gays and lesbians—meaning that the institute was producing lots of gay and lesbian linguists.

Language training at Monterey for the most critical languages, including Arabic, Farsi, Chinese, and Korean, can take up anywhere from a year and a half to two years of a servicemember's enlistment, costing the government a pretty penny and making those servicemembers into valuable public assets. So when Nathaniel Frank kept coming across linguist after linguist who had been discharged pursuant to DADT, he began to see a potentially valuable new line of argument to use in the then-dormant public debate over DADT. When the news broke in 2002 that seven Arabic linguists had been fired at one time from the Defense Language Institute because they had been found to be gay or lesbian, Frank had brilliantly pushed the story out to the mainstream media and succeeded in shining a bright national spotlight on this practice of spending millions of dollars training critically needed linguists and then discharging them because they were gay or lesbian.

Frank would go on to find and interview dozens more gay linguists and intelligence personnel, including yours truly, for his book, and this roster of highly qualified, taxpayer-trained, critical personnel was at the Palm Center's disposal in the summer of 2008 when the witness panel for Congresswoman Davis's hearing was being assembled. However, SLDN wasn't too keen on giving away witness seats to potential witnesses who were seen as another organization's contacts. When Belkin threatened to submit his own list of witness recommendations to the subcommittee staff, Aubrey Sarvis, SLDN's executive director, freaked out and tried to convince Belkin not to go around SLDN. Belkin, however, was adamant, knowing that the witnesses he had to recommend, including the Marine Corps general and some of the highly skilled discharged Arabic linguists who had enthralled America several years before, were right up there with anyone SLDN could produce and should at least have a chance to be considered by the subcommittee staff.

But Sarvis still wasn't about to let the Palm Center take one or more of those coveted witness slots. He finally convinced Belkin to submit his separate witness recommendations through SLDN. Belkin, however, remained highly skeptical that any of his witness recommendations would ever make it beyond Sarvis's inbox, and he was very likely right.

One organization that SLDN could not brush aside in this process was the Human Rights Campaign. Several factors worked to ensure that HRC got one of the three pro-repeal witness slots by default: HRC had much more extensive contacts and had done much more work on

Capitol Hill over the years; it had a much larger bank account; and it had nearly exclusive control of the most widely known DADT advocate of them all, Eric Alva.

Alva was a solid choice for a witness at this historic hearing. No one else had the mainstream name and story recognition that he did at the time, and the fact that some of his unit members knew or suspected he was gay when he was injured on the first day of the Iraq War was a powerful testimonial to the argument we always put forward: that no one would care if they knew they were serving and fighting alongside gays. It was just a fortunate coincidence for us as a community that the best person that HRC could come up with was actually a solid witness recommendation, because few would dispute that HRC would still have been pushing one of its own exclusive assets for one of the witness slots even if that person hadn't made the best, most convincing, or most qualified witness. The opportunity for organizational promotion, media, and political prominence would have just been too tempting for the organization to pass up.

Although this scenario didn't come to pass with HRC at this particular hearing, there is a very strong case to be made that it did with SLDN. As mentioned earlier, Aaron Belkin at the Palm Center was actively lobbying to get excellent witnesses considered from his own contact list, but, according to Belkin, SLDN's Sarvis was still resistant. It's unknown whether SLDN even put forward more recommendations than the two who were ultimately selected for the remaining pro-repeal witness slots, but of those two witnesses, only one was solid; the other was a less-than-optimal recommendation as a witness for this hearing.

The stronger of the two was Major General Vance Coleman, who was called to make the case for repeal from the perspective of a flag officer. Major General Coleman, a retired army two-star, began his thirty-plus-year military career as a private in a segregated unit before being selected for Officer Candidate School and rising through the officer ranks through desegregation and beyond. While Major General

Coleman was a formidable witness, he was not the *most* formidable witness we could have put forward as a community. The Marine Corps general that Belkin had access to would have made a much stronger candidate to make the same case, but Coleman had two characteristics that Belkin's Marine Corps general did not. First, Major General Coleman was a member of SLDN's Military Advisory Council, which meant that SLDN could claim "SLDN Advisory Council Member Testifies Before House Armed Services Committee."

Second, Coleman was African American. The hearing was scheduled to coincide with the date on which President Truman had issued Executive Order 9981, which required the armed forces to end the racial segregation of its units. Clearly the hearing architects planned to play up the issues of civil rights and fairness at the hearing, and having an African American witness in Major General Coleman, and a Latino witness in Eric Alva, played right into that goal. Unfortunately, the civil rights parallel would turn out not to be one of our stronger lines of argument in the debate, whereas addressing the Marine Corps culture and concerns would have been.

In keeping with the strategy of highlighting the civil rights parallels, the third witness was a woman, retired navy captain Joan Darrah. Darrah was—go figure—a member of SLDN's board of directors and a diehard SLDNite. Although she was a very nice person with a distinguished navy career, she was nowhere near one of the best candidates for the extremely limited witness slots at the first-ever hearing on DADT repeal. While Darrah had a great story that played well with the media—she had been in the area of the Pentagon hit on 9/11, and had she died, her lesbian partner would not have been notified of her death—this was nevertheless not the story that those we needed to convince at that time in the political arena needed to hear.

The main problem was bringing up partner benefits. Darrah's story was mainly about the fact that her partner could not receive recognition or benefits because of DADT. But a repeal of DADT would not have fixed most of her issues, since the military would still have been prohibited from providing benefits for gay and lesbian partners by the Defense of Marriage Act (DOMA). Furthermore, one of the biggest arguments our opponents successfully used against us with moderates was the "slippery slope." In other words, if you repeal DADT, a pretty moderate request, that would surely lead to the provision of benefits to their partners, a seemingly more extreme request. We always struggled in the public and political DADT repeal discourse to defer the question of that possibility for fear of alienating moderate support, or support from those who were OK with simply allowing gays and lesbians to serve but who were not yet OK with giving benefits to same-sex partners or with (gasp!) gay marriage. Yet here SLDN was putting forth someone whose main talking point highlighted exactly this possibility. There were certainly hundreds more well-qualified individuals with distinguished service records who could have served that witness role at our first-ever opportunity to make the case for repeal in the House, but none would have the opportunity that afternoon because of organizational territorialism and politics.

(Coincidentally, Servicemembers United would later go on to build the first initiative to reach out to and support the partners of gay military personnel. And while this angle was always intriguing to media, it never helped us any with the moderate or conservative lawmakers whose votes we desperately needed to secure repeal.)

On the other side of the table were the opposition witnesses. Since the Democrats controlled the House and, therefore, its committees and subcommittees, the pro-repeal side got three witness slots while the anti-repeal side—in this case the Republicans—got only two. And there was really only one organization for them to go to for opposition witness selection: the Center for Military Readiness (CMR). "CMR" is almost always said with a smirk, because it is really just code for our community's archnemesis, the leader of the opposition, Elaine Donnelly.

Donnelly is quite a character, and I still to this day can't help but admire her fervor and persistence. Whereas some of the most vociferous issue opponents are still able to remain friendly off camera, Donnelly would have none of it. I have tried many times over the years to throw on the Southern charm and chat her up, and I once even politely invited her to lunch, but she always coldly refused to engage. She declined my lunch invitation via e-mail by saying that others in our community had previously been so mean and rude to her that she just didn't want to take the chance.

Given the intensity of Donnelly's opposition to gays in the military in any capacity whatsoever, not to mention her lies and distortions of fact, it's not hard to imagine how frustrated and angry folks in our community must have grown with her over the years. A protégé of staunch antifeminist conservative Phyllis Schlafly, Donnelly founded and ran CMR largely as a one-woman show from an upstairs bedroom—the "Center," apparently—of her home in Livonia, Michigan, according to one of her organization's advisory board members with whom I met and talked at length about her operation in 2007.

Donnelly herself is a staunch ideologue who also uses CMR to advocate for keeping women out of combat, cockpits, and any other significant militaristic role in the armed forces. She has never served in the military, and her only connection to the defense world at all is a brief stint she served on the Defense Advisory Committee for Women in the Services (DACOWITS). But her policy positions are often so extreme that much of our legitimate opposition was afraid even to be associated with her and CMR. However, Elaine Donnelly was one of the few people left who would forcefully advocate for keeping gays out of the military, so she was always the go-to person for media and for the organization of opposition witness lists for congressional hearings.

For the hearing in 2008, Donnelly of course recommended herself as a witness, but she also brought with her a retired army sergeant major named Brian Jones. I'm sure Jones had seen rough combat in his day, but he appeared totally unprepared for the onslaught of truth and reason brought upon him that day by our allies on the

Military Personnel Subcommittee. By the end of the hearing, I actually felt sorry for him. It just looked as if he had been lured into being there by Donnelly and her hype about the righteousness of her cause, with which he sympathized. But over the course of the hearing he got thoroughly embarrassed by the inconsistencies of his own positions and arguments, and the irrationality and insanity of hers. After that day, we never again saw Sergeant Major Jones appearing in the DADT repeal fight in any significant way.

Donnelly was, of course, in rare form. Always poised and erect with perfectly Aqua-Netted hair, she is the real-life embodiment of everything that comedy personality Betty Bowers mocks. While anyone can rightfully accuse her of twisting facts and data to suit her reactionary agenda, no one can accuse her of not knowing inside and out the facts that she's artfully twisting. Despite her seeming lunacy at times, Donnelly is a formidable opponent for our community, and she has single-handedly carried the flag for the opposition to gays in the military for two decades.

While she may have thought she performed well at that hearing, no one else agreed. One Democratic committee staffer even remarked to me that they might have to help find a good opposition witness for the Republicans next time because the Democrats just tore Donnelly to shreds, and the Republicans wouldn't participate next time if they had to sit through that sort of roasting again.

During the roast, one lawmaker who really stood out above the rest was a conservative freshman Democratic congressman from Pennsylvania named Patrick Murphy. Murphy, a former army officer, had been the first Iraq War veteran elected to Congress, and his credentials made him an automatically credible authority on military personnel issues. Given his relative conservatism on some issues, though, the community had been rather nervous about where he might come down on the issue of repealing the DADT law. As a Blue Dog Democrat, if he came out against us it would have been a huge negative blow to our momentum.

However, Congressman Murphy launched immediately into an aggressive line of questioning against Donnelly at the subcommittee hearing. In a classic moment in DADT history, Murphy asked Donnelly rather bluntly why she thought American servicemembers weren't professional enough to serve beside openly gay men and women like the members of our allied militaries already do. It was his first public shot at DADT and its opponents, and it turned out to be an atomic bomb. Congressman Murphy would later go on to put those skills to work for the cause of DADT repeal in a much more substantive and involved way and with the same serious, aggressive demeanor and highly credible authority as he did that day in late July 2008.

After that first hearing wrapped up, the American political world went from being 99 percent consumed with the presidential election to 100 percent consumed. The stakes were make-or-break for many issues, given the sharp contrast that had been drawn between Republicans and Democrats, but on DADT the contrast could not have been clearer. "It's working, my friends. It's working," became a favorite refrain of Senator John McCain with respect to DADT during his presidential campaign, whereas Senator Obama had promised to be a "fierce advocate" for gay rights and equality during his.

Jarrod and I spent election night with two close friends and SU supporters in Charleston, South Carolina. Earlier in the evening we had attended the near-victory party of another friend, Linda Ketner, who was running for Congress in that district. Ketner lost that night but only by about thirteen thousand votes, which was a huge accomplishment in itself considering the fact that an openly gay woman was running against a four-term incumbent male Republican. But even though that smaller historic victory wasn't to be, a greater one occurred that same evening on a national scale.

As we relaxed in our friend's traditionally southern home on a marsh inlet in Charleston, the place where the Civil War began, we watched the first African American get elected to the presidency of the United States by an overwhelming margin of victory. And given

Senator, now President-elect, Obama's campaign promise to be a "fierce advocate" for gay rights and his public loathing of the DADT law, everyone's expectations were also high that night that DADT's days were now numbered. Election night in 2008 was truly a milestone for many people and on many levels. Hope was indeed in the air.

6

* * * * *

"SERVICEMEMBERS'
MILESTONE"

The election of a pro–open service presidential candidate for the first time in American history ushered in a sense of optimism and expectation within the gay military community, as it did within the wider gay community on other issues and within the even wider progressive community on a portfolio of progressive issues. As of January 20, 2009, we finally had a pro-repeal president combined with a pro-repeal party in control of both chambers of Congress, as well as a solid majority of Americans in favor of the repeal of the DADT law. In theory, the "low-hanging fruit" of the gay rights movement should have been within quick grasp, but the reality of politics, especially the strange world of defense politics, was about to set in.

That same winter, my mother caught a bad case of pneumonia that quickly deteriorated into respiratory failure. She spent a month in a coma at Duke University Hospital, and I spent nearly a month by her side while living out of a hotel in Durham. Despite being anoxic for hours, a condition that would kill most healthy youth, my mother made a complete recovery with no brain damage. After her miraculous recovery and my subsequent move back to Washington, I ended up driving back down to Durham several times to go with her to her follow-up medical appointments. It was on one of those late-night drives from Duke back up to the Beltway that I began thinking long and hard about what to do next with Servicemembers United.

We had built up a great young organization that had already contributed substantially to reinvigorating the DADT repeal movement. Without our efforts, there would have been virtually no grassroots work and nearly no proactive media campaign going on at the time, especially at the local and regional level across the country. More important, those actually affected by DADT would have continued to have no part in planning and strategizing the repeal movement. We would have simply continued to be puppets, carefully stage-managed by the puppet masters when it was convenient, as long as we promised to behave and say exactly what we were told.

What I feared most, however, was that despite how much we had done already to push the repeal movement along, if we went back to our private lives there was no one around to pass the torch to. While we were able to easily recruit young troops and veterans to get involved on an ad hoc basis, these people had lives and always went back to them after doing what we asked of them. And although they kept coming back and doing advocacy work again and again whenever we would ask, no one else was in the unique position that Jarrod and I found ourselves in, once again, to commit to leading a major advocacy effort full time.

Jarrod and I had both just finished up all of our course requirements for graduate school in December 2008 and were both now able to take on full-time work again. So in early February 2008, as I drove north on I-95 heading back to Washington late one night, I came to the realization that if we were going to dive back into the DADT repeal movement full time, then we were going to have to go big or go home. The stakes were now higher. A reputation for creating high-profile, high-impact events and initiatives preceded us, and a window of opportunity existed that never had before. I realized that if we were going to take Servicemembers United to the next level—indeed, if we were going to take the gay military community and those impacted by DADT to the next level—we'd have to open a real, physical, full-time office in Washington, DC, and significantly scale up our operations.

I would be lying if I denied that the thought of diving back into this work full time and making this sort of personal, financial, and reputational investment and commitment frightened me. But the thought of leaving this window of opportunity to the civilian lawyers and academics and professional activists frightened me too. They had always "controlled" our issue, and I firmly believed that those actually affected by DADT should at least have a seat at the table in Washington, if not call the shots on the issue entirely. If we didn't do this now, I knew it just wasn't going to get done. So somewhere on a desolate stretch of interstate south of Richmond, I made the decision to go all in and open a DC office for Servicemembers United. There would be no turning back. It was DADT repeal or bust.

I knew absolutely nothing about office real estate when I started searching for space for SU later that week. Luckily, a few good contacts quickly led me to a number of great options to check out and several reliable donors pitched in to help fund our start-up costs. The following month, we settled into a small but brand-new space on the third floor of a beautiful modern building on I (as in the letter "I") Street in northwest Washington, just two blocks from the White House. While we would scale up to a larger office space on the same floor a year later, 1725 I Street NW became our home for the remainder of the DADT repeal fight.

Those first few months in the new SU office consisted of many long days and late nights to get the organization off the ground and running there in the heart of the lion's den of Washington. Seventeen- and eighteen-hour days were common in the spring of 2009, so we were lucky to have a twenty-four-hour 7-Eleven just a few blocks away on the western edge of George Washington University's campus, at which I became a frequent customer and a connoisseur of Mountain Dew Slurpees to keep me awake.

Back in those days, fundraising to acquire the resources to build a real organization and put it to work took up more than three-quarters of my time as executive director. I hated fundraising, but we were lucky to have developed some great relationships with many people through our work across the country over the past few years, and we had never before asked most of those people for money. So when we finally did come rolling up to cash in, many were happy to donate. Some even asked us what took so long for us to ask them for help. It wasn't until the foundation grant money started coming in, however, that I was finally able to reduce the amount of my time spent fund-raising to below one-quarter and actually concentrate on doing what I loved and did best—organizing, recruiting other young vets to get involved, creating unique and high-impact projects to draw atten-tion to our issue, and helping to push the DADT repeal movement forward.

By late spring, after working proactively to develop relationships with their political reporters, Servicemembers United had started attracting the attention of the DC-area LGBT and progressive media outlets. One of those publications, *Metro Weekly*, wanted to come by SU's new office one day, take some photos of our staff of three work-ing, and do a small feature on our opening of SU's first full-time DC office. When the article, entitled "Servicemembers' Milestone," ran a few weeks later, the reporter immediately received a furious call from SLDN's communications director, who scolded him over the piece. He seemed to take issue with the article's characterization of the DADT repeal movement and how various organizations fit within that move-ment as specialized components of the wider community. I had char-acterized SLDN as a legal services organization at its core, one that was staffed primarily by lawyers and professional activists (which it always was), and Servicemembers United as a grassroots-based organization staffed by veterans that was now moving into the legislative and policy arena. SLDN's PR shop evidently wanted to keep the myth alive that SLDN covered every prong of the movement sufficiently and was the only face and legitimate representative of the gay military community. SLDN also took issue with the reporter's characterization of Servicemembers United as the nation's largest organization of gay and lesbian troops and veterans—which it now was. The next time I saw that reporter in person, he confided in me that SLDN's call was the nastiest he had ever received in response to a story in his life as a journalist.

Despite that article's overall accuracy about SU and the wider DADT repeal movement, there was one factoid in there that was a little off: the article referred to me as a former army "intelligence director," the biggest bump in rank and position that any reporter ever unilaterally bestowed upon me, then or since. But reporters were always getting the details of everyone's story wrong in one way or another, and it never bothered me in the slightest. I always admired their ability to listen to fast-talking sources and interview subjects, furiously take notes, and get 95 percent of their stories right in the end.

Typically, the errant detail was rank or age or occupational specialty description. The most common factual error was to refer to my specialty as "linguist" instead of human intelligence collector, which was an easy mistake to make since I was also multilingual. The next most frequent was to confuse my or others' former rank, usually by referring to me as an intelligence "officer" when I had actually been an enlisted soldier. It's an innocent enough mistake for most reporters, who are largely unfamiliar with the military and know that personnel who perform similar jobs in organizations like the CIA and FBI are often referred to as "officers." Still, I had to laugh when the *Metro Weekly* piece promoted me to the army's "intelligence director." Back pay, anyone?

Another reporter error was less frequent but more concerning: misquoting. As far as I know, I was only misquoted a handful of times in six years, and only two of those times are worth noting. The first was back in spring 2006, very early in our first national tour, the Call to Duty Tour, when a reporter in Providence, Rhode Island, decided to fill in some details in a story he was writing about our swing through his state. Rhode Island had a moderate Republican senator at the time who was an excellent target for our style of grassroots advocacy work, so we couldn't help but stop off in the state for an event while passing through New England. Naturally, our stop brought coverage from the *Providence Journal*; I distinctly remember rushing that interview, being quick with him, and staying vague on some details so as to not prompt more questions and to ensure that I got off the phone quickly. To my surprise, when the story came out the next day, the reporter seemed to have filled in some of the gaps in my interview with a few "extra" details of his own.

The inserted details were innocuous—things like the locations where certain conversations and events had taken place and specifics about what was said in conversations with fellow servicemembers when I was in the army, details I didn't remember disclosing in our quick phone conversation. And, strangely, the details weren't that far off from the truth in the end. I don't know if the reporter took a few lucky guesses or did research to try to figure out those details from other interviews I had given, which weren't that many at the time. Regardless, all I could really do was laugh.

Another incident of minor misquoting that didn't bother me too much but which did resurface later in a rather serious setting involved a visit to the White House and a conversation with the president. By the summer of 2009, we had managed to establish pretty good relations with the new administration. We were seen as "behaving" as an organization at the time, simply because we weren't making useless noise to try to push the president to make one of the same mistakes Clinton did—that is, take on the DADT issue in his first few months in office. Instead, we had what we saw as a more realistic strategy of laying the final groundwork in 2009 for supporting legislative repeal in 2010. So while SLDN, in the absence of a real plan or strategy of its own, was jumping up and down and "calling on" the president to do this or that immediately, Servicemembers United was quietly building resources, building our network of advocates, and planning our nationwide grassroots strategies for a more realistic push. But in the eyes of the administration, we were "behaving," and as a result, despite our very recent entry onto the Washington stage, we were enthusiastically invited, along with other national organizational leaders, to the White House that summer for the first LGBT Pride Month party, a significant gesture in that first year of the administration.

The event itself was nice, albeit a little cliché. After an hour or so of mixing, mingling, and enjoying the DJed Madonna remixes throughout half of the main floor of the mansion, President Obama entered the East Room and delivered remarks to the crowd of two to three hundred members of Washington's "professional gays" corps. Jarrod and I happened to be along the president's entry and exit route, so as he briefly greeted partygoers while exiting the East Room, I managed to get in a quick conversation with him.

I introduced myself and told the president that I had been one of those intelligence trainees who was discharged under DADT right after 9/11 and that I also now spoke Arabic but couldn't go back in. I also told him that our community wanted to see the DADT issue done sooner rather than later, to which the president responded, "I'm trying, I'm trying," in a rather exasperated tone. I found out later that just moments earlier along his exit route from the room, Victor Fehrenbach, one of SLDN's clients and spokespersons and Aubrey Sarvis's date to the party, had caught the president for a few seconds as well and had said something similar.

When I later recounted details of this exchange over the phone to another reporter, he summed it up in his article on the LGBT Pride celebration by saying that I had told the president that I was "one of those Arabic speakers" who had been discharged under DADT. This was a simple enough mistake for a reporter to make, given the convoluted nuance of my story, but it was technically incorrect. I was quite careful never to claim to have been an Arabic linguist (human intelligence collectors were actually a step above linguists, because they went through both linguist training and human intelligence/counterintelligence training), nor would I ever claim to have been an Arabic speaker when I was in the army. (I didn't learn Arabic until two years after I got out, although I did still learn it at taxpayer expense, through DOD's National Security Education Program, thank you very much.) But journalists would nevertheless often get confused about these nuances.

Such demotions and promotions were inconsequential in the grand scheme of things, but years later, when the Log Cabin lawsuit challenging the constitutionality of the DADT law finally went to trial, the Justice Department would attempt to use this particular misquote against me.

7

* * * * *

EXECUTIVE OPTIONS

By the spring of 2009, the stars were beginning to align for some movement on the DADT issue. A pro-repeal candidate had taken the White House, pro-repeal leadership controlled both houses of Congress, public opinion was overwhelmingly in favor of repeal, and those who had actually been affected by the issue had finally stepped forward to demand a seat at the table in Washington. We viewed 2009 as the natural period in which to finish our capacity-building efforts in preparation for 2010, which seemed the natural and most realistic year for legislative action. However realistic, though, that still wasn't fast enough for many, and there was a muted but steady drumbeat for our new "fierce advocate" president to do something on this issue sooner.

At the time, President Obama had a great excuse for not taking personal action on the DADT issue: Congress had to act first. DADT was a law passed by Congress, and legislation to repeal that law had to come from Congress and then over to the president's desk to sign it into law, which he would surely do. This enabled the president to dodge the random calls for him to do something on DADT during the first few months of his presidency. In May 2009, however, President

Obama's insulation evaporated when Aaron Belkin of the Palm Center proposed a unique and interesting idea that caught on in the gay and progressive communities like wildfire and which, from that point on, succeeded in placing the responsibility for doing something about DADT personally upon the president.

Dr. Belkin had dug up an obscure law from the 1980s that authorized the president of the United States to suspend certain other laws pertaining to the expulsion of military personnel from active duty in times of national emergency, with "national emergency" defined as any time the reserve forces were called up. Back in the 1980s when this law was enacted, it certainly may have taken a national emergency to call up the reserve forces for any extended period of time, but in the post-9/11 world the reserve forces were in a constant state of activation. According to Belkin and his colleagues, that technically meant that the president could issue an executive order suspending enforcement of DADT.

As the progressive community embraced this new "executive order option" as a valid way to end DADT, they eviscerated the Obama administration's strategy of passing the buck to Congress on this issue. But while the liberal masses quickly lined up to start calling on the president to exercise his executive authority to stop the discharges, and Belkin made an attempt to get other DADT repeal movement leaders to back his new proposal, not everyone on the pro-repeal side was persuaded of the wisdom of this approach.

I personally thought that Belkin's proposal sounded idealistic but naïve—like something that a political scientist with little practical experience in politics had come up with because it looked good on paper. I knew that it would never fly in Washington—the Pentagon, in particular, wouldn't let it happen in a million years. To me, its value as a policy proposal would be strictly limited to pressuring the president, who in turn would have to be more proactive in pushing Congress and the Pentagon to act in order to help alleviate the pressure on himself. With limited bandwidth and limited but growing capital, I certainly wasn't going to put all of SU's eggs in this very flimsy basket and abandon the capacity-building and grassroots efforts we were gearing up for in anticipation of legislative action in 2010.

The reasons behind SLDN's opposition to the executive order option, however, ran a lot deeper. According to at least one SLDN board member, Belkin attended one of the organization's board meetings to present the idea and try to solidify the group's public support for his proposal. But he went in with two strikes against him: first, the fact that the executive order option originated with the Palm Center and not SLDN, and second, the fact that it could potentially be seen to undermine or at least slow down the legislative repeal effort. SLDN as an organizational entity tended to strongly prefer that its initiatives and assets reign supreme, even if they were not necessarily the best for the issue and the community. It wasn't necessarily a malicious thing but rather a pathology that is common among some hypercompetitive niche organizations and interest group communities.

Finally, at the board meeting, some SLDN board members were reported to have been quite angry and upset that Belkin wanted to push this option; his shaky performance before the board meant he struck out with SLDN. From then on, SLDN not only refused to substantively support the executive order option but also sometimes actively worked to undermine it as an alternative to the legislative repeal route.

Aaron Belkin and his colleagues were not against full legislative repeal, and although many others saw the executive order option as undermining that approach, Belkin saw it as perfectly complementary. As the theory went, once open service became a reality via executive order and the dire predictions of DADT supporters did not come to pass, support for keeping the ban in place would naturally fall apart and Congress would inevitably be driven to repeal the already-defunct DADT law. But however plausible Belkin's assumptions seemed, there was still a real threat that Congress would fail to follow through with the actual repeal. Lawmakers might reason that the executive order had already provided a perfectly fine solution, so why stick their necks out and reignite the issue? This, of course, would leave open the very real possibility that a future chief executive could come along and rescind the executive order, a common practice at the beginning of new administrations, especially when the opposing political party returns to power.

Belkin was especially incensed by those who disagreed publicly that his executive order proposal would make sound policy. But while it was true that some had purely political reasons for not favoring his strategy, there were also those who had no dog in this fight, like *Washington Post* editorial board member and columnist Jonathan Capehart, and those who truly and passionately believed that the legislative route was the best way to go, like Iraq War veteran and DADT repeal hero Congressman Patrick Murphy. In a fit of frustrated fury, Belkin shamefully took to the media to blast those very men and others for not supporting his plan. Servicemembers United was spared from this assault, because the organization wasn't in the habit of publicly criticizing the plan, primarily because we knew it had absolutely no chance of ever being adopted.

(Later, as support among key influencers in the repeal movement failed to materialize, Belkin and his Palm Center colleague, Nathaniel Frank, would argue that they never really thought that this proposal would actually be adopted but that it was only ever intended to be a pressure tactic. However, those of us who encountered the ferocity with which Belkin and company lobbied for this option to be supported and adopted, both publicly and privately, would beg to differ with that rewrite.)

HRC's involvement in the executive order drama is a bit of a story of its own. By this point, HRC still wasn't really a major player in the repeal movement. Most of the substantive work that it claimed to have done on the DADT issue had been done primarily by Servicemembers United and its contacts. The only thing HRC had to insert itself into the DADT debate was near exclusive control of Eric Alva, who after doing a round of national media about his own personal story and testifying at the subcommittee hearing, was just making the HRC dinner rounds to raise funds for the organization. When the issue began to simmer a little in the spring of 2009, HRC had virtually no in-house expertise on DADT or the military—Antonio Agnone had left HRC after about a year—and its staff consisted mostly of liberal activists, none of whom understood Pentagon politics or even the gay military community.

HRC, being closely tied in with the Democratic Party and the administration, tried very hard to stay out of the executive order debate for as long as it could. Internally, there was an understanding that the organization would not support Belkin's proposal, because the administration did not support it and did not want it to be supported. HRC as an organization was publicly mum on the executive order option until MSNBC's Chris Matthews put HRC president Joe Solmonese on the spot one day on *Hardball*, asking if the president could issue an executive order to suspend the DADT law.

Solmonese was on with Lorri Jean, the head of the Gay and Lesbian Center in Los Angeles, who, not having been involved in this issue thus far and knowing little if anything about the proposal's mechanics and viability, said that of course the president should immediately issue an executive order suspending DADT. As Solmonese would later tell me and others in an understandably frustrated tone, he then had no choice but to side with Jean. He certainly couldn't be seen as opposing something that many in the gay community, especially the far left of it, thought was a no-brainer that should be done immediately. So, boxed into a corner on the air, Solmonese responded that "he can and he should." Almost immediately, back at its headquarters, HRC's legislative, policy, and communications staffers rolled their eyes and conceded to one another, "Well, I guess we're supporting the executive order now," according to those who were there.

SLDN, meanwhile, wasn't doing much in the political arena. Besides several moderately effective e-mail advocacy campaigns to promote the House repeal bill, the group was essentially just "calling" on the president to "do something" in the abstract. What seemed strange to those of us who knew defense politics a little more intimately was the insistence by Aubrey Sarvis that the president put repeal language in his fiscal year (FY) 2010 defense budget. In fact, only literal fiscal issues really go into the document that is technically referred to as the "defense budget"; since DADT had no quantifiable cost, its repeal was not a line-item issue that could be inserted into the budget. The repeal would instead be expected to appear in the Pentagon's subsequent policy transmittals, the series of legislative proposals that the Pentagon wants included in the annual defense authorization bill, which follow the release of the budget over the following several months.

Although very few caught the mistake at that time, I knew what Sarvis meant to say but didn't seem to know how to say correctly. The "budget" misunderstanding would resurface again in 2010, when I would actually move to correct the mistake on the public stage so that our community wouldn't keep shooting itself in the foot by asking for the impossible and giving the White House an easy dodge. But in 2009, SLDN's "calls" on the White House to do this and that were so powerless and impotent that the mistake did no damage.

The real pressure came from the Palm Center's executive order proposal. The liberal masses were demanding that their "fierce advocate," who on the campaign trail had lamented the immense damage that discharging Arabic linguists was doing to our nation's security, live up to his words and stop those discharges with the stroke of his pen, the Pentagon be damned. But pressure was also starting to build on HRC, as the largest gay organization in Washington, to use the money, influence, and political capital that it had amassed in the gay community's name to get substantively engaged and truly put its weight behind the full legislative repeal of DADT. Solmonese's slip-up on MSNBC had actually bought it a little time, but HRC's relative absence from the repeal movement was becoming more and more evident as that slow simmer continued toward the summer.

Another pressure point on HRC exploded out of the blue: in a bombshell report, the *Daily Beast's* Jason Bellini claimed that all along, HRC had been lobbying Capitol Hill offices, especially House leadership, not to move on DADT in 2009. Citing unnamed Democratic staffers and referencing a "slip" by Senator Charles Schumer of New York, Bellini's accusations blew up the blogosphere and riled the progressive community. Aaron Belkin stepped forward on Michaelangelo Signorile's radio show to say that he too had heard that HRC and other groups were actively lobbying Democratic offices to dial back on DADT in 2009. While this may have been true, I never personally witnessed it happening, and if I had I certainly never would have supported or stayed silent about an organization lobbying Congress to hold back legislative progress. While we may not have had a realistic shot at legislative action in 2009, it certainly wouldn't have been wise to try to hold back members of Congress who wanted to help push the ball forward for us. Regardless, by the late spring of 2009, the pressure on HRC to start looking helpful on DADT repeal had become enormous.

David Smith, HRC's vice president for programs and the person who truly made the political decisions on the organization's behalf, approached me in late May about finding someone with military credentials whom HRC could hire on a temporary basis. He stressed the temporary nature of the position and actually turned down some good candidates because they would have had to quit their current jobs and relocate, which they were more than willing to do. It seemed that HRC just needed a good show-hire, something to hold up as evidence that they weren't stagnant on DADT. They had tried the show-hire tactic in the past when community pressure and restlessness heated up around transgender issues and HRC was caught doing too little, and it had worked, to an extent. Now they hoped it would work again.

One of the candidates I forwarded to Smith to consider was Servicemembers United's own Jarrod Chlapowski. Jarrod had impeccable DADT credentials, having served in the army and cofounded the largest gay military group in the country by membership, Servicemembers United. Jarrod was also an attractive male with a deep voice who still maintained stereotypical military bearing more than four years after leaving the army. He was the perfect mollifier for HRC, so Smith hired him immediately and began touting him to the organization's base as HRC's new "military consultant." This arrangement was also ideal for Servicemembers United, as it gave us access to the inner machinations of HRC and provided us with a much better pressure point to try to get HRC, the largest and best funded gay organization, out of first gear on DADT.

As Jarrod got to work making the rounds on behalf of his new employer, I didn't waste any time using the fact that Servicemembers United's cofounder and number two was now in house at HRC, and as far as we were concerned this arrangement wasn't going to be temporary. Some serious groundwork still needed to be done before we as a community would be prepared to push DADT forward legislatively in 2010, and HRC was the only organization that had the serious cash to invest in the effort. SLDN pulled in several million dollars each year, but it just didn't seem to be interested in rolling out any sort of serious national-scale effort to put a shot of energy into the movement. And with as much as SLDN paid for its staff, operating expenses, and legal services, they wouldn't have had the spare cash to invest even if Aubrey Sarvis had known what to do on that front. Servicemembers United itself, a relatively young organization that had only opened its Washington, DC, office a few months earlier, certainly didn't have the cash to put behind a major national campaign. If we had been around for fifteen or twenty-five years like the other organizations, we surely would have built up quite an operational war chest by then, but that kind of money didn't come in matter of months or even a few years.

What Servicemembers United did have was talented and aggressive leadership that wasn't willing to just ride the wave of others' work or wait on the administration to get around to doing something. And we also had a limitless supply of recent veterans who could aptly be the face of and make the case for DADT's repeal at the grassroots level, in the media, and throughout Washington.

This was truly a time when our community had to put up or shut up, because the stars were continuing to align and a window was clearly about to open up to take the DADT issue across the finish line or die trying. But without the cash to put a serious national ground game into action and round up the votes, we were going to miss our chance. And that national ground game wasn't going to come quick. It was going to take time to build up to the level needed to support the political game when the ball started rolling in Washington.

Over the summer I met with HRC's Smith again to start trying to get his organization to seriously invest in the DADT issue sooner rather than later. I calmly but passionately explained to him that 2009 was the time to begin laying the groundwork for the DADT repeal fight and that waiting until 2010 to start ramping up would be too late. I pleaded with him to commit at least a half-million dollars to DADT within HRC's budget, an amount equal to or even less than amounts they'd committed to far less concrete projects and priorities. I even offered to help raise half of that for HRC if the organization could at least provide an initial investment in raising the issue's profile and building the army of advocates needed to move forward. And once again, I wasn't asking to take any of the credit for this. The proposal was to have all of this fall under HRC's brand so that they could get their much-prized credit for work that they had financed, even if it wasn't work that they actually did.

As I also mentioned to Joe Solmonese over dinner one night in Orlando, HRC had a well-defined and well-funded religious and faith program, a university-oriented unit, and a workplace equality project, and there was no reason why they shouldn't have a well-funded "military equality project" too. Solmonese said that he completely agreed with me, but I knew that as the ceremonial head and fundraiser-in-chief he wasn't really the one who made these things happen. Smith, the one who could have made it happen, simply responded to my pleas by saying that when the time came and DADT came to the fore, HRC would simply "do what it does." When asked what that meant exactly, he never did articulate a clear answer, at least not to me.

As Jarrod kept pressuring HRC to scale up from the inside and to use him as more than just a token, I kept up the pressure on Smith and company from the outside. We stuck firm to our claim that at least $500,000 was needed in 2009 to build the type of operation that our community needed to fight for repeal and secure the votes in Congress early on. But we also kept our offer on the table to raise half the money ourselves if they would invest at least $250,000. Instead, Smith came back to us and said that HRC would spend one-tenth of that amount and asked us to use it to do another tour—but to only five or six cities that were important to HRC for other reasons.

If you ask HRC how much they spent on DADT in 2009, they have a funny way of papering over their paltry commitment at that time. As they've done before in other instances when they've tried to inflate the numbers to look like they're doing more than they are, they would count in the salaries of certain employees—who would have had to be paid anyway, regardless of what issue they were working on—and they would recategorize other expenses—again, line items that would have been spent anyway and which have only a dubious connection to DADT, if any at all—to claim that they too fall under DADT-related expenditures for 2009. However, anyone who rejects "fuzzy math" wouldn't be fooled. To paraphrase a certain former commander-in-chief: "Fool me twice . . . we can't get fooled again."

Twenty-five thousand dollars to do a few measly events in the half-year leading up to 2010, the primary purpose of which was to mollify the renewed calls for action and to please donors, was typical HRC style. But in the absence of anything else going on, Jarrod and I knew that if we didn't take it and run with it, nothing would get done in 2009 to lay the groundwork for 2010. So run with it we did. We took that $25,000, and instead of doing five events, as originally requested, we did nearly *twenty* events, and we still didn't manage to spend the whole budget. That just served as further proof to us that we could at least take advantage of HRC's financial waste to get more groundwork done for DADT—by diverting their excess to more events, more media, more recruiting, and more pressure. But imagine what we could have done in 2009 with ten times those resources. Would the fight the following year have ended up being that hard, that close, or that long? Coulda, woulda, shoulda, right?

8

* * * * *

A NEW QUARTERBACK ON
THE FIELD

After Marty Meehan, the original lead sponsor of the DADT repeal bill in the House, left Congress to become the chancellor of the University of Massachusetts at Lowell, Congresswoman Ellen Tauscher stepped up to lead the repeal effort in the House. I've always maintained that while Tauscher was a tough and formidable opponent in any fight she took on, she wasn't the ideal lead on this particular bill. The district she represented was situated in the greater San Francisco Bay area, which added fuel to our opposition's most oft repeated talking point about "San Francisco values" and a new "San Francisco military." However, in June 2009, Congresswoman Tauscher also left Congress to take up the position of undersecretary of state for arms control and international security. The following month, Congressman Patrick Murphy stepped forward to take over as the lead sponsor of the DADT repeal bill in the House.

Despite the fact that he was a relatively junior member of the House, Congressman Murphy was a man of impeccable stature on

Capitol Hill. After graduating from law school, Murphy, an army JAG officer, went on active duty and taught constitutional law as an instructor at West Point before volunteering for deployments to Bosnia and Iraq. Murphy was a member of the US Army's prestigious 82nd Airborne Division before going on to become the first Iraq War veteran elected to Congress. It was Congressman Murphy who had become the man of the hour in the July 2008 DADT hearings in the Military Personnel Subcommittee of the House Armed Services Committee, effectively shutting Elaine Donnelly down with his very first question and immediately becoming a hero of the repeal movement. Murphy was highly credible in defense circles and was quite passionate about ending DADT. He spoke with authority, eloquence, and conviction, emotions buttressed by his own personal experiences serving in the modern military, including with gay servicemembers. We could not have asked for a better steward heading into a critical period in which we all knew we finally had a realistic shot at moving DADT repeal legislation.

Congressman Murphy's takeover of the Military Readiness Enhancement Act coincided with the start of our new tour, which had been christened the Voices of Honor Tour after a series of other names we tossed around internally failed to surpass the cheesiness threshold (not that this one did by much, but it was the best of the bad naming choices we could come up with on short notice). We were set to make our tour launch announcement at the National Press Club in Washington on July 8, 2009, which provided a perfect opportunity to invite Murphy to join us and simultaneously announce his takeover—or "quarterbacking," as he put it—of the repeal bill. This marked a turning point in momentum for the bill and the issue, and it was also a strategic and tactical turning point for DADT repeal advocacy.

Servicemembers United had pioneered the strategy of having those actually impacted by the DADT law step up to take control of the advocacy effort on the DADT issue, as opposed to just using those affected as showpieces and puppets while others controlled the strategic direction of the movement. Specifically, SU used young, recent veterans, many fresh from active duty, as the face of the repeal movement. These were people who could talk firsthand about serving in Iraq and Afghanistan, serving openly among the "*Will & Grace* generation" of troops, and often defying DADT and serving openly without becoming a detriment to unit cohesion, morale, or combat readiness.

We had the option to use active duty troops, too, and while many active duty servicemembers were active SU members and even leaders, we chose to focus on recent veterans, who had more flexibility to handle the demands of advocacy. Active duty troops simply couldn't get away to do the sheer volume of work that needed to be done across the country, and while we used them sometimes for anonymous media pieces, they couldn't speak openly or provide verifiable testimonials without running the risk of being fired pursuant to DADT. They also had to deal with the well-established impropriety of active troops speaking out publicly on political issues. So recent vets who could speak on the record and advocate passionately did more than 95 percent of the advocacy work, without question. Without them, our issue would have continued to be represented only by civilian lawyers, professional activists, and academics.

At this point, however, Servicemembers United began systematically pushing for our straight servicemember and veteran allies to join us on the road to campaign for DADT's repeal. While current gay and lesbian servicemembers couldn't publicly campaign for the repeal of DADT without risking their careers, straight servicemembers technically could, especially members of the National Guard and Reserves, and straight veterans certainly could. We began insisting on having a straight ally with military experience at every new event possible, a change that the media quickly picked up on. At the launch of our new tour at the National Press Club, CNN actually did a full segment on our use of straight vets to advocate for repeal.

The Voices of Honor Tour, originally conceived as a five-stop tour, quickly turned into a much bigger event series in the hands of Jarrod and me. Our first event was a press conference in Philadelphia in front of Independence Hall, again with Congressman Murphy. Joining Murphy, Jarrod, and me were Steve Vossler, a straight army veteran and a staff member at Servicemembers United; Philadelphia resident Joe Soto, a Naval Academy graduate and a very early supporter of Servicemembers United's work; and Anu Bhagwati, the head of a then-new organization called Service Women's Action Network and a co-organizer of our very first public event ever: our trial by fire at Harvard's Kennedy School back in early 2006. But instead of doing just the one press event in Philadelphia as originally planned, Jarrod and I turned that trip into four separate events—not to mention a much more cost-effective trip.

It just didn't make sense for us to go to the expense and trouble to travel to a city, especially when we later had to fly across the country for these, to do only a one-hour event once we got there. We figured if we were going to be in the Philadelphia area anyway, why not also do a town hall–style event there, plus two more events across the river in New Jersey, which had a few moderate Republican congressional districts that we were targeting for support on the repeal bill? From then on, at every scheduled Voices of Honor Tour stop possible, we spent an extra day or two in the area and turned one event into three or four, a strategy that paid off significantly in terms of media coverage, local advocates recruited, and pressure generated on a wider array of lawmakers.

The early groundwork we were laying with Voices of Honor in the summer and fall of 2009 turned out to be critical to the repeal effort. We were literally out putting troops on the ground in battleground states such as Missouri, Florida, Indiana, West Virginia, and Nebraska as others were still just talking back in Washington. While some questioned why we were off gallivanting in such places, we would have the last laugh when the support of those states' senators turned out to be the critical last few votes desperately needed to get repeal through the Senate, particularly the all-important Senate Armed Services Committee (SASC). Nevertheless, there were still important battles brewing on other fronts.

A good, longtime friend of mine from South Carolina, a surgeon named Dr. Chad Rubin, had been a delegate to the American Medical Association for the American College of Surgeons for a number of years. He was a strong supporter of Servicemembers United's work and a shrewd and active politico himself within the medical community. During one of his trips up to Alexandria, Virginia, for an American College of Surgeons meeting, we met for dinner one night and the conversation turned to DADT. I happened to mention to Chad the routine talking point that doctor-patient confidentiality was virtually nonexistent in the military because of DADT. If a gay or lesbian servicemember had to come out to his or her doctor in the course of seeking treatment, the physician could report that servicemember to the command and put an end to his or her career.

Indeed, this very scenario had happened with doctors, psychiatrists, and chaplains numerous times in the past, and the stories still circulated within the gay military community as a warning to be careful what information one revealed even to seemingly trustworthy figures. And to the detriment of gay and lesbian servicemembers, fear of being outed by a healthcare provider sometimes led them to delay treatment for serious conditions such as potential exposure to sexually transmitted diseases; to find a civilian clinic or doctor to see at considerable out-of-pocket expense; or even to forgo treatment for chronic ailments such post-traumatic stress, one symptom of which is often relationship problems.

As a doctor, Chad was appalled to hear that DADT interfered with provider-patient confidentiality and endangered some servicemembers' health. He immediately thought to ask if we had ever considered approaching the American Medical Association (AMA) to suggest a resolution against the DADT law. While he assured me that the AMA was traditionally very conservative, he was certain that even the coalition of Republican-leaning physicians would be equally outraged at any law that threatened the sacrosanct relationship between a physician and his or her patient. And a resolution from the powerful AMA would carry a lot of weight in Washington. It seemed a long shot, but it was one that Chad convinced me was worth pursuing.

Chad returned home to South Carolina and did some research for me, and within a few weeks he forwarded me an administrative contact for the AMA's GLBT Advisory Committee. Little did I know that this small coalition of gay, lesbian, bisexual, transgender, and ally doctors had been struggling to get traction on gay issues within the normally conservative association. So when I reached out to them cold on this issue in mid-2009, they quickly invited me to join them for their committee meeting at the AMA's interim policy conference in Houston in November.

Rear Admiral Al Steinman, the retired director of health and safety for the US Coast Guard who had done advocacy work with us around the country for years, was scheduled to join me in Houston for the "DADT and Healthcare Issues" briefing that I had put together for the AMA conference in November. In addition to being a senior retired military officer who carried the natural prestige of age and rank with him, Al could also speak as a physician. And while I could always hold my own before any audience when talking about the ins and outs of the DADT issue from a policy perspective, I was glad that Al was going to be there to back me up and lend some weight to my medical arguments, given that they were, after all, being offered by a twenty-eight-year-old nonphysician.

In the end, though, Al couldn't make it to Houston because of a last-minute family issue, and I had to tackle the AMA all by myself. Fortunately, the association's GLBT Advisory Committee was very friendly and welcoming, and although several of them later admitted that they were amused and a little confused by my youth, they thought the issue was ripe enough to push forward immediately. I had originally gone to Houston for a day with the intention of just bringing the committee up to speed on DADT and its impact on healthcare with the hope that they would pursue a resolution from the full AMA the following year. Instead, the committee decided to try to push a resolution through the organization right then; in fact, two of the committee's leaders, Dr. Jennifer Chaffin and Dr. Paul Wertsch, had taken the preemptive step of submitting a draft resolution ahead of time in order to allow the issue to be brought up immediately should the committee decide to move forward. Sure enough, I was asked to stay in Houston to help usher the resolution through to the full AMA House of Delegates later that week. My surgeon friend Chad, who had been coaching me on what to expect, was as surprised as I was.

The first step, however, was to get the draft resolution—a modest one that actually only called for a plug to the provider-patient confidentiality hole in the DADT law—adopted by the reference committee to which it was assigned. Since I wasn't a doctor, the GLBT Advisory Committee had to obtain special permission for me to testify before the reference committee, but my unique credentials on the issue under consideration ensured that I was granted an exception. Although I ran over my allotted time, prompting a stern warning from the reference committee chair about sticking to the schedule, I managed to squeeze in every argument I could think of related to DADT's negative impact on servicemembers, their access to and quality of healthcare, and the sacrosanct provider-patient relationship in front of the packed ballroom of physicians. I even encouraged the reference committee to consider going beyond the draft resolution before it and calling for full repeal of the DADT law as the best solution to its many flaws.

While numerous other doctors lined up after me at the "for" microphone to testify in favor of the draft resolution, only one person patiently waited to speak at the "against" microphone in the middle of the room—a colonel in full military dress uniform clearly representing the Department of Defense. When his turn came, however, he preceded his remarks by joking that he wanted to temporarily rename his microphone the "other considerations" microphone instead of the "against" microphone, prompting light laughter from the crowd.

Despite our fears of what this DOD representative might say to thwart our effort, he surprisingly just asked the reference committee to consider the conflicts that military doctors face in trying to be oath-abiding physicians and also in trying to serve their commands and the laws and regulations under which the Defense Department must operate. Fair point, I thought.

After the reference committee finished its business, it took all draft resolutions within its jurisdiction under consideration in private. And thus began the long, tense wait for what the reference committee would do with our rather modest (in our terms) but rather radical (in terms of the conservative AMA) resolution that sought to at least put another dent in the DADT law by pointing out yet another of its flaws. Even if the reference committee decided in our favor, we would still have to hold our breath as its package of resolutions went before the full AMA House of Delegates, at which time our resolution could easily be pulled out and tabled, virtually killing it. With ample representation present from the military medical establishment, we were certain that we had several uphill battles still left to go.

Despite its controversial nature, the DADT resolution was so far going mostly unnoticed by the true conservative ideologues within the AMA, because a far greater threat, in their minds, loomed elsewhere. In another reference committee, the AMA's doctors were engaged in all-out warfare over their board of trustees' controversial approval, prior to this policy convention, of President Obama's healthcare reform bill. This move, which gave a significant boost to what they called "Obamacare," outraged many within the conservative AMA and threatened to split the organization during this very meeting. As we waited on our reference committee to decide the fate of the DADT resolution, I spent several hours sitting in on the back and forth over the evils of "socialized medicine" and the future of the AMA. It was quite a time to be in Houston, to be involved with the AMA for a brief period, and to have a front-row seat to the fiery politics of another active interest group community with a lot on the line.

When our reference committee finished its deliberations and a verdict finally came, we were in for another big surprise. They had completely revamped the draft resolution on DADT—but for the better. Instead of the modest call to simply plug the provider-patient hole, the reference committee recognized the overall chilling effect that the DADT law had on access to and quality of care for gay and lesbian servicemembers, and it recommended complete repeal of the outdated law as the only real remedy for the policy's many maladies. And when it came time for the package of resolutions in which the DADT resolution was embedded to come before the organization's full house of delegates, the entire package sailed right through without a single objection, not even from the Pentagon's representatives.

Later that November came more direct DADT grassroots groundwork in America's heartland, including more events, media, and organizing in some very red states like Nebraska. By this point we had established great relationships with many organizers and influencers in that state, which was growing more and more critical. We got to know Lincoln quite well, in addition to Omaha, Kearney, and even the rural town of North Platte. (Don't ask! We got the pivotal vote in the end, didn't we?)

Meanwhile, SLDN, in the absence of any real plan of its own for building real support on the ground in key states, had spent most of the year simply "calling" on the president to put repeal language in his budget, which clearly wasn't going to happen in the absence of a real ground game to back it up. Those hollow calls really rattled the White House, since there wasn't much it could do in 2009 to allay them even if it wanted to at the time. Even more problematic for the administration was the Palm Center's executive order option, which offered a more concrete proposal for movement on the issue, however unrealistic. The White House truly hated the fact that it had become hard to explain why that proposal wouldn't work, even though the Palm Center itself was now claiming it knew that it wouldn't. In the end, the president just had to endure a severe beating in 2009 on DADT.

The only two major players in the DADT repeal movement still in the good graces of the White House at the end of 2009, for very different reasons, were Servicemembers United and HRC. SU was still favored because we hadn't spent the year pushing for solutions that couldn't be done in reality or that wouldn't succeed if they were attempted. Instead, we spent the year steadily building support for repeal in key battle-ground states where persuadable House members and critical Senate Armed Services Committee members resided. HRC was favored because it had spent the year waiting to see if DADT was even worth investing in, so of course it had refused to put any significant pressure on the administration unless it was backed into a corner, say, on day-time television. (Although, because Jarrod was still in-house at HRC as a "temporary" employee, we at least managed to wrestle some resources away from their large advertising, marketing, promotional, and staffing budgets to get some significant work done on the issue.)

The seemingly acquiescent nature of Servicemembers United, however misinterpreted, ended up garnering us a coveted invitation to one of the first 2009 White House Christmas parties. So on December 15, I joined several hundred guests, including other organizational leaders who were assumed at the time to be "behaving," celebrities, senior administration and military officials, and the First Family for an elaborate holiday celebration throughout the main floor of the presidential mansion. Unlike the LGBT Pride celebration at the White House back in the summer, this mainstream event was much larger, allowing partygoers full run of the first floor. Although I attended alone, I ran into a number of people I knew, like Iraq and Afghanistan Veterans of America's executive director, Paul Rieckhoff; the chairman of VoteVets, Jon Soltz; and many others whom I knew of but didn't know personally, like the Reverend Al Sharpton and megachurch leader and televangelist Joel Osteen.

Near the very end of the party, I also ran into HRC president Joe Solmonese. We chatted for a few minutes before I asked him bluntly if we could meet for just fifteen or twenty minutes sometime before the end of the year to talk about significantly scaling up HRC's commitment to DADT repeal. I expressed some grave concerns about HRC having waited until it was way too late to invest resources in this issue that was becoming increasingly likely to jump to the fore of the national policy agenda soon. I also specifically asked if just the two of us could meet and talk alone, without other senior HRC staff there who might turn out to be part of the problem with the organization's lackluster commitment thus far.

Joe agreed to meet with me before he left for his holiday vacation and even scheduled a day and time to make it happen. However, when the time came for us to talk, his assistant e-mailed to cancel and reschedule for after the new year. When early 2010 came around, the same assistant reached out to cancel again and said that she wasn't able to reschedule this time. DADT was on the verge of exploding onto the national stage as the biggest LGBT federal policy battle ever, and the Human Rights Campaign's president didn't even want to be bothered to talk with the leader of the country's largest gay military group, HRC's only true partner organization on DADT, about increasing HRC's paltry commitment to the issue.

But soon thereafter, HRC did want to talk about DADT, and they wanted to be right out front in doing so—when representatives of several of the gay community's biggest political and organizational donors called for an unusual meeting with organizational leaders and senior staff involved in the DADT issue. It was mid-January, and I had been scheduled to go to Miami for a few events, but I postponed the trip by one day to stay in Washington for what I was told would be a rather informal meeting with donor representatives and the other organizations—including SU, SLDN, HRC, and the Palm Center—to talk about where we were as a community on DADT. When we arrived at the meeting that Wednesday morning, January 13, we discovered that the donor reps were actually looking for more concrete answers on what resources were required and what needed to be done to get ready for the anticipated upcoming fight.

I'll have to admit that I felt rather unprepared for such questions, and I wished that I had been forewarned about what we would be discussing. It seemed only natural to me that a coalition of savvy, multimillion-dollar gay foundations should have had the good sense to inform meeting participants of the full purpose of the meeting ahead of time, in order to maximize its effectiveness and better utilize each group's and each representative's time. Apparently the gay donor community could sometimes also be as dysfunctional and disjointed as the gay organizational community it supported.

Despite the fact that some of us had been caught unprepared, a surprising dynamic unfolded that yielded some serious insight into the attitudes and allegiances of the various organizational actors in the DADT repeal movement. HRC, led at the meeting by David Smith, strongly argued against pressuring the administration on DADT. He exclaimed repeatedly that HRC had "studied this White House," a curious phrase that stuck out in my mind for a long time, and that it had concluded that the Obama administration would not respond kindly to our community drumming up pressure around DADT now.

Aaron Belkin joined Paul Yandura, a political adviser to gay phi-lanthropist Jonathan Lewis and later an organizer within the direct action group GetEqual, in leading the charge against the seemingly impotent strategy advanced by HRC. Belkin argued that his execu-tive order proposal had generated significant public pressure already and that the White House was feeling the heat on DADT, a situation that would lead them to act in some way sooner than they otherwise would. Yandura strongly and passionately agreed with the need for public pressure on the White House, at one point angrily lashing out at lobbyist Robert Raben, who was very closely tied with both HRC and the Obama administration and whom Yandura perceived to be urg-ing support for David Smith's unbelievable no-pressure strategy. Thus, two distinct camps emerged from this meeting, and the representa-tives who attended from each organization and foundation surely left with a realization that there would be two distinct approaches in the DADT repeal activism to follow.

The donor meeting seemed to grow into much more, however, in the minds of those who began getting bits and pieces of information about it. Some in the gay media and blogosphere made it into quite the mystical spectacle, a perceived "secret" meeting with "big gay donors" on the "fate" of DADT. Some of them wasted little time coming up with grand theories about the gay mafia and its invisible hand in the political marketplace. Despite the reports, the meeting actually wasn't a secret. I was never asked to hide the fact that the meeting took place, nor was I ever asked not to disclose who attended the meeting, and I'm sure other participants weren't either. In fact, many who were there soon disclosed their presence publicly when asked, and both HRC and SLDN had allowed several midlevel staffers to sit in on it who would have never been allowed into one of our real high-level or private DADT meetings. As fun as it would be to think of this meeting in such grandiose terms, it simply wasn't the case.

In the end, the missing critical piece of information during that whole strategy discussion was what the White House was prepared to do on DADT in 2010. If the administration stepped up and put its entire weight behind repealing DADT that year, then perhaps the HRC suggestion that we "behave" and play along would work. However, if the administration wasn't 100 percent committed, then surely public pressure would be needed to push it along. While no one from the White House or the administration was present at that donor-organizational meeting, we would soon be in receipt of the missing puzzle piece.

9

★ ★ ★ ★ ★

STATE OF THE UNION AND SECRET MEETINGS

Tuesday, January 26, 2010, was the day we found out that the DADT repeal movement was about to kick into overdrive. Late that morning, Brian Bond, deputy director of the White House Office of Public Engagement and the de facto White House liaison to the gay political community, called me to confirm that the president would be mentioning DADT in his first State of the Union speech the following day.

It wasn't clear exactly what the president would say at that point. The White House was pretty good at giving us a heads-up about things that were about to happen with our issue, but they never divulged too much detail. This practice of keeping us at arm's length could not have been more frustrating, especially given the fact that we were desperately trying to help the administration accomplish one of its stated campaign goals—the repeal of DADT. Despite its name, the White House's Office of Public Engagement neither dealt directly with the general public nor truly engaged anyone. But at least they did usually tip us off about the major things that were about to happen, and we were grateful to at least be thrown those bones from time to time.

Bond was not able to talk long, despite the barrage of questions I could not help but throw out about this potentially game-changing news. "How long is the president going to talk about the issue? Is he going to set out a timeline? Is he going to call for repeal this year or next?" I eagerly asked. He wasn't able to give me much more than the general intelligence about the issue's inclusion in the speech, but I am not sure if that was because that information had just not been shared with him or because he was just staying tight-lipped about it. White House staffers were often under gag orders from higher-ups, and this appeared to be one of those times.

Bond was also involved with coordinating the guests invited to sit with Mrs. Obama in the First Lady's box during the State of the Union speech before Congress. When I found this out at the end of the conversation, I joked that he should try to arrange for my seat within the box to be as close as possible to Michelle herself. After I hung up the phone, it occurred to me that the subtle message of having a gay veteran sitting with the First Lady at the State of the Union address was not such a crazy idea after all. The First Lady's box is often populated with exemplary Americans who embody issues that the president will be mentioning in the evening's address. I immediately e-mailed Bond to follow up on the phone conversation and to seriously push for the strategic placement of a gay veteran or two in the First Lady's box during the speech. I argued that this would also be an excellent way to send a subtle message that would be virtually undetectable to the mainstream public but a strong signal of support to the gay community on DADT.

At the time, the White House needed to throw as many bones to the gay community as it could. The community had become quite disenchanted with a president who had campaigned as a "fierce advocate" but who had appeared to become significantly more moderate once in office. And this feeling of disappointment was not just isolated to the gays. Latinos, another important constituency, were quickly becoming disenchanted as well, as were women, labor, veterans, and other groups that were important to the president—and the progressive community in general.

Unfortunately, the gay veteran spot in the First Lady's box at the State of the Union speech did not materialize that first year. Bond explained that all the spots in the box had already been filled by that time, but why they had not previously thought to fill at least one seat with a gay veteran for this extraordinary moment for the gay community, I do not know. They always seemed to forget about us and promise "next time." If only candidate Obama could still have been around to advise President Obama on how to truly be a "fierce advocate." However, Bond assured me that there would be future opportunities for that down the road.

By later that afternoon, news of the issue's inclusion in the speech had reached the media. I got an e-mail out of the blue from a senior opinions editor for CNN.com who invited me to pen an op-ed for placement the following day about the meaning of the speech for the DADT issue. I still do not know how this editor came across my name, but I assume he had seen me mentioned, profiled, or quoted in previous pieces on CNN. A reporter from CNN's Washington bureau had become a pretty good social acquaintance of mine by that point, after we worked together on a significant article on gay and lesbian military partners in December. In addition to giving me the best gossip from all over Capitol Hill and CNN's Washington bureau, he was pretty good at pushing out the DADT issue to other CNN producers, bookers, and editors, too. However the opinions editor came across my name, I was honored to be asked to weigh in on the speech via a platform as high profile as CNN.com.

I watched the State of the Union speech from home that night on my couch, with my laptop out to diligently take notes for the short-notice op-ed that I had committed myself to for the next morning. It was a speech of many news-making moments, like Congressman Joe

Wilson yelling "You lie!" in response to one line and Supreme Court justice Samuel Alito mouthing "Not true" in response to another. But the DADT portion of the speech finally did come, and somehow it managed to rank right up there with the more sensational lines in the news headlines that followed. It was a brief mention—just one sentence—but an important one: "This year, I will work with Congress and our military to finally repeal the law that denies gay Americans the right to serve the country they love because of who they are. It's the right thing to do."

Many progressives were elated with the president's speech. To them, the president had committed the full force of the presidency to getting DADT repealed *that year*, and they intended to hold him to that commitment. But few seemed to pick up on a minor nuance in the president's remarks, and I wondered aloud immediately after the sentence was uttered whether "this year" was meant to apply to "repeal the law" or "work with Congress and the military." I hoped for the former, but I feared the latter—that the intent was to only *start working* on it this year. The difference was huge.

On the one hand, the administration clearly knew what it was doing when it inserted those two words into that sentence. They did not have to do that. They did not even have to include a mention of DADT in this speech at all. Every community and group was gunning for a mention of their issue in the State of the Union, and I feel confident that with all of our competing priorities the White House could have gotten away with not mentioning this issue at all. Sure, there was pressure to mention some gay issue, but there was no consensus that it needed to be this one at that time.

On the other hand, it seemed like political self-mutilation to bring up the issue, insert the words "this year," and get an important community's hopes up if it didn't really mean *and bring it to fruition* this year. A mistake like that seemed like such blatant shortsightedness; clearly, if the community's expectations did not materialize, the backlash would be far more damaging than the short-term gain. Surely all the president's men (and women) were smarter than that.

The mistake seemed so rookie that we all assumed at the time that the president must have meant "this year" to apply to "repeal the law." Whether he meant us to take it that way or not, the fact that he still said it gave us a powerful advocacy tool—a way to hold his feet to the fire, as he had asked us to do. And with that one line, the issue exploded earlier than any of us had expected.

It would not be a stretch at all to admit that the DADT repeal community was caught off guard by how quickly things took off after the State of the Union address. Later that week, we learned that on the following Tuesday, Senator Carl Levin, chairman of the Senate Armed Services Committee, was going to redirect to the DADT issue an hour of the three-hour block of time that he had scheduled to talk with the secretary of defense and the chairman of the Joint Chiefs of Staff about the defense budget request. At long last, we were going to get our first Senate hearing on DADT in seventeen years. And immediately following this news came a White House summons. Some of us DADT repeal advocates (not all) were being called to the White House for an ultra-secret meeting—one that would later turn out to be quite the spectacle for the progressive media and the blogosphere.

That weekend I finally reached Brian Bond again to try to get the dish on the ultra-secret Monday meeting. White House staffers were kept on notoriously tight leashes leading up to big administration announcements, much to the dismay of issue advocates who needed to get in touch with administration staff for assurances or with questions leading up to those announcements. But I at least managed to get Bond on the phone long enough to find out that the ultra-secret meeting was about to be not too ultra-secret anymore. Chris Neff, the Palm Center's "DC liaison" who did not even live in DC, had somehow found out about the meeting, to which he was not invited, and, according to Bond, was threatening to expose the meeting with DADT repeal activists if he was not added to the invite list. Bond relayed that Neff had called him up and left a voicemail saying, tongue in cheek, that he understood that there was going to be a meeting about DADT at the White House on Monday and that it clearly must have been a mistake that he was left off the invite list. He rhetorically asked Bond if he should show up or if he should go to the media instead.

This infuriated all of the White House staff involved in the meeting, but it infuriated me even more. The Palm Center touted itself as a nonpolitical think tank that did not engage in activism, yet here was one of its staff members threatening to derail a sensitive political meeting because he was not invited to it. That certainly was not the first example of a pro-repeal organization cutting off its nose to spite its face, and it would not be the last. It was not the first or last for the Palm Center either.

No one could quite figure out how the Palm Center had found out about this meeting, but many of us strongly suspected it was through the Raben Group. Gay DC lobbyist Robert Raben, a former assistant attorney general under Clinton, had been invited to the meeting, and the Palm Center had at times been a client of the Raben Group. Also, Raben had given Neff temporary office space to use while he was visiting DC for a few weeks, so Palm was physically collocated with Raben at the time. The connection was not hard to make. But Mark Glaze, a principal at the Raben Group, strongly denied that it was Raben who had spilled the beans about the meeting. In fact, Raben Group staff roasted Palm Center staff via conference call about that whole ugly incident after the fact, according to one participant who was on the call, and Neff was ejected from his temporary pro bono office space at the Raben Group soon thereafter. Glaze and Raben reportedly feared that Neff's collocation convicted them of leaking the details of the meeting to Neff. In many of our minds, it certainly did.

Monday morning was chilly, and I forgot to wear a jacket for the walk over to the White House. I always assumed that a suit jacket was enough of a jacket before stepping outside during winters in DC, but the cold air always reminded me how wrong I was—just in time for me to be too far away to go back in and get an overcoat. The walk to the White House was only about two and a half blocks from the Servicemembers United office, just down 17th Street, so I made it without getting frostbite.

Appointments for meetings in the Eisenhower Executive Office Building (EEOB), a part of the White House compound, usually required you go to the southwest gate of the compound to enter the grounds, then go up the gigantic stone staircase on the south side of the building. EEOB is by far my favorite building exterior in all of Washington. It is massive and majestic, but unfortunately it's almost always under renovation. The scaffolding continuously hides the ornate masonry and plentiful minicolumns that adorn the building's entire towering facade.

This meeting was to be held in the Secretary of War suite inside EEOB. The building used to house the War Department before the Pentagon was built, and the Secretary of War suite contained a large conference room with what appeared to be period furniture in it, which gave it a sense of official charm, although the chairs around the conference table were modern, leather, and, thankfully, comfortable.

As was often the case, I was the only one at this meeting who had ever even served a day in the military, much less served under or been impacted by DADT. It never ceased to amaze me that the affected constituency would not even be directly represented by one of its own if not for my presence at these meetings on DADT. And if anyone else at the meeting from the advocacy community had their way, I would not have been there either, nor would any other gay veteran. Those of us actually in the gay military community had had to elbow our way to a seat at the table from the very beginning, and we still had to fight to remain there.

The only reason I was there was because of the benevolence at the time of Brian Bond. I had cultivated an acquaintanceship with Bond, and he thought that I, and gay veterans in general, had a right to be represented. When details of the meeting came to light weeks and months later, many thought that HRC had gotten me in. Nothing could have been further from the truth. If it were up to HRC, I would never have even known the meeting took place, and neither would any other gay veteran or servicemember. Bond was responsible for including Servicemembers United in that meeting, and in future meetings with the administration as well.

One person who was conspicuously absent from this meeting was Aubrey Sarvis, the executive director of SLDN. It was quite a major and noticeable slight for Sarvis to be excluded, and the exclusion was arranged by the White House to send a clear message that administration officials, including and especially deputy chief of staff Jim Messina, were still quite angry at Sarvis over his 2009 "calls" to immediately include the DADT issue in the "defense budget." At the time, Sarvis's error went largely unnoticed and was of little importance within the repeal movement, but anyone who knew anything about the Defense Department's budgetary process recognized the ignorance on display right off. At one point, gay longtime congressman Barney Frank even went off on a gay political radio program, *The Michelangelo Signorile Show*, about people ignorantly calling for repeal language to be put in the defense budget.

As I had been saying to anyone who would listen at the time, DADT was not a budgetary item. No one seemed to understand that, and the gay community usually defaulted to SLDN for rhetoric back then. So for months the community looked like idiots calling for DADT repeal language to be put in the "budget" rather than in the Defense Department's legislative policy transmittals. And when the language was not in the budget, they went crazy again, which further reinforced their ignorance in the view of all who actually understood defense budgeting and politics.

Sarvis's astounding lack of expertise helps explain why the administration excluded him from the first big meeting of 2010. It was not just because he had called on them to do something; he had called on them to do something that was not remotely realistic for the first few months of the new presidency. Not only did it embarrass the administration, but it was not even possible for the president to take the called-for action to alleviate that embarrassment. In fact, Bond said that Messina was so angry with Sarvis that he didn't want him anywhere in the building for the foreseeable future. Sarvis would later have to work hard to reingratiate himself with the White House staff.

The White House meeting convened with a rather common cast of characters for the gay community but a rather uncommon cast given that this was DADT and not any other gay political issue. Present on the gay community's behalf were me, as executive director of Servicemembers United; Winnie Stachelberg, senior vice president for external affairs for the Center for American Progress (CAP); David Smith, vice president for programs at HRC; and gay DC lobbyists Hilary Rosen and Robert Raben. From the administration were Jim Messina, White House deputy chief of staff; Melody Barnes, director of the White House's Domestic Policy Council; Tina Tchen, director of the White House's Office of Public Engagement; Brian Bond, the openly gay deputy director of the Office of Public Engagement; John Berry, the openly gay director of the Office of Personnel Management; and a few other White House staffers whom I did not know at the time.

Messina, as the administration's senior point person on the DADT issue, led the meeting. The primary purpose of us being there seemed to be for them to confirm for us that Secretary of Defense Bob Gates and Joint Chiefs chairman Admiral Mike Mullen would be testifying the following day before the Senate Armed Services Committee on the topic of DADT. He hinted that these top two Pentagon officials would be testifying in a direction favorable to us, but he would not go into any specifics because of the leak that had already come out of the invited group (when Chris Neff of the Palm Center learned of the meeting). His hesitancy to bring up the content of the testimony, which I thought was understandable in light of that leak, severely limited the potential value of having these busy individuals in one room at the same time.

Although Messina would not talk about the upcoming testimony—the most he would say at the time was that the details of exactly what Mullen and Gates would say were "still being negotiated"—members of the advocacy community piped up to ask about what other actions the administration might take now in light of the president's State of the Union remarks. David Smith of HRC asked Messina directly if repeal language would be included in the Pentagon's budget, still using that erroneous terminology that SLDN had popularized; knowing what he meant, Messina humored him. In a rather abrupt, clear, and direct shutdown, Messina responded, "Repeal language will not be included in the budget." A shell-shocked Smith, who was sitting beside Rosen and directly across the table from Raben, actually restated Messina's answer in question form, "It won't be in the budget?" and an even more resolute Messina reiterated, "It will not be in the defense budget."

This represented a clear and undeniable signal that the White House might be working "with Congress and our military" this year on DADT, but the president would not be including that language in the Pentagon's policy transmittals for the authorization bill, which would have been the most surefire way to position DADT repeal language to pass Congress *this year*. Messina even went so far as to bring out the "two wars" argument, saying that the fact that the military was still engaged in combat in Iraq and Afghanistan at the moment was one of the reasons why they couldn't move on the issue immediately. I was especially surprised to hear him use that misguided argument, given that it was straight from our opponents' talking points tip sheet. I suppose he thought that talking about us being involved in two wars in a room full of activists who, other than me, had never even been in the military would help shut down backtalk, but it only served as further evidence of White House doublespeak on the DADT repeal timeline.

This exchange, which took place toward the end of Messina's time in the room, literally caused my jaw to drop. I was just stunned. Millions of progressives—and nonprogressive supporters of repeal—had taken the president's State of the Union remarks on DADT at face value, thinking he had to put the weight of the administration behind this effort if he wanted to get DADT repealed *this year*. Although I was more shocked at this stunning pronouncement, I was at least glad that the White House was not going to lead us on about this. Clearly they had been negotiating with Gates and Mullen over what they would and would not support, and inclusion of repeal language in the Pentagon's policy transmittals this year must have been where they drew the line.

Messina left this meeting early to go meet with the president, but Barnes, Tchen, and the others stayed behind to continue the conversation with us. My jaw dropped again when Barnes indicated that the administration would be open to hearing other strategies and plans for moving forward on DADT, if there were any. Here we were, supposedly with the crew inside the White House that was working and strategizing on how to best go about repealing DADT, and none of them seemed to be aware of the alternative proposals that we had already sent over—ideas on delayed implementation, phased repeal options, and so on. Since Bond was supposed to be the conduit for such communication, I incredulously looked his way, wondering how anyone in the room could pretend that other options had not already been presented. He motioned for me to speak up to Barnes, so I did just that.

I nervously blurted out a quick synopsis of a few other options the administration had that would have been more palatable to the Pentagon but still accomplished the goal of ending DADT once and for all. Barnes listened closely while other repeal advocates seemed confused, and she said they would be open to considering such options. I was still reeling on the inside from the newly discovered fact that they had not already considered such options—that evidently they had never even been forwarded the proposals and white papers that I, and surely others, too, had sent Bond the previous year.

When the meeting wrapped up, I was still floored by the meeting's other bombshell, Messina's assertion that they had already decided not to include repeal language in the 2010 Pentagon policy transmittals. But to me, the situation represented a challenge. Evidently to Smith and others, it represented defeat. As we walked out, Winnie Stach-elberg remarked to Smith that they now needed to figure out if they wanted to go after the Employment Nondiscrimination Act (ENDA) instead of repealing DADT in 2010. Smith, recognizing after glancing back that I was walking closely behind the two of them on the side-walk, did not respond.

When Smith returned to HRC's offices, he immediately called a meeting with his relevant staff to relay to them what had transpired at the White House meeting. According to two HRC staffers who were in that huddle, Smith rather bluntly informed them that the White House had already decided what it was going to do, and if they, mean-ing HRC, did not go along with it then they would essentially get cut out of the process.

I had a bit of a different take, however. I was deeply disappointed, but I saw the situation as the administration showing us its poker hand. Messina could have told us that a repeal in the policy transmit-tals remained a possibility, and/or that they were still negotiating with the Pentagon on the idea. That would likely have caused us to go softer on them than we otherwise would have—after all, you do not want to tick off someone you think is still actively working with you. But now that I knew they were not going to do it, I knew it was OK to encour-age a more aggressive stance against the White House's position.

A short time later, when I realized that the White House wasn't going to reverse course on those transmittals, I thought someone finally needed to sound the alarm for the community that this was going to be a harder fight than the administration and others were leading us to believe. But there was no way I could go on the record about it; the administration was known to retaliate harshly for not playing by their rules or not being complicit in whatever they wanted to do, and we were just at the very beginning of our work with them on DADT. So I agreed to go "on background" with journalist Kerry Eleveld of the *Advocate*, anonymously disclosing the troubling news out of that White House meeting.

Kerry then went to David Smith at HRC to ask about the revelation from an "anonymous meeting participant." In a characteristic move, Smith flat-out lied on the record to Kerry, claiming that Messina and company were "noncommittal" about putting DADT repeal language in the authorization bill transmittals, despite the fact that Smith himself had gotten Messina to repeat a firm denial. Following that, lobbyist Robert Raben, whose firm was also paid significant sums by HRC and relied heavily on cozy ties with the administration to service its clients, similarly spoke out to obscure Messina's comments. And when everyone within the "establishment" started quickly going after Eleveld to try to figure out if it was I—the newcomer without a blood loyalty to their incestuous circle of gay political operatives— who had leaked the information, even trying to pull the "It's only his word against everyone else's" line, Kerry pointed out that even if I was her first source, her article cited multiple sources to corroborate the story.

As one of the few people who knew what the truth actually was, I was astounded that these men would be willing to lie in such a brazen manner. Sure, they felt pressure from the White House to shoot back at the leaked revelations and play along in order to stay in the president's good graces, but I wondered how they would back out of their lies if someone had been just crazy enough to secretly record that meeting. With the technology to do that and get away with it cheaply and readily available, I was surprised that such ostensibly smart people weren't more careful when putting their reputations on the line like that. Of course, the language didn't end up in the defense transmittals for the authorization bill in the end—shocker!

The tricky part now for the advocacy community was that the administration could claim all day long that it supported DADT repeal. After all, the president had explicitly said so many times, and he had even included a call for repeal in the State of the Union address. But if he supported repeal *this year*, then he should have included repeal language in the Pentagon's legislative policy transmittals. But no one was talking about that. Activists were unintentionally giving the White House a complete pass because of their lack of understanding of the process. They would call on the president to support repeal of DADT, and the president would say that he already did, which was true. Then they would call on him to put it in the "budget," and he or his surrogates would say that DADT repeal was not a part of the budget, which was also true. The missing piece, of course, was why he was not putting it in the administration's defense policy transmittals that accompanied the budget. I decided it was time to personally remedy this hole in the activist community's understanding and rhetoric.

Over the next several months I wrote op-eds and guest blog posts about the distinction between the budget and the policy transmittals, and how the proper question was whether the president would insert repeal language into those transmittals. I began explaining this distinction to the senior staff at other pro-repeal organizations, including HRC, CAP, and SLDN, at our weekly DADT coalition meetings. And I began reaching out to the all-powerful gay and progressive blogosphere and media circles to educate them on the difference so that they could specify the correct mechanisms for presidential action in their writing.

In one particularly comprehensive op-ed for the *Huffington Post*, entitled "The LGBT Community's Raised Consciousness on DADT," I argued that the LGBT community on the whole was in a state of evolution in its understanding of DADT and how to properly pressure the president. This concept of a collective or community-wide understanding was unique, but it accurately reflected the growing widespread acknowledgment that if we were going to be more effective advocates and a more successful interest group community, we all needed to get smarter on this complex issue.

In addition to the traditional gay media outlets, including the *Advocate*, the *Washington Blade*, and *Metro Weekly*, and their enterprising political reporters Kerry Eleveld, Chris Johnson, and Chris Geidner, respectively, the blogosphere also became a powerful medium for education of and communication with the masses. The blogs, which often openly blended journalism and activism, played a particularly important role in keeping the progressive community informed about what was happening on the public stage and behind the scenes. Of particular note were the political blogs *AMERICAblog*, run by the always caffeinated John Aravosis and his much more laid-back counterpart Joe Sudbay; *Pam's House Blend*, run by North Carolina based blogmistress Pam Spaulding; and even lighter sociopolitical blogs like *Towleroad*, *Queerty*, and others. These latter blogs, even though they could be more gossipy and even salacious at times, nevertheless served very important roles in the gay political fights because of their mass appeal and their reach beyond just the gay political community.

This mass education and rhetorical correction campaign worked quickly, to my surprise, and soon many gay journalists, bloggers, and politicos were talking and writing about "transmittals." The final proof to me that I had succeeded in helping the community figure out how to really pin down the White House on its commitment was when the hard-core activist arm of the community, the folks involved in the new direct action groups that were springing up, changed their public calls on the president from "support repeal of DADT," to which he would always get a pass by responding that he already did, to "insert the language." To this, he certainly could not say he already had. Even if he would not change his mind, at least the pressure was more intense, because now we were actually asking for the right thing.

10

* * * * *

BOMBSHELL HEARINGS

On February 2, 2010, the morning following the meeting with Messina and company, activists and reporters packed a Senate Armed Services Committee hearing room, where the secretary of defense and the chairman of the Joint Chiefs of Staff were scheduled to give their annual testimony on the Pentagon's budget and policy requests for the following fiscal year. Jarrod and I occupied the second and third spots respectively in the front row, just to the right of the center aisle. It was a great vantage point from which to witness the history that was about to be made, but first we had to get through two hours of regularly scheduled testimony on budget, equipment, and other personnel policy issues.

The defense budget hearings were supposed to last three hours, but Senator Carl Levin, the committee chairman, had agreed to redirect the third hour of those hearings to the DADT issue. Senator Kirsten Gillibrand, who at the time had been facing potential Democratic primary challenges to retain the Senate seat to which she had been appointed when Hillary Clinton vacated the seat to become secretary of state, readily claimed credit in public for getting Senator

Levin to schedule the hearings on DADT, but in reality the scheduling was more the product of an agreement between avidly pro-repeal Levin, the White House, and the Pentagon than anything that one of the most junior senators in the chamber had orchestrated.

While Senator Gillibrand was suddenly very vocally supportive on gay issues in light of potential Democratic primary challenges in heavily Democratic New York State, her actual contributions at the time were more talk and less substantive action. But she was certainly trying; it was just that her junior status in the Senate at the time impeded her influence. HRC's political director, a straight woman who had come from the pro-choice community, even joked that HRC was trying to find ways to give Senator Gillibrand credit for something to help her out in the election, and since she was already claiming to have convinced Senator Levin to schedule a hearing on DADT that they were just going with it.

Some of the gay and progressive activists in the room seemed to be struggling to stay awake and attentive during the first two hours of the hearing that day, as senators questioned the senior defense leaders on a wide range of other important but rather dull issues. One random matter disposed of by the committee during this first part of the hearing, since a quorum was present, was the confirmation of several of President Obama's political appointees to high-level Pentagon positions. One of the names I heard quickly rattled off and voted on by the committee was Douglas B. Wilson, who had been nominated by President Obama to be the new assistant secretary of defense for public affairs.

I had been introduced to Doug the previous year by Paul Rieckhoff, the executive director of Iraq and Afghanistan Veterans of America. Doug had a long and storied career in politics, having served as a foreign policy adviser to former senator Gary Hart and as a diplomat with the State Department before working on President Clinton's reelection campaign and then securing an appointed position in the Pentagon as the principal deputy assistant secretary of defense for public affairs under then–secretary of defense Bill Cohen. During the Bush years, Doug had gone back into the private and nonprofit sectors. Although he made his permanent residence in Delaware with his partner, Doug and I arranged to meet for breakfast one morning at the University Club in Washington to become better acquainted. He mentioned over breakfast that morning that he had not been able to do as much as he wished he could have done during his stint in the Pentagon in the 1990s, and he hoped he would have the opportunity to do more to help the gay military community again in the future.

After his confirmation that day by the Senate Armed Services Committee and subsequent confirmation by the full Senate chamber, Doug would indeed go on to do more to help our community than anyone would ever know. As one of the highest-ranking political appointees in the Defense Department when the DADT issue resurfaced in 2010 and played itself out, he played a central role in the long and arduous process and was of great help to our community along the way, while never once crossing the line of impropriety. Some within DOD's leadership, including the secretary of defense himself, would later suspect Doug—and some political opponents would even accuse him—of strategically leaking favorable but confidential information to our side and to the media, which just didn't happen, despite our best efforts.

After two hours of committee business, including those nominations and other mundane matters, the first portion of the Senate budget hearing came to an end, and the energy level in the room became noticeably more electric. Secretary Gates and Admiral Mullen had chosen to give separate opening statements for the second part of the hearing rather than wrap their statements on DADT into their earlier opening remarks, so this portion effectively functioned like a completely separate and independent hearing just on the DADT issue alone.

Secretary Gates went first, giving a positive but relatively safe set of remarks. He acknowledged that the president had laid out a goal of working with Congress to repeal the DADT law and said that he fully supported that goal. This was without a doubt a remarkable opening, but thereafter Gates stuck with a sort of technocratic approach, announcing the details of a high-level working group that he had tasked with looking into the issues and potential challenges surrounding the repeal of DADT. While this obstacle to moving forward was somewhat predictable, what concerned me about the announcement of the working group was the length of time that Gates wanted it to span—virtually the rest of the calendar year.

This immediately stood out to me as problematic. While I had proposed and even lobbied for a commission of some sort in 2009 to help build political cover for repeal, I envisioned the life of that working group in the range of three to six months at the maximum, and it should have begun the prior year in order to allow Congress to move forward on legislative repeal in 2010. But if the White House and the Pentagon wanted to do a study group for that long in 2010, the working group's work and legislative action could not be pursued sequentially if we intended to get DADT done this year. Instead, they would have to be pursued simultaneously. But the simultaneous approach didn't jibe with Messina's blunt message to us privately the previous day that the administration would not put repeal language in the defense policy transmittals for that year, which would have been the easiest and surest way to jumpstart legislative action. Even if the working group's work continued through the end of the year, the administration knew—and if they hadn't known before, I at least had flat out told them—that there were safe ways to structure repeal language so that it didn't take effect until the working group finished its study. While options were starting to narrow, the road ahead was coming into sharper focus, even if those around us hadn't picked up on that yet.

One additional item that Gates announced before he finished his opening remarks was his intent to change the Defense Department's interpretation of the DADT law to eliminate some abuses in its application during the law's remaining life. This was especially important and helpful, because after more than a decade and a half on the books, the law had deteriorated to a state of arbitrary and capricious enforcement—even the policy's architects claimed to not recognize it anymore in practice. In fact, in 2006 I spoke with one of those architects, then-senator John Warner of Virginia, and told him the circumstances surrounding how I was outed within my unit and later discharged. Senator Warner immediately leaned over to his longtime aide and softly asked, "That's not how we intended this thing to work, is it?" So finally, after seventeen years, Gates promised to have more details on a narrower and "fairer" application of the law within forty-five days.

Next came the chairman of the Joint Chiefs. Admiral Mullen also started out his remarks by going in a positive but safe direction, acknowledging support for the plan that Secretary Gates had just laid out for reviewing the issues and challenges related to the repeal of DADT. Interestingly, he seemed to be speaking on behalf of all of the Joint Chiefs, necessitating a least-common-denominator statement of support for the process rather than the goal. But even this was quite significant, as he wasn't outright opposing a thorough and comprehensive review of the policy or simply repeating the bogus congressional findings from 1993, such as the infamous, unilaterally determined "fact" that "homosexuality is incompatible with military service," as military leaders had always done.

Admiral Mullen would still be considered a pioneer had he stopped right there. But, of course, he didn't. About halfway through his opening remarks, Admiral Mullen went from fair-minded pioneer to a true hero of repeal in the hearts and minds of millions of Americans.

Mr. Chairman, speaking for myself and myself only, it is my personal belief that allowing gays and lesbians to serve openly would be the right thing to do. No matter how I look at this issue, I cannot escape being troubled by the fact that we have in place a policy which forces young men and women to lie about who they are in order to defend their fellow citizens. For me personally, it comes down to integrity—theirs as individuals and ours as an institution. I also believe that the great young men and women of our military can and would accommodate such a change. I never underestimate their ability to adapt.

Still sitting there in the middle of the front row of the public audience seating, I turned to Jarrod and said, "Oh my God. He just made history." And while Admiral Mullen went on to again stress the importance of a thorough and deliberate process, and even the need, for reasons known best to him, to involve military families in that process, the personal journey he took out onto that limb in front of the Senate Armed Services Committee and all of political America changed the course of events on DADT.

The question-and-answer period began, and true to form, Senator John McCain began his infamous things-aren't-going-my-way crankiness right out of the gate. When Senator Levin announced that he had to restrict the first round of questioning to three minutes in order to fit all committee members in at least once while the secretary and the chairman were able to remain on the Hill, Senator McCain balked. When Senator Levin reminded him that his staff had received the witnesses' schedules in advance, he grumpily complained that he hadn't seen it. "You're the chairman," Senator McCain finally mumbled before allowing the first round of questioning to begin. But that wouldn't be the end of Senator McCain's theatrics that day. As ranking member, he went second after the chairman, Senator Levin. It soon became clear that Senator McCain wasn't actually interested in hearing much testimony that day, because as soon as he finished hearing the line of questioning he was interested in, he stormed out of the hearing room and didn't bother to return.

Senator McCain would get his time to gloat soon, when the four service chiefs were each called to testify before the same Senate committee. Although Admiral Mullen had communicated the Joint Chiefs' collective agreement that a comprehensive study would be worthwhile and had spoken only for himself thereafter, the chairman clearly disagreed on a personal level with the other chiefs about the need to repeal the DADT law, even for the sake of integrity—"theirs as individuals and ours as an institution," as Admiral Mullen had put it. In their testimony, the service chiefs gave Senator McCain and our other opponents the ammunition they needed to keep fighting, at least for the time being.

Our opposition also got another round of ammunition from another group of flag officers—hundreds of them. In response to the growing list of more than one hundred retired flag officers that the Palm Center had gotten to sign onto a joint letter supporting the repeal of DADT, the first round of which he had given to Servicemembers United to release at our "12,000 Flags for 12,000 Patriots" event on the National Mall in 2007, Elaine Donnelly and her Center for Military Readiness quickly began assembling their own list of flag officers who were staunchly opposed to repeal. We always knew that there was majority support among the older retired veterans for keeping DADT, so we were certain when Belkin was ready to go public with his list, initially of twenty-eight officers, that Donnelly would not be far behind with a larger list. But it was somewhat surprising to us that she waited so long to release her counter-list. Evidently she was preparing quite a sizeable list, and many of the target signers weren't the e-mailing types.

When she finally released her own list, which she entitled "Flag and General Officers for the Military," Donnelly had astonishingly assembled over one thousand signatories. This was undoubtedly a damaging hit for us, but we at Servicemembers United had some suspicions about Donnelly's list right off the bat. One of the names on the list was footnoted as having been signed by the general's widow, and a simple search revealed that he had actually died before the statement was written. This prompted us to put together a research team to look into a sample of the other names on Donnelly's list. SU staffer Dylan

Knapp headed the effort and recruited a group of SU volunteers to help with the digging. And without even having to dig far, we struck gold.

The SU research team's findings were released in March 2010 in a report that we called "Flag and General Officers for the Military: A Closer Look," and they neutralized Donnelly's powerful weapon. Some of the initial facts we discovered by looking at the names were to be expected. First, most of the signers were very old. The average age of our inquiry sample was seventy-four, and the oldest signer had been born in 1911 and had entered military service in 1930. Few of them had served in the military when DADT was in force, and an even smaller number had served during the current century. Second, some of alleged signers were found to be dead, including the one who was footnoted as having been added later by his widow because he "would want his name added." But even for that entry, we soon found out that even prior to his death this general's health had deteriorated to the point that he had probably lost the ability to communicate as far back as 2003.

Armed with this information, we had enough to reduce the list's overall credibility and dispute the associated claims that Donnelly based on her influential petition, but more was to come. PBS's *NewsHour* had covered Donnelly's release of the list shortly after it came out, and one of the generals they contacted to ask about the list expressed surprise at seeing his name as among the signers, claiming that he had never agreed to be listed. But *NewsHour*'s outreach to signers was extremely limited and conducted under a deadline; we now had the bandwidth to try to verify a slightly larger number of signers.

Our sample for basic Internet research had included two hundred of the names on the list, but we decided to try to reach out personally to a more manageable sample of signatories. We attempted to contact thirty signers directly and were successful in reaching eight of them. Of those eight, three of the generals who appeared on the list denied the legitimacy of their inclusion on Donnelly's list. One told an SU staffer, "I do not wish to be on any list regarding this issue," while another remarked, "I do not remember being asked about the issue." A third said to us, "I have never agreed to represent either side of this issue." Yet another signer, who was not included in our sample, told Chris Johnson of the *Washington Blade* (then temporarily called the *DC Agenda*), "I do not believe there should be any limitations based on sexual orientation."

Donnelly's list also turned out to be somewhat scandalous. Signatories who were happy to be listed included a general who had been involved in covering up the administration of a potentially unsafe anthrax vaccine to troops, another who had a history of publicly making racist remarks as late as 1993, another who was forced to step down as the head of a school for at-risk youth after his own program was found to be scandal-ridden, and much more. After Servicemembers United released the report, MSNBC host Rachel Maddow featured our revelations that night on her television show. After that, politicians' public references to the "Flag and General Officers for the Military" list were noticeably reduced, and Donnelly's best weapon against us had been effectively neutralized. But we still had a long way to go.

As events rapidly unfolded in those early weeks of 2010, it started becoming obvious to those of us with a view on both sides of the curtain that the administration had made a deal with the Pentagon. In exchange for senior defense leaders' support for repealing the DADT law, the president would allow the Pentagon to spend all of 2010 doing an extensive and expensive study to help build both cover and consensus. After the study period concluded and Congress and the public had time to digest the results, then legislative action to repeal DADT would be pursued in 2011 as part of the normal defense authorization process for the following fiscal year. As I would later tell many frustrated activists when they lamented that the administration did not truly have a plan for DADT, as of early 2010 they finally did have a plan. That plan was just to do their study in 2010 and pursue legislative repeal in 2011.

Unfortunately, the administration's plan would have been disastrous; it would have resulted in DADT still being the law of the land
to this day. What they didn't count on way back in late 2009 when this
plan was being formulated was the potential for one chamber of Congress to change hands after the 2010 midterm elections. For most of
America, that possibility didn't start to materialize until the spring of
2010, and many believe that it didn't really sink in for overly confident
senior administration officials until well into the summer.

Despite rapid progress and support on the Senate side on Capitol Hill now, we still didn't even have a Senate repeal bill at this time
equivalent to the Military Readiness Enhancement Act in the House.
Senator Joseph Lieberman had long been our community's target for
spearheading this effort in the Senate, but Lieberman didn't want to
go through the trouble to introduce a repeal bill in the Senate only to
have the administration lollygag along and cause the bill to stagnate in
the upper chamber for months and years as it had in the House. While
we were pushing Lieberman to make the leap, he and his staff begged
the administration for some sort of solid commitment that they were
going to support bringing the bill through to fruition that same year.
But the administration gave the senator's office no clear answers,
another troubling sign, and pressure from our side was mounting. So
Senator Lieberman made the call to move forward with the bill, the
White House be damned.

Servicemembers United worked with Senator Lieberman's office
for some time on the details of the bill's introduction. So did representatives from HRC, SLDN, CAP, and Third Way (a growing moderate
political think tank), but we seemed to be the only ones who had an
issue with the proposed name of the new Senate bill. Senator Lieberman's office wanted to call it the "FAIR Military Act of 2010," with the
acronym FAIR standing for "Fairness and Improved Readiness." However, SU staff were aghast at the obvious potential for mocking in the
blogosphere and even in the wider mainstream military community:
all you had to do was put the letter "Y" on the end of that acronym and

you had enough fodder for jokes and right-wing headlines for years to come. As an alternative, Servicemembers United recommended calling the bill the "Military FORCE Act of 2010," with FORCE standing for "Fairness, Operational Readiness, and Cohesion Enhancement." However, that name was ironically deemed too militaristic and aggressive, and in the absence of any other catchy acronyms available at the last minute, the senator opted for just naming the bill after its House counterpart: the Military Readiness Enhancement Act.

The Senate bill itself was identical to the House bill as well, in all provisions except for one. Senator Lieberman, being the centrist from Connecticut he was, had recently clashed with the state's ultraliberal community when he was defeated in the Democratic primary in his last reelection bid for the Senate seat he had held since 1988 (he subsequently ran as an independent and won reelection anyway). Like other moderate and conservative Democrats, and nearly all Republicans, Senator Lieberman had always objected to the practice of Ivy League schools banning or refusing to support ROTC programs on campus, first because of antiwar sentiment and then, allegedly, because of anti-gay discrimination within the military. But many gays in the military didn't even support this misuse of their community by elite universities and faculties as an excuse to continue to discriminate against the armed forces on campus. Many thought that the senior defense leadership perhaps wouldn't be as socially conservative as it is today had liberal Ivy League schools cultivated and supported officer training programs on campus and filled the ranks over the preceding decades with more Ivy League–educated officers.

Regardless, the impending end of DADT seemed to provide a perfect test of whether these elite universities really were using the gay military community as a prop to mask antimilitary sentiment, so Senator Lieberman sought to include a provision in his version of the repeal bill that stuck a finger in the eye of these elite schools—including Connecticut's own Ivy League member school and the senator's alma mater, Yale. So an extra provision was added that required the secretary of defense to prepare a report soon after the repeal of DADT went into effect on whether America's universities that did not host ROTC programs had taken any steps after the repeal of DADT to reinstitute those programs on their campuses. When we were briefed on this provision by Senator Lieberman's staff, none of us advocates had any problem with it, and thus a Senate bill was finally ready to be introduced.

As was the case with most of these public events on the DADT issue staged by politicians, all that was left was to find a veteran or two to appear at the bill introduction press conference. All political operations in the United States—campaigns, elected officials, their offices, and so on—quickly become skilled in the art of using servicemembers and veterans as props for political purposes, and our allies are no exception. While sometimes the use of a member of the military or a veteran is appropriate, the practice is often carried out in poor taste, especially by members of Congress and their offices. This time, however, I would agree that it was appropriate to highlight someone who had been affected by DADT at the press conference announcing the Senate DADT repeal bill.

Other than Jarrod, who was still an in-house consultant at HRC at the time, HRC only had one person to use for anything related to DADT, and that was Eric Alva. But Eric was a little overexposed in the media by that point, and HRC didn't offer him up for Senator Lieberman's press conference. SLDN lobbied Lieberman's office hard to use one or two of its Military Advisory Council members—who were straight, retired flag officers. I found their choice a bit odd, so I proposed using a gay veteran who had either served under DADT and left the military because of it or had been discharged pursuant to the policy. We submitted a list of three candidates and their bios for the prominent spotlight position, and from that list the senator's staff chose former air force officer Mike Almy.

Almy had been a virtual unknown in the repeal movement before I recommended him to Senator Lieberman's office. Almy was a competent speaker with a compelling story, and he looked good on camera, although this would be his first foray into the public spotlight. He had been a major in the air force serving in Iraq only a few years before when another servicemember who had been sent in to replace him in his billet discovered some e-mails that Almy had written on a government computer that evidently revealed that he was gay. Almy wouldn't discuss or disclose the specific content of the e-mails he had sent, so I distinctly asked him on two different occasions to at least assure me that there was nothing inappropriate in them or anything that could be considered a liability for our community and our issue if it eventually came out, especially given the fact that they had been written on a work computer.

Almy swore up and down that the discovered e-mails that had prompted such harsh treatment from his command and led to his eventual discharge under DADT were completely innocent and appropriate, and with those assurances in hand I felt comfortable moving forward with my recommendation. Little did I know at the time, however, that perhaps my definition of what sort of e-mail was "appropriate" and "not a liability in any way" differed wildly from Almy's definition.

The bill introduction event took place on March 3, 2010, and it went off without a hitch. From that point on we finally had ourselves a companion bill in the Senate to the repeal bill in the House, which had first been introduced back in 2005. Things were now progressing quite nicely. Mike Almy landed a spot on MSNBC's *The Rachel Maddow Show* that night, and at each of these events he maintained the carefully crafted and repeated story that he had been treated "like a common criminal" by the air force simply for being gay after the fact was discovered inadvertently in his "private e-mails." And from there, despite the fact that SLDN had not previously been willing to recommend or consider him for any prominent role before, after I plucked him from obscurity and gave him a public platform, SLDN eagerly jumped in and made him their pet project from then on.

I had offered to hire Almy as a principal at SU immediately after I recommended him to Lieberman's office, which would have given him a substantive role in the DADT repeal movement, but he wanted to retain the ability to pull a paycheck from SU and try to get one from SLDN simultaneously. When I found out that he was trying to double dip, I withdrew the generous offer to work for SU, and he thereafter went to work part-time for SLDN in a much lower role, basically as one of their media puppets. It had always been a theme of SU's to put those impacted by DADT in significant (i.e., decision-making, strategy-shaping) roles within the DADT repeal movement and to combat attempts by organizations like HRC and SLDN to relegate those actually affected by the issue to stage-managed puppet roles. But not everyone was up for greater levels of responsibility within the movement, and some were comfortable being relegated to less meaningful roles in exchange for a greater share of the public spotlight and the social perks that came with it.

Two weeks later, on Thursday, March 18, 2010, the biggest circus of all pulled into the station in Washington in the form of another Senate hearing on DADT. But instead of a substantive one, in which our side got to put forward several of the many, many experts who could testify convincingly about the existing evidence that DADT was enacted for bogus reasons to begin with (like Dr. Nathaniel Frank), or that current empirical evidence showed no correlation between the presence of openly gay troops and deteriorations in unit cohesion or morale (like Dr. Laura Miller of RAND), or that there were plenty of retired military leaders who thought that the repeal of DADT would actually be a good thing (like any one of the 125 generals and admirals who by then had signed on to the joint letter saying as much), we instead were only allowed a stunt hearing. The Senate Armed Services Committee staff, in what was ultimately a naïve and patronizing decision, wanted to replicate what was already out on the public record a million times over—a few typical stories of people being discharged.

Now, I will be the first one to say that putting a face on the issue and showing America what kind of talent it was losing because of the DADT law was a key element in our ultimate victory, and Servicemembers United had even pioneered this as a systematic strategy at the local, regional, and national levels. But by that point, and as a result of our work, there was no shortage of stories of those who had been discharged. I strongly disagreed that our community's one chance to select our ideal witnesses to make a forceful case for repeal before some of the most politically savvy people in the country should be wasted with boo-hoo stories. But, alas, both the committee staff and SLDN did want to use this once-in-a-generation opportunity in such a manner, and our lone objection was overwhelmingly overruled.

But even if they were going to use our one shot at a double-sided Senate hearing for boo-hoo stories, I simply couldn't believe that Aubrey Sarvis would insist on putting forward only SLDN's own legal clients at the expense of much better options for witnesses. One of their proposed choices was Mike Almy. With the stakes much higher going into a Senate hearing, which unlike a one-sided press conference could include fierce opposition cross-examination, I once again asked Mike, and now Aubrey too, if there was any way in which someone could construe the content of the e-mails in question in Mike's discharge story as a potential liability to our community and our issue. Once again, Mike assured me that their content could in no way be construed to be a liability, a position for which Aubrey vouched. So although I still objected to not using a stronger category of witnesses at this hearing, like experts in military sociology and group psychology, I was at least satisfied at the time with using Mike for this hearing, based on those explicit assurances.

I was never sold, however, on SLDN's second witness, and I think her inclusion was a classic example of SLDN's preference for using its own assets even when it wasn't necessarily best for the issue. Jenny Kopfstein had been a client of SLDN's for a number of years and was a plaintiff on SLDN's failed lawsuit challenging DADT in the courts. She seemed nice enough, but she wasn't an ideal spokesperson for our issue or our community. In addition to not being very polished, she readily admitted to having *intentionally* outed herself to her command, knowing that she would surely be discharged from the navy as a result. It was a story line that sometimes appeared in DADT repeal advocacy but was the most unhelpful to the repeal movement overall. Despite this liability, SLDN aggressively pushed her on the committee staff over our strenuous objections.

In the end, the hearings went fine, as expected, but there is no way to measure the damage that was done by deliberately putting forward a less-than-ideal witness. Likewise, we will never know how much more we could have been helped in the repeal fight by stronger witnesses, especially those who were issue experts or straight flag officer allies with impeccable credentials—the very kinds of people that opponents like Senator McCain said they wanted to hear from.

While we didn't bother to attend this show hearing ourselves, Servicemembers United did make a unique contribution to it. At many congressional hearings, the major interest groups and community representatives are offered the opportunity to submit written testimony for the record to supplement the in-person witness testimony. These written submissions rarely if ever actually get read by the members of the committees to which they are submitted, but it's a nice symbolic gesture. This would have been a more appropriate way to submit testimonials from discharged gay veterans, but since we already had those going on that day in person, most other organizations just used their written testimonies as a way to promote themselves and rehash the same old arguments for repeal that we had been repeating for years.

Servicemembers United, however, turned over its written testimony submission to its active duty members. Since those currently serving under the law were not allowed to speak out about it, we gave them our organizational platform at the hearing to finally have their voices heard on the record before Congress. In all, we submitted over twenty pages of anonymous testimonials from actively serving gay and lesbian troops on what it was like to serve under DADT, the challenges and burdens they faced on a daily basis, and what repeal of the DADT law would mean for them.

We weren't able to utilize active duty servicemembers very often at all, but since these testimonials had to be anonymous anyway, we were more than happy to turn over the platform to them and get their diverse and passionate voices on the record in a congressional hearing. Our written testimony is one my favorite things that we did that year, but few people even noticed it. Still, we remain very proud of being the only organization to give a diverse range of active duty gay and lesbian troops a true voice before Congress during the DADT repeal fight, even if it was only symbolic.

11

* * * * *

CELEBRITIES ON THE STAGE
AND SOLDIERS AT THE GATE

While the second DADT hearing on Capitol Hill was taking place on March 18, another stunt got underway just a short walk down Pennsylvania Avenue. In the large plaza in front of DC's City Hall called Freedom Plaza, the stage was set, literally, for comedienne Kathy Griffin to appear at a "Repeal DADT" rally that was being organized by HRC. But holding this rally on the same day and at the same time as the second Senate hearing of 2010 on DADT was by no means HRC's choice, and the senior staff loathed having to be involved in such an ill-planned stunt.

A week earlier, Kathy Griffin had just unilaterally announced that she was going out to Washington, DC, and holding a rally for repeal. This pronouncement caught nearly everyone who worked on the DADT issue by surprise—particularly since her frivolously scheduled event directly overlapped with the hearing, a nightmare media and logistical conflict that no one with any sense in Washington would have allowed had they had any say. Griffin was shooting the latest season of her reality-based television series for Bravo (which would end up being the last before it was canceled), and it must have seemed like a good idea to Griffin and her California-based production team to incorporate the hottest political issue of the day into the show.

According to several senior HRC staffers, virtually no one within HRC's leadership wanted to divert the time and resources to Griffin's poorly timed event, but they quickly decided to take control of it and make sure a good show happened—both to keep their celebrity supporter happy and to make sure that such a high-profile event didn't completely flop during a critical week for repeal advocates. They also didn't mind the easy branding opportunity, nor the chance to be featured again on Griffin's TV show. But it was not a unanimous decision; internally, HRC was split, and one senior staff member even quit over the utter ridiculousness of the whole affair.

Ultimately, although Griffin's decision to insert herself into the events going on in Washington that week was, without a doubt, incredibly selfish, there was nothing any of us could do to stop it. Unfortunately for Griffin, however, her stunt ended up somewhat backfiring on her, as neither she nor the two pro-repeal witnesses at the Senate hearing turned out to be the star of the day.

Before the rally, Griffin went over to Capitol Hill and actually sat in on the first part of the Senate hearing, which was open to the public. But after apparently becoming bored and not liking what she was hearing, she disrupted the proceedings with a brief vocal outburst from the audience seating area, then stormed out and headed for her conflicting event. The outburst was loud enough for even the witnesses sitting at the front of the room before the panel of senators to hear her, although they were facing the opposite direction. Without turning around to look, they were left wondering what the disturbance behind them was all about, as one of the witnesses, Mike Almy, later told me.

By the time Griffin arrived at Freedom Plaza, an elaborate raised stage and an expansive information booth for HRC had already been constructed. A fairly large crowd had also begun assembling, the result of both heavy promotional work done by HRC in the days leading up to the rally and the curiosity of hordes of DC-based professionals who wandered out of their offices and into the plaza on their lunch breaks. Since HRC had taken the lead on organizing the rally and Jarrod was off in Indiana doing another event that day, the organization asked me if I would address the assembled crowd. Despite my doubts about the wisdom of the whole event, I reluctantly agreed to speak, alongside Eric Alva, Joe Solmonese, and a few others, before Griffin took the stage for her "performance."

Shortly before the rally commenced, I called Jarrod in Indiana to report on how it was shaping up. Jarrod, who had been at HRC for more than nine months at this point, had become quite fed up with the wait-and-see attitude that HRC's senior leadership took toward the DADT issue. He was having to fight hard for every penny spent on DADT advocacy work, and he felt strongly that he worked within an organization that not only didn't care too much for working on repealing DADT but also had an astounding level of ignorance about and even disdain for the military itself. I told him that the plaza was beginning to fill up but that the ridiculousness of the event seemed just over the top. I offered to text him photos after we hung up—including one of the drag queen in a camouflage-colored tutu and bra standing in front of me.

Jarrod warned me especially to watch out for any attempts that Kathy Griffin might make to get the crowd to salute. He said that the previous day at HRC's headquarters, she had said that she wanted to instruct the crowd to wave flags with their right hands while saluting together with their left hands. The catastrophic problem with that scene, as anyone with the slightest knowledge of military custom would know, is that saluting is always done with the right hand only. Luckily, Jarrod was there to correct them all the previous day, but he rightly feared what other mishaps this publicity-hungry celebrity would cause as our years of hard work hung in the balance. I didn't even bother telling him about her outburst at the Senate hearing that morning.

As we waited backstage for the rally to start, scores of attendees lined the rope cordoning off the open-air backstage area, chatting with several of us over the rope line. One of those I spoke to there was Dan Choi, an Iraq War veteran who spoke Arabic quite well and who was the first in a series of gay and lesbian servicemembers and veterans to publicly come out on *The Rachel Maddow Show*. Curiously, he had come to the rally in his full US Army uniform. Another gentleman, also in uniform, was with him, although I didn't recognize his friend. As Eric, Joe, Kathy, I, and others made our way toward the steps on the side of the stage, Dan managed to pull Kathy aside for a few moments to talk to her. I continued on to the side of the stage, but looking back I could see the two of them engaged in an intense conversation. Suddenly, Dan crossed the rope line and came into the backstage area, with Griffin helping him under.

Dan had asked Griffin directly if he could join her on stage, and she had agreed, to the surprise and consternation of everyone there from HRC. Dan then joined the rest of us over by the stage's side steps, where, ironically, an angry Joe Solmonese leaned over and quietly said to Choi, "This better not be a joke." Dan defiantly responded to Joe that this issue wasn't a joke to him. Then, after the rest of us had spoken but just before Kathy prompted Dan to join her on stage, Dan leaned over to me and whispered in my ear, "I'm going to get arrested at the White House today and I want you to support me." He then bolted up the steps and onto the stage with Kathy Griffin.

Dan had already become somewhat of an anomaly within the DADT repeal movement by insisting on remaining an independent activist. Most of the movement's public figures succumbed to attempts by organizations like SLDN and HRC to control them, and while they may have appeared to be speaking and acting for themselves, most were actually being carefully stage-managed and told what to do by their handlers. Aubrey Sarvis had tried to get Dan to become an exclusive asset of SLDN, even asking him to sign a ridiculously restrictive exclusive representation agreement, which Dan later showed me. But he, like Jarrod and myself and a few others over the years, refused to become a marionette. Instead he joined forces with one organization or another for single events or initiatives but clearly remained in charge of his own schedule, agenda, and message.

The only organization that Dan aligned himself with for any length of time was Knights Out, a new and small organization for LGBT West Point alumni, but that affiliation would be relatively short-lived as Dan grew frustrated that no one else in the association wanted to do any serious work to forward the DADT repeal movement. Instead, they were content to ride on Dan's coattails. Of the three LGBT service academy alumni organizations, Knights Out had become the most recognized only because of Choi's association with it in the beginning, but even it never played a significant role in the repeal movement. (In defense of the other alumni groups, they intentionally eschewed involvement in the politics and instead focused on serving as a social and support network for LGBT alumni of those institutions, a fine goal in and of itself.)

As Dan took the stage, he immediately brought some seriousness to the Kathy Griffin rally, telling Griffin, surely with an eye to Solmonese too, "You're great at telling jokes, but this is not a joke." For the next ten minutes, he energized the crowd by railing against the injustice of DADT in a rousing and historic speech. He then pledged that at the end of the rally, he'd go stage a spontaneous protest in front of the White House, less than two blocks away. At the end of this announcement, he turned to Griffin and those of us to the side of the stage and asked if we were with him. "Kathy Griffin, are you with me?"—to which she instantly replied, "Of course." Then came "Joe Solmonese, are you with me? Eric Alva, are you with me? Alex Nicholson, are you with me? Will you all go with me?"

Each of the people he called out either answered in the affirmative or gave a thumbs-up in full view of the cameras, and the crowd cheered as he enlisted them to join him too. Everyone on stage except me, however, would renege on that public commitment, despite the fact that I was the only one of them who knew of Dan's intention to get arrested. Admittedly, I had no clue how or why he planned to get arrested. All I knew was exactly what he had whispered in my ear in the seconds before he took the stage.

Months later, I would watch the episode of Kathy Griffin's reality show that covered these events and be utterly appalled to see that she and her producers had blatantly lied to viewers about that whole incident, especially relating to why Griffin didn't follow through on her promise ("Of course!"). Griffin said in her show that she had a commitment to stay with the hundreds assembled in the plaza for the rally and finish the event, so she couldn't possibly have gone with Dan to the White House. However, as the unedited video clearly showed, Dan had pleaded for the crowd and Griffin to join him at the *end* of the event. He even waited around for a good ten to fifteen minutes after the event ended for Griffin and the others who had promised to join him, but they refused to go.

After so much talk by Kathy Griffin about supporting our movement and our community, it became abundantly clear that 100 percent of her involvement was for selfish reasons only, not just the 95 percent that many of us had previously suspected. She turned an important day into a clown show and blatantly lied about her willingness to join Choi for a more meaningful peaceful protest. And then she went on the air and lied again in a pitiful attempt to absolve herself of responsibility. Things could have gone a lot differently that day, and I held out hope at every turn that they would. But ultimately, Griffin chose to take the coward's way out, and she owes Choi and the rest of our community a major apology.

Despite being snubbed by Griffin, Solmonese, and the others involved with HRC, Choi, along with scores of rally attendees, proceeded the two blocks to the north side of the White House property. Although I didn't know him at the time, I later learned that the other person in uniform with Choi was Jim Pietrangelo, a former army captain who had been discharged under DADT and who had been a plaintiff in SLDN's lawsuit challenging the constitutionality of DADT in the First Circuit Court of Appeals. Pietrangelo had later become disenchanted with the SLDN legal effort and separated himself out from the other group of plaintiffs in the case in order to pursue his own legal strategy, which ultimately ended when the US Supreme Court declined to hear his appeal. (SLDN, meanwhile, had ceased to pursue its case after failing at the appellate level, refusing to submit their case for Supreme Court review.)

Once they arrived at the fence directly in front of the White House's north portico, Choi and Pietrangelo wasted no time getting down to business. After a brief speech, both men jumped up on the ledge bordering the wide sidewalk—a detail that would become quite consequential later on—and handcuffed themselves to the White House fence. As a stunned crowd cheered, Choi continued to address them as the Secret Service scrambled to respond. Some of the gay and progressive media from the rally had already wandered over to cover events as they unfolded, and they were soon joined by other members of the media who filtered out of the White House pressroom as the crowd grew. The resulting shots of Dan Choi and Jim Pietrangelo became iconic, representing not only the growing frustration within the DADT repeal movement but also a wider progressive frustration with a White House that had promised far more than it delivered.

Dan and Jim were assisted by a feisty young lesbian mother of two from Fresno, California, named Robin McGehee. McGehee had become an unlikely national-level activist for LGBT equality when the parent-teacher organization at the school one of her children attended forced her to resign as its president because of her involvement in the protest movement against California's anti–gay marriage referendum, Proposition 8. Newly energized, McGehee had gone on to help organize several highly successful regional and national equality initiatives, including the Proposition 8–related Meet in the Middle event in central California and the National Equality March in Washington, DC, in 2009. After the National Equality March, which was as much an anti-"Gay Inc." initiative as it was a populist call for more federal action on LGBT equality issues, McGehee became involved in a follow-up effort to continue the momentum. The march had demonstrated an intense and widespread yearning for a more aggressive and representative LGBT lobbying and advocacy effort on the national stage, so after the march McGehee and several fellow activists, including Kip Williams, Paul Yandura, Dan Choi, and others, banded together to form a new direct action advocacy group called GetEqual. Choi's White House fence event would launch not only a new phase in the DADT repeal movement but also a new, more aggressive, and uncompromising organization—one without which, I would argue, we likely could not have won the DADT repeal fight in the end.

The Choi/Pietrangelo/GetEqual White House event electrified a large portion of the progressive community and helped refocus pressure on the president to do more to get DADT repeal pushed through in 2010 instead of waiting until 2011. But the activists and advocates' timetable for seeing the repeal of the DADT law come about conflicted with the timetable that the Pentagon wanted and had agreed to support. The president was, therefore, stuck between senior leaders in the Defense Department, whose support we all needed in order to make this happen, and the progressive political community, to whom he had implicitly promised that repeal would come *this year*. The problem was that the White House clearly didn't intend to follow through on that promise and instead was deferring to defense leaders' desired timetable.

Just over a month later, on April 20, Choi and Pietrangelo were back in handcuffs on the White House fence again, along with four other uniformed protestors, all veterans. The pressure and the protests were growing, and just two weeks later, on May 2, yet another group of activists chained themselves to the White House fence. This time Choi and Pietrangelo weren't able to join them. They were under a court order from their second protest to stay away from the White House perimeter until their cases were resolved in court. But Dan and

Jim were still present for the action. They had been across the street in Lafayette Park just moments before the fence chaining, speaking out at a rally also organized by GetEqual.

About a week before, New York–based activist Justin Elzie, a Marine Corps veteran who had become involved with GetEqual and who had also been a prominent figure in the 1993 fight for gays in the military, had reached out to me about speaking at an event they were planning to hold in Lafayette Park on Sunday, May 2. I was admittedly a little nervous about joining a GetEqual protest, as my role within the repeal movement had always been more of a veteran organizer and inside-the-room negotiator and strategist. But two days before the event, Defense Secretary Robert Gates released a stern letter to Congress asking it not to move on DADT repeal until well after the Pentagon's study was completed and released in December. Things were getting seriously bogged down, especially since it was starting to look like the House of Representatives might flip to Republican control after the November elections, and I was personally growing increasingly frustrated.

I had no interest in getting arrested, but I was ready to become a little more belligerent in my public rhetoric. At the last minute, I told Elzie that I would be happy to join them and speak at the rally. Jarrod agreed to join in as well, a move that was nervously sanctioned by HRC, as did Aubrey Sarvis from SLDN and a number of other veteran activists from across the country, including Brett Stout from New York, Evelyn Thomas from San Diego, and several others.

As the rally got under way on Sunday afternoon, former Democratic National Committee chairman Howard Dean happened to be simultaneously attending another event nearby. When gay DC communications consultant and activist Lane Hudson saw him at the event, he told Dean about the GetEqual rally in front of the White House and invited Dean to walk over with him. We were about halfway through the rally when, to everyone's surprise, Hudson and Dean walked across Lafayette Park together and joined us at the front of the staging area. Dean spoke to the assembled crowd briefly, but his support for the pressure campaign on President Obama and his impromptu presence at the rally immediately raised the media profile of the event.

Speaking of media, the previous evening Jarrod and I had attended several receptions that are held annually in conjunction with the White House Correspondents' Association dinner. Although the ritzy Washington event is more for socializing and being seen, Jarrod and I used the opportunity of our presence there to converse with and pin down several key senators and top administration officials on DADT. We thanked Senator Susan Collins for her continued support on the issue and joked with Tina Tchen, director of the White House Office of Public Engagement, that it was good to finally run into her somewhere other than at a conference table. At the typically conservative *Washington Times* reception, we surprised Massachusetts's Republican junior senator, Scott Brown, by chatting him up about defense issues and then switching to the topic of DADT in what he surely thought would be a no-liberal-politics zone.

We took a break to snap photos with Betty White and talk about St. Olaf before running into the president's chief of staff, Rahm Emanuel. I spoke with Emanuel briefly about our strong desire to see DADT repeal pushed through in 2010 before asking him what he thought the issue's chances were of succeeding at that point. Emanuel thought for a second before saying that he thought repeal still had a 30 or 40 percent chance.

The following day at the rally, I seized on that encounter to rail against the White House's clear lack of intention to proactively push DADT repeal through that year. "You know why it's not 60 to 80 percent?" I asked, pointing toward the White House behind me. "Because *they* don't support us right now. There's more they can do and they *know* it."

After I spoke, Dan Choi took to the bullhorn to finish off the rally and energize the crowd for the grand finale. But before he could finish, the rally audience became distracted by something going on behind Dan and the rest of us. In another preplanned civil disobedience action, of which most of us at the rally (myself included) were unaware, six more people suddenly chained themselves to the White House fence. I think the group commenced the action a little earlier than they had planned, because Dan was still speaking when they finished handcuffing themselves to the fence and began chanting. It appeared to annoy Dan a little that he hadn't been able to give his remarks and wrap up the rally, but he nevertheless graciously deferred to the new cadre of activists he had inspired. Both he and Pietrangelo had to watch the action from Lafayette Park, however, because they were still under court order to not approach the fence.

While Jim Pietrangelo had been a veteran for some time, it was quite remarkable that Dan Choi was doing all of this while he was still technically in the military. Dan was a member of the New York Army National Guard and was still drilling the entire time he publicly protested the DADT law, often in uniform. The fact that he spoke out and engaged in protests, and especially the fact that he engaged in civil disobedience while wearing his army uniform, really angered a lot of people both in and out of the military, including some LGBT servicemembers and veterans. The question "What do you think of Dan Choi?" was often immediately posed to me when someone found out that I was involved in the DADT repeal movement. It was a delicate question, because if they asked, then they usually had a strong opinion one way or the other.

I was always careful to acknowledge and respect people's frustrations with Dan doing activism in uniform, especially when those frustrations came from other gay servicemembers who thought that our community was being poorly represented by the act. But at the same time, I was also quick to point out the enormous amount of attention and pressure that Dan was generating for the movement, without which we would have had a much harder time pushing repeal legislation through against the grain in 2010. As Dan once told me about his activism in uniform, he knew that he wouldn't make headlines for the issue if he were chained to the White House fence wearing jeans or a suit.

Indeed, hundreds of other activists protesting for liberal causes chained themselves to the White House fence, but I never saw their arrests making mainstream headlines or the images accompanying lead stories. Choi's protests were indeed controversial, and such tactics do pose legitimate questions about the propriety of political activism by active duty troops, but it is nevertheless undeniable that those photos of Dan, Jim, and others on the fence in front of the White House in uniform became iconic images of our community's frustration with the pace of progress in the spring of 2010.

It's also important to remember that Dan Choi wasn't the only active duty servicemember engaged in public activism on the DADT issue—despite what other publicity seekers would later claim—nor was he the only controversial one. Victor Fehrenbach, an air force lieutenant colonel who had faced discharge proceedings under DADT since 2008, was also on active duty the entire time he publicly advocated for repeal. Fehrenbach had been forced to out himself to air force authorities when he came under investigation for allegedly raping a civilian man. Fehrenbach admitted to being gay in the course of the investigation but strongly denied that any sexual contact with the man in question was nonconsensual. The investigation results concluded that the allegations had been false and baseless, but Fehrenbach was nevertheless left with the threat of discharge for admitting that he was gay.

Victor eventually chose to go public about his situation in order to help in the fight against his discharge. He became a favorite guest on *The Rachel Maddow Show*, the same program on which Dan Choi had first come out publicly, and during his long and drawn-out discharge process SLDN began publicly stage-managing him. However, Victor's late-blooming wild side soon began to show up in the public domain, leading many to conclude that he too could be a liability, a ticking time bomb for the gay military community and the DADT repeal movement.

Vic presented well in the media and his story was compelling, but after coming out and going public for the purpose of saving his air force career, he began chastising others for not coming forward and speaking out as well. It was a hypocritical accusation: in his then-eighteen-year career, Fehrenbach himself had never once made an effort to fight for the repeal of DADT until he was forced to go public to try to save his own career and retirement check. But he went so far as to call at least one former army officer a coward for not also becoming an activist, despite the fact that the veteran in question wasn't able to do so in his current job. And Fehrenbach's other friends and acquaintances often found themselves on the receiving end of profanity-laden rants on public social media websites as well, even after Vic had been asked to stop because the recipients' other friends and relatives—even their children—could also see such posts.

Vic didn't seem to care about the very public nature of his own social media platforms either, often posting profane and sometimes seriously disturbing things for the whole world to see. In one especially irresponsible episode, Fehrenbach used his Facebook profile to rant against the Log Cabin Republicans; he even encouraged his followers to go up to that organization's executive director and "punch him in the face." When people pointed out to Vic that such inciting language was inappropriate and a potential major liability, he followed that up by writing that perhaps they should resort to "Second Amendment remedies" instead. That phrase, widely understood as a reference to gun violence, had been popularized by Nevada Senate candidate Sharron Angle—a fact that was pointed out frequently on *The Rachel Maddow Show*, on which Victor Fehrenbach often appeared.

12

* * * * *

OLD PARTNERSHIPS

The growing restlessness within the progressive community in the spring of 2010 put a whole new level of pressure on HRC, which up to then had only been substantively involved in the repeal movement to the extent that Jarrod and I could wrestle a few thousand dollars from them here and there. But now, as the need for action grew critical, that level of participation looked wholly inadequate, especially since GetEqual was doing far more to push the issue forward than the largest LGBT lobbying group in the country.

HRC had a major board meeting scheduled for that spring, and the organization knew it would need a field plan to do more on the DADT issue in order to appease its board members. Since that plan did not exist, David Smith asked HRC's national field director, Marty Rouse, to come up with one on short notice. Marty then turned to Jarrod and asked for help, making clear that if he provided it, a more extensive and thoughtful plan could be created later. So the "plan" was hastily thrown together about a week before their board members began arriving in Washington. After making it through the board meeting, HRC didn't give the field plan much more thought or attention, and the final plan ended up being not much different from the thrown-together original.

HRC's efforts took the form of yet another tour in coordination with Servicemembers United, Voices of Honor II, at which both Jarrod and I rolled our eyes, then readily agreed to execute. As with Voices of Honor I, we took HRC's money to do a set number of events around the country and stretched it much further by scaling back on the typical HRC extravagance. We returned to all of the key target states that were the homes of the moderate members of the Senate Armed Services Committee and hit them hard with events, publicity, local vet recruiting, and extensive lobbying both locally and back in DC.

SU's work in these key states over the past few years had started to pay dividends, especially in the numbers of both gay and straight veterans we were able to recruit who were then willing to get active locally during the Voices of Honor II campaign. Their support was critically important; it was one thing for gay and lesbian Americans who had no connection to the defense world to call and write and scream and yell for senators in these conservative states to support repeal of DADT, but when those who had actually been in the military made those same demands, they became much more credible and influential in the minds of moderate and conservative senators and representatives.

As more public attention focused on our efforts, HRC also invested significant sums of money in branding the work that Jarrod and I were doing around the country—with the HRC label, of course. But what we found quite hilarious was that their new slogan for the issue, "Repeal DADT Now," was the opposite of what they were pushing behind the scenes with the White House and even at times on Capitol Hill. I even once heard HRC's political director tell one moderate senator's staff, "Now, if you see us pushing publicly on this, it's because we have to for our members." Such a counterproductive statement, which was clearly intended to let the senator's office know that HRC would put on only a facade of outrage for its members if that senator didn't move ahead on the issue, was just the tip of the iceberg.

I will, however, give HRC full credit for finally activating its vast e-mail list in a consistent manner and deploying its team of staff field organizers into our key target states to help with the grassroots effort that spring, which did bump up the volume of generic public activity around the DADT issue at this crucial time. Even though veteran constituents held the most influence with members of Congress on defense personnel issues, thousands of calls and e-mails from non-military constituents certainly helped supplement our work. But HRC largely refused to use its membership to target the White House, and we desperately needed pressure on the Obama administration to bring the Pentagon along on a simultaneous legislative strategy (the Pentagon study plus repeal legislation in 2010) instead of the consecutive legislative strategy (study in 2010 and then legislation in 2011) that they and the Pentagon really wanted to stick with.

Another thing that HRC did agree to do, which was also very helpful in the end, was to underwrite an unprecedented servicemembers and veterans "lobby day." HRC often held a smaller lobby day in conjunction with its annual national dinner, but the lobbying effort was always an afterthought to the huge socializing and fundraising opportunity that was the dinner itself. We, however, just didn't have much time to raise funds, having been thrust into the political battle quicker than any of us had anticipated. But we did understand the value of bringing a sizable chunk of our members and supporters—particularly our veteran advocates from across the country—to DC, where they'd spend a day receiving detailed updates and training and then a long day hitting the Hill and demanding immediate legislative action on DADT. The event was organized jointly by SU and HRC—and by that I mean it was organized primarily by Jarrod and me, since he was still in house at HRC. Why SLDN had never done something like this escapes me.

On May 10 and 11, 2010, three hundred gay and lesbian service-members and veterans and a handful of straight veteran allies came to Washington for the first and only National Veterans Lobby Day on DADT. This was the first time that hundreds of Servicemembers United members had been together in one place, and it could not have come at a more important time for the DADT issue. As it turned out, we were just two weeks away from the most critical set of votes on the DADT repeal bills, the full House floor vote and the Senate Armed Services Committee vote, and this historic gathering of LGBT veterans and servicemembers in Washington proved to be a major bump for the community and the issue immediately preceding these votes.

The first day of the event consisted largely of meetings, trainings, and issue updates designed to give the participants a deeper base of knowledge with which to lobby their members of Congress the following day. HRC and the contractor it hired to schedule the Hill visits wanted the participants to stick to generic talking points on the issue and focus more on "telling their stories," but I found this approach atrocious. While spoon-fed talking points would suffice for, and even be helpful for, the typical civilian who supported repeal and wanted to lobby for it, this tactic was far too simplistic for a body of participants who had served for years or even decades in the military and understood defense policy better than any of HRC's senior staff did. And since lobby day participants would be meeting with congressional defense aides with prior military experience themselves, in addition to more senior aides and actual members of Congress, simplistic talking points just weren't going to cut it. These offices had also already heard all of that before, and it would already be listed on the fact sheets in front of them; just hearing it again from another set of people, even if they were constituents, wasn't going to do anything for us or for the issue at this late stage in the game.

This was a major tactical difference between HRC and SU: we believed our members were capable of more substantive engagement with congressional offices than the superficial recitation of talking points. Jarrod and I had sat in on many lobbying visits with HRC's senior political staff before, and we had seen how ineffectual their very passive style of lobbying was. We, on the other hand, advocated a much more substantive, engaged, and responsive style of lobbying, and we'd witnessed firsthand the greater levels of respect and cooperation it garnered. Over time, we could see real progress being made. But our approach seemed novel to HRC, which appeared to believe that when it came to lobbying and constituent contact, its members could do little more than function as tick marks on a spreadsheet in a member's office. Even Aubrey Sarvis at SLDN suggested to me that we should have our participants stick to basic talking points.

As for the advice to simply "tell your story," that phrase had become a disgusting cliché. Just like with talking points, members and their staff had already heard sob stories for years. Years before, they might have been legitimately ignorant of the plight of gays and lesbians in the military, but by now, *no one* remained unaware, and the tactic of telling boo-hoo stories was simply ineffective. Those who truly needed lobbying weren't interested in hearing why someone wanted to join the military or when they realized they were gay. They wanted to hear about the more practical stuff, like how straight colleagues felt about finding out someone in their unit was gay, or how the older veterans back home would react if their senator voted in favor of repeal, or whether the Pentagon study would be able to provide sufficient political cover in their home states. Hearing how someone came out to their mother at seven wasn't an effective lobbying tactic on DADT.

Despite the overwhelming pressure to go with a least-common-denominator approach, I insisted on more substantive and nuanced training for our lobby day participants. This meant that we conducted an entire half-day of detailed legislative and political updates for participants the day before their actual Hill visits.

Then, on the morning of the scheduled lobbying visits, an HRC lobbying consultant addressed the group and did an hour-long seminar on how to lobby. I sat in on this session to see if what he had to say was worth the time and money, and I was quite frustrated at what I heard. The consultant once again told the group to focus on a tactic we already knew would not work anymore—"tell your story." Here was someone who knew less about the military than even HRC's staff, telling these three hundred people to go to the Hill two weeks before the most critical votes on the issue in seventeen years and tell boo-hoo stories. Luckily, we had armed them the previous day with more nuanced, substantive, and aggressive tactics, and I felt confident that the group appreciated being given credit for being capable of more and would use those higher-level tactics to make us proud on the Hill.

Another thing that I had insisted on adding to the schedule that previous day was a group visit to both the White House and the Pentagon. For our supporters who arrived early May 10, I arranged for a group of vets to meet with staff members of the Pentagon's DADT study group—known as the Comprehensive Review Working Group on DADT—and for another group of servicemembers and veterans to meet with some midlevel and senior political staff at the White House.

When I pitched the idea to the Working Group at the Pentagon, they were eager to rearrange their schedules so that their senior staff could meet with our vets. The Working Group had been conducting group meetings with thousands of servicemembers all over the world, but they couldn't get the perspective of gay servicemembers or engage our community about the impact of repeal because of the restrictions of the DADT law itself. But we were able to offer them a unique opportunity to talk to a diverse range of gay and lesbian veterans, many of them very recent veterans. The series of meetings at the Pentagon that morning turned out to have a major impact on the Working Group—although a similar future meeting I also arranged for them would turn out to be even more critical and game changing.

While the group of vets met with the Working Group at the Pentagon, an even larger group of gay and lesbian vets and servicemembers was meeting with the Obama administration's political staff in a small auditorium within the White House compound. We all knew that this meeting would be tough for the administration, but we also knew that there was no way they could turn down my request to meet with our group and talk about where we were and where we needed to go on DADT. For all of my other complaints about him, I have to give props to Brian Bond for helping me arrange this historic meeting at such a delicate moment in the DADT repeal fight, and for ensuring that it took place on White House grounds, a meaningful detail for them and for us.

The congressional lobbying effort the next day also seemed to go off without a hitch. This was the sort of stuff—White House lobbying visits by gay and lesbian troops and vets, meetings between recent gay and lesbian veterans and the Pentagon Working Group, LGBT troops and vets substantively lobbying congressional members' offices in person—that absolutely needed to happen in the weeks leading up to the critical DADT repeal votes of May 2010. But it still astounds me that without us, without Servicemembers United, it would never have happened. Neither HRC, CAP, nor the Palm Center ever could have pulled off this sort of activity, and SLDN certainly wasn't doing any of it itself. Our five groups were the only ones substantively involved in the DADT repeal effort nationwide—four of us in Washington—and without SU none of this critical work at the critical hour would have ever been done, much less the years of extensive grassroots work around the country leading up to it.

National Veterans Lobby Day was one of the biggest events we organized, and it turned out to be one of the most potent events of the entire DADT repeal movement. But it was also one of the last events we did with HRC. Throughout our entire time working with that group—and doing much of its DADT repeal work for it—HRC, and specifically its field director, Marty Rouse, had broken agreements left and right. That pattern of dishonest behavior began to increase in early 2010 during the Voices of Honor II campaign, and it climaxed with the Veterans Lobby Day event. Throughout Voices of Honor, HRC had readily agreed to certain terms and conditions in order to secure our cooperation, but when the time came to honor those agreements, the organization often fell far short. Some of these breaches were minor and just annoying, but others left a bitter taste in our mouths.

Servicemembers United had carefully crafted its reputation for genuineness over the years by refusing to do things for the wrong reasons or in ways that were inconsistent with our image, values, and objectives. Since SU hadn't had much time to build up a fundraising base, we also always strove to do more with less money and to stretch out the money we had. As executive director, I had even made a personal commitment not to accept a salary from the organization until after DADT was repealed; I preferred to reinvest the board-approved salary for me back into the organization to allow us to do more advocacy while things were hot. I had other sources of personal income, but it was nevertheless unprecedented for the head of a major national organization working on one of the hottest national policy issues of the year to refuse to accept one penny in salary until our overarching policy goal was accomplished. (I would still love to see the heads of even a few of the other political and charitable organizations make a similar pledge to the one I did. If they did, perhaps then we would have higher quality, more principled, less partisan, and truly independent leadership at some of these organizations. Not all organizational heads and senior staff are infected with pathologies, but it is a serious problem in the LGBT community that many undeniably are.)

We were constantly fighting with HRC to do things in more efficient, productive, and meaningful ways rather than in the flashiest and quickest yet most hollow ways. We weren't interested in just checking a box but in making progress and not hurting the issue in the process. But that wasn't always consistent with HRC's many and often conflicting goals. If we weren't fighting HRC's field department to keep the focus on gay and lesbian servicemembers and veterans, then we were fighting them to hold events in more appropriate and relevant venues, as previously agreed. One time, I even had to fight HRC's Rouse tooth and nail to not hold a joint DADT event at a Holocaust memorial.

When I refused to budge, Rouse finally relented and agreed to move the event location. In the end, though, the event was held in that location anyway, and Rouse just apologized to me after the fact for "forgetting" to switch the venue.

By the time we were planning the Veterans Lobby Day, we had watched HRC violate many agreements, not just with SU but with other organizations as well. So we went to great lengths to explicitly set out a branding agreement for this event. There could not possibly have been a more solidly understood and acknowledged agreement: everything related to the Veterans Lobby Day event would be branded jointly as SU and HRC. Yet when the event rolled around, I found myself having to take precious time out of my limited day to call out and correct violations of this simplest of agreements. For instance, final drafts of documents would be approved by SU for printing with both organizational names and logos on them, and suddenly the actual printed product would only have HRC's name and logo on it when it arrived.

At one point, Rouse had ordered hundreds of Veterans Lobby Day lapel pins with only HRC's name on them, and he begged Jarrod not to tell me about them. When I accidentally found one of them one day, Rouse had to confess that he had spent an enormous amount of money ordering these lapel pins in explicit violation of the agreement, and he only reluctantly agreed to dispose of them. However, during the event he kept coming back to Jarrod and asking him exactly how mad SU would be if they just distributed them to attendees anyway. When Jarrod cautioned him against doing that, Rouse kept probing him about whether I would be just sort of upset or outwardly angry if he did it anyway.

I also had to battle Rouse over a rather small expenditure, for a bus to take a group of vets over to the Pentagon for the meeting with the Comprehensive Review Working Group. Many of the people going to the meeting weren't familiar with DC or its Metro mass-transit system, and one of the meeting sites wasn't even accessible by Metro. We

had planned to hire a coach bus to take the group over to the Pentagon together for this historic opportunity, but before the day came,
Rouse's extravagant and wasteful spending habits began to surface,
and he came under pressure from within HRC to make some cuts.
However, he also wanted to add more events during the lobby day
period to cater to HRC's donors and board members. So in a move
that astounded nearly everyone who found out about it, Rouse tried to
cut out funding for the bus to transport our vets to the Pentagon while
adding in an extra (and more costly) reception for HRC members and
donors. And at first he succeeded in unilaterally making this change
to the schedule, until I "anonymously" leaked the unbelievable story
to the gay blogs and media.

When the story got out, the entire community was incensed and
the blogosphere blew up, and HRC had to immediately put its PR spin
machine into overdrive. HRC's communications director, who had
just been promoted into that position after their previous one got fed
up and quit, issued quick statements denying the allegations and saying that there had never been any funding committed to a bus in the
first place. He peddled this response enthusiastically, reaching out to
individual blogs and LGBT publications—and calling me an outright
liar in the process.

But how dumb must an organization be to call someone a liar in the
public sphere when it knows good and well that he has concrete, documented proof of the claim being made? This incredibly shortsighted
move only prolonged the story, because I subsequently released copies of the internal e-mails between HRC and SU in which the funding
for the vets' transportation had unquestionably been committed to. In
fact, ten different people had been copied on the e-mail, so I just didn't
understand how they could be so arrogant as to think that they could
actually get away with lying. That was HRC.

One interesting side note to that story is that the e-mail I leaked
wasn't even the most damning one I could have released. But it was
the only one that proved the case on which ten other people were cop-

ied too. And although those responsible for the incident within HRC knew exactly who had leaked it, many others weren't sure which of the recipients actually did. Some thought it had been a disgruntled employee within HRC, since most of those on the e-mail were lower-level HRC staffers. But alas, no one within HRC had spoken up, even anonymously, about the blatant lies that were being told by their communications department and senior staff. It took someone outside of the organization to blow the whistle on them and force them to do the right thing.

Had the incident gone on for just one more day, it looked increasingly like either GetEqual or Dan Choi himself might have stepped up and offered to pay for the Pentagon transportation costs. Dan had e-mailed me when he heard about the blow-up to ask how much the bus was going to cost, and I'm almost certain that within about twenty-four more hours, one of HRC's archrivals would have stepped up to cover the costs. But in the end, with the truth out there in black and white, HRC was publicly shamed into restoring the bus's funding.

This was the sort of lack of integrity with which we had to contend throughout the course of our partnership with HRC. Some of these battles I won, and others I lost, but certainly not for lack of trying to fight them. All the while we were also fighting with the administration and pushing the DADT issue forward on Capitol Hill, so it was doubly stressful on me, Jarrod, and all of SU. At times it seemed that no one was happy with the way things went, whether decisions made were for our community's own good or not.

By the summer of 2010, I had begun begging Jarrod to leave HRC and come back over to SU. At first he was hesitant to give up the well-placed position within HRC, but the pressure, the backstabbing, and the integrity issues eventually got to him, too, and he did quit and return full time to Servicemembers United. His resignation e-mail to the senior staff, which he disseminated widely for the record via BCC, was hard-hitting and scolding, but it was also undeniably genuine and accurately reflected some of the exact same fundamental problems with that organization and its leadership that I and many others had experienced.

ALLCON:

Follows is a two week notice of my intent to terminate my employment with the Human Rights Campaign.

This decision has not come easy. But then again, it has.

I accepted employment at the Human Rights Campaign with the intention of both utilizing HRC's existing resources to reach a broad audience in a short period of time, as well as to utilize my upstanding reputation in the military community to help build a solid DADT repeal advocacy program going forward. I soon found, however, that resources would be artificially restricted.

Given a small budget of $25,000 with an initial request to organize only five events (compared to the field budget—a department which, for example, was given a budget of $50,000 merely for web advertising for a non-substantive and ineffective 'No Excuses' campaign) it was clear the task I was given was not intended to accomplish much towards repealing DADT. Instead, my role was to function as a public token to appease frustrated board members.

This is a mantle I have consistently refused to wear. Even with minimal resources, I created twenty events instead of five, with $5,000 to spare, gathering the most media HRC has ever gained for a series of public events. Because accomplishing this feat required bucking HRC bureaucracy repeatedly, instead of receiving positive recognition for my work, an environment of distrust and passive-aggressive attempts to reduce my role in the organization resulted, and has persisted continuously.

This environment, while difficult, has only developed into a toxic one over the last few months. Communication with the legislative team is not shared. My own sharing of intelligence—shared by me despite lack of reciprocity—is not responded to, and organizational plans to use the intelligence I provide are not shared unless that sharing is compelled. The development of a field plan to deal with the final few weeks before the full Senate vote was created without my consultation, and the resulting product will inevitably prove to be a colossal waste of resources and energy that could have been avoided should the funds have been directed more effectively. Communications on the issue typically have cynically utilized Joe Solmonese and Eric Alva, although utilizing existing talent in the organization such as myself would have created much better results in both the LGBT community with which HRC is rapidly declining in favor, and in the mainstream.

In effect, my role has been reduced to even less than the token role in which HRC had originally intended to place me, and my talents, knowledge, and efforts could go much farther in ensuring a successful vote in the Senate on this issue as it approaches. Ultimately, I am in a position in which I cannot be creative and effectively utilized, and HRC's organizational and self-promotional interests continue to ensure that my potential impact on this issue is reduced.

I would be a traitor to every veteran and active duty service member faithfully relying on me to represent their interests if

I were to continue in this position longer than necessary.

My involvement in the "Don't Ask, Don't Tell" issue has always been personal and selfless, never self-serving. I cannot say the same for many that work in this organization. There are times when I have been proud to have been associated with the Human Rights Campaign. Today is not one of them.

I am stepping down as Public Policy Advocate (DADT) as of two weeks from today, June 25, 2010. My last day will be Friday, July 09, 2010.

And with that, Jarrod unilaterally terminated his employment with HRC and returned to SU. Finally, the same duo who had helped resurrect the DADT repeal movement in 2005 and 2006, who had helped keep it alive at the grassroots level through the doldrums of 2007 and 2008, who had worked together to open a full-time SU operation in DC and give those actually impacted by DADT a voice and a seat at the political table in Washington starting in early 2009, and who had worked in tandem to hold together a delicate and frustrating but productive partnership between two of the most prominent LGBT organizations in late 2009 and early 2010, were reunited at the helm of SU for what we hoped would be the final stretch of this epic war.

13

★ ★ ★ ★ ★

THE AMENDMENT AND
NOT-SO-SECRET MEETINGS

Congressman Patrick Murphy and Senator Joseph Lieberman introduced identical DADT repeal amendments to the National Defense
Authorization Act (NDAA) in late May 2010, surprising much of the
public with the amendment's language, a vast departure from the original two versions of the Military Readiness Enhancement Act. Prior
to this point, MREA had remained largely unchanged since it was
first introduced in 2005, consisting of a virtually immediate repeal
of DADT and an affirmative nondiscrimination policy. MREA represented the ideal position of the pro-repeal community, not surprising given that the bill was written in part by the staff of a pro-repeal
organization, SLDN.

Unfortunately, although by the spring of 2010 the original MREA
could very likely have cleared the full House of Representatives, not
enough groundwork had been laid for it to pass through the gauntlet
of the Senate Armed Services Committee. Perhaps more important,
the Pentagon did not support the bill in its original form, and Penta-

gon support would be a must in order to gain the support of a critical mass of senators. Rather than passing the full bill in the House and having it amended and watered down in the Senate, the lead sponsors in each chamber agreed to go with a least-common-denominator version of the bill to ensure that it would not be "conferenceable" if passed.

All legislation that passes both the House and the Senate must go to a conference committee to work out the differences between the two chambers' versions of the bill. Then, an identical final version must be agreed to by both chambers before it can go to the president to be signed into law. If a certain provision or amendment within a larger piece of legislation is identical in the versions passed by each chamber, that provision is said to be "nonconferenceable"—it does not need to be worked out by the committee and must remain in the final version of the bill untouched. One of the dangers of having provisions that are similar but not identical is that the conference committee can further alter them or cut them out altogether. Given that the conference committee for NDAA (the chairmen and ranking members of each of the two Armed Services Committees) consisted of three opponents of repealing DADT and only one supporter, it was strategically necessary that the DADT repeal amendment passed by the House be identical to the DADT repeal amendment passed by the Senate. If one word, or even one punctuation mark, was different, the provision became conferenceable and would face certain death.

As mentioned earlier, the two original versions of MREA were already slightly different in language. When the two bills were merged into one to make the provision nonconferenceable, however, the final amendment language indeed retreated from the strong stance of the original MREA bill. Of the three concessions it made, I agreed that two of them were necessary. First, the immediate-repeal provision, declaring that the repeal of DADT would take effect almost immediately upon the law going into effect, was turned into a delayed-repeal provision. That simply meant that repeal would take effect at some future point in time, not as soon the president signed the bill into law. This concession was necessary to get the Pentagon on board, as the top brass felt more comfortable having sufficient time to adjust to the policy change rather than having it imposed swiftly. In truth, they surely could have handled a swift imposition, but not all of them realized that. The bottom line was that their support was critical, and they believed that they needed a little time to prepare for the change and finish their study. Thus, a delayed-repeal structure, which Service-members United had begun advocating privately in 2009 and publicly in early 2010 as the only realistic model that the Pentagon would accept, was adopted in the final amendment.

Second, the trigger mechanism for the law going into effect was turned into a floating and conditional trigger rather than a fixed trigger. In the original MREA legislation, the act that made the new law go into effect was the president's signature. Even in the delayed-repeal models that we put forward, the trigger for the law's effective date was concrete and written into the legislation. In one of our proposals, for example, the effective date for repeal within various categories of military job fields was tied to the passage of time—within six months for the supposedly easier job fields to integrate, within twelve months for the supposedly tougher fields to integrate, and within eighteen months for all the rest. In all of these alternate proposals, the effective date, or trigger, was set in stone ahead of time by law.

What made most people uncomfortable about the second concession was the fact that the trigger, rather than being set in stone, was never technically guaranteed at all. Instead, it was tied to a certification, signed by the president, the secretary of defense, and the chairman of the Joint Chiefs, confirming that the recommendations made by the Pentagon Working Group were sufficient to ensure a smooth transition. That gave the Pentagon the power to dictate how long it would take to put the new policy into effect, and it actually gave them veto power over doing so if they decided they just didn't want to. Although that scenario was unlikely, even next to impossible, the gay community had a deep mistrust of the Pentagon because of how badly the military had historically treated gays and lesbians.

Many, especially those who remembered this history firsthand, actually went ballistic over this concession. Certain blogs and activists decried the "deal" as a betrayal. They could not understand how the pro-repeal organizations could be united in supporting such a concession. They called it non-repeal and denounced Gay Inc. for being its typical self-interested, self-preserving, self-screwing self. But this time around, one thing about their argument just did not make sense, not even to them: Servicemembers United was endorsing this provision, and no one truly believed that an organization founded by gay troops and veterans, led by gay troops and veterans, and representing the interests of gay troops and veterans would do something to screw over gay troops and veterans including themselves. No one doubted for a minute that an organization like HRC, the epitome of Gay Inc., might do something like that, but not Servicemembers United.

Our endorsement, along with SLDN's, was critical to legitimizing this concession, and the new repeal amendment as a whole, to the gay and progressive communities. But the idea for this second concession did not come from Servicemembers United. It did not come from SLDN or HRC either. As soon as I saw it in writing, weeks before it was announced publicly, I knew it was brilliant and I wished that I had thought of it. But the conduit through which it came was Winnie Stachelberg at the Center for American Progress. To my knowledge Stachelberg hadn't come up with this idea herself either, and it likely didn't even come from within her organization, but CAP nevertheless was the organization that was given the proposal to vet, to present to our coalition, and eventually to present to our allies in the Senate, namely Senators Joseph Lieberman and Carl Levin, for their buy-in.

Stachelberg had been with HRC for eleven years, serving as their political director and then as the vice president of the HRC Foundation before she went over to former White House chief of staff

John Podesta's new progressive think tank, the Center for American Progress. Winnie's former ties to HRC and CAP's close ties with the administration—Podesta was also the head of the Obama transition team—meant that Stachelberg got roped into the inner DADT circle with us. She often supported HRC's positions in the coalition, which is why they liked her being there, but she was actually pleasant and personable, which is why I liked her being there too.

Others outside of the inner circle, however, did not understand why Stachelberg was a part of DADT repeal deliberations. She and CAP did not have a constituency, they argued, and their close ties to the Obama White House meant that she was inherently distrusted by bloggers and many independent activists. But I often defended Stachelberg's involvement in our coalition. Even though I grew to trust her less as time went on, I still liked her, and I thought she was a lot more of a decent human being than many of the others involved. And we needed some pleasantness to balance out the lack thereof elsewhere in the coalition.

When Stachelberg introduced the idea of the conditional trigger to the rest of us in the inner DADT circle at a meeting in Senator Lieberman's office in early May, I immediately perked up and thought we had found our magic key. This trigger mechanism was a perfect match for the requirements of the Pentagon, which wanted control over the rate of change—and desperately wanted to hold off the start of that change until after their nine-month-long review was completed. As far as I was concerned, this option of passing the repeal law now but stipulating that it would only take effect when the top defense officials gave the go-ahead was brilliant. Once legislative repeal was locked in, Congress would be out of the picture. Then, as soon as the chairman and the secretary were ready, they would sign off on the certification, and of course the president would too, and we would be done. This seemed like the perfect solution to pick up the last few votes we needed on the Senate Armed Services Committee in order to proceed. And as it turned out, it was.

But Dr. Aaron Belkin at the Palm Center had a change that he wanted added in: a third and wholly unnecessary concession. Aaron was not directly involved in the repeal movement's politics, but he certainly thought he was abreast of them, and he seemed to desperately want some sort of fingerprint on the final version of the legislation. Belkin began almost unilaterally lobbying to have the nondiscrimination language taken out of the bill, and as he was so good at doing, he began manufacturing momentum for this idea. He wrote an op-ed in its favor for General John Shalikashvili, whose *New York Times* piece in support of DADT repeal had been so influential, then got General Shali's son to get Shali to sign off on it. Belkin began declaring in public that we did not have the votes for repeal without removing the nondiscrimination language, but he would not have known whether we did or not. He was never in the room with the coalition, and no one else associated with the Palm Center ever was either. He did not know the vote count directly from Senate offices. His information was second- and third-hand at best, yet here he was unilaterally giving away the coveted nondiscrimination language that ensured that the military could never again revert to any sort of antigay policy.

All of us who were actually working on the political parts of DADT repeal were furious. We knew that taking out the nondiscrimination language would not pick up one single vote—the two concessions we'd already made picked up the votes we needed on committee—and we hoped that Belkin's lobbying effort had not foreclosed upon our options for keeping that language in. But once your interest group community puts a concession out on the table, or someone on your side unilaterally puts it out there for you, it's hard to walk it back. What the White House and the Pentagon essentially did was to take all of the concessions that had been publicly floated, read the writing on the wall, and reluctantly agree to support a repeal amendment that included all three of them.

We found out that the White House and the Pentagon were finally going to agree to support the new repeal amendment when we were summoned to yet another meeting at the White House on Monday, May 24. Foreshadowing their slightly greater level of cooperation, this meeting took place in the West Wing, in the Roosevelt Room to be precise, instead of in the Eisenhower Executive Office Building. I had only been in the West Wing once before, and I entered through the entrance across from EEOB then. This time, I entered through the gate directly north of the West Wing. Since I had never been through this entrance before, I had no clue which door of the actual building to go into, so at first I accidentally walked into the press briefing room. The only reason I recognized I was in the wrong place was because it looked almost exactly like the press briefing room from the TV series *The West Wing*, and for a moment I secretly hoped I would see C. J. Cregg come around the corner and make a witty comment. A jovial reporter hanging out by the door quickly picked up on the fact that I was lost and told me that the West Wing lobby was the next door down.

A tall, sharp marine opened the outside (correct) door for me, and another marine opened the second door inside. I wondered immediately if they knew why we were there and what they thought about DADT. When I got inside, I noticed that I was one of the last to arrive. Waiting in the lobby already were some of the usual suspects, including David Smith and Joe Solmonese of HRC; Winnie Stachelberg of CAP; Aubrey Sarvis of SLDN (this time he was actually invited); and Tobias Wolff, a law school instructor who had volunteered on the Obama campaign and who was clearly there to serve as the administration's cheerleader-in-chief. After a few awkward hellos, I joked with Aubrey that we had a bit of a Romeo and Juliet situation on our hands, as one of his staff members had started dating one of mine. He laughed and said that he was never up on those things.

Brian Bond soon came out to greet us and ushered us into the Roosevelt Room. Since the room was an enhanced-security area, we had to leave our cell phones outside. We then had a good ten minutes or so to chat awkwardly among ourselves and with the few White

House staffers who were minding us. While the others commented on the various paintings that adorned the wall, my eye quickly darted to a glass-encased Medal of Honor that was on display in the southeast corner of the room. Although I could not see the detail of the medal itself from that far away, I recognized the characteristic light blue ribbon from which Medals of Honor always hung.

I have been in the Roosevelt Room several times now, and I have yet to wander over to that display case and see whose medal that is. I am always in awe of the incredible sacrifice and selflessness required to earn that honor, and I even get a little emotional when I hear the Medal of Honor talked about on the news. Some of the people in that room were completely oblivious to being in the presence of the nation's highest and most sacred military honor, but there they were, and there I was.

We were eventually joined by deputy chief of staff Jim Messina, who apparently was still running the DADT issue for the White House; Tina Tchen, director of the Office of Public Engagement; and a few folks from White House Counsel's office. Chris Neff, the Palm Center's "person in DC," was strangely permitted to join us by phone from Australia, where he was living.

The meeting was rather quick and tense. Tchen first told us that news of the meeting had already leaked, and that the White House press office was getting calls from *Politico* asking if they could confirm that a meeting with gay activists was taking place. It occurred to me then that putting us all in an enhanced-security conference room and then having someone dial in from Australia seemed like a huge contradiction and a huge confidentiality risk, politically speaking. For all we knew, the caller could easily record the entire meeting on the other end of the line, and on the other side of the globe. That would actually have been useful, given how quickly the participants had started lying after the previous White House meeting.

After the customary confidentiality admonishments, Messina rather coldly informed us that the White House would be issuing a statement later that day regarding the new repeal amendment that had been proposed. The statement was clearly an attempt to reluctantly jump on board a fast-departing train. But it would not even come from the president in the end. It would come from Peter Orszag, the director of the Office of Management and Budget. Having an administration official not involved in the DADT issue send the White House's position out in the form of a letter was obviously meant to downplay the significance of the tepid and reluctant endorsement.

When we tried to press the White House staff for more—a guarantee of an administrative nondiscrimination policy after legislative repeal, for example—all we got was "This is where we are right now." The message was clear: the administration was now on board, but they were not happy about it. They were upset that we had pushed them onto the train a year earlier than they wanted to get on board. And they were not going to provide any additional fuel for that train or make us feel better about the ride ahead.

Orszag's statement was soon followed up with an equally tepid statement of support from Secretary Gates and Chairman Mullen, although it was still one we could work with. Their statement said that although they would have preferred legislative action after their nine-month study had been completed, they could support the new proposed amendment.

It was completely incomprehensible that all of these men would not fully support this amendment. Gates and Mullen had testified before the Senate Armed Services Committee that they both supported the president's goal of ending DADT. This amendment did that, and it did it when, and only when, those two men specifically said the military was ready. If they said it was ready after the study was finished, they would be allowed to make that change happen. If they did not think it was ready for another fifty years, they could block the change for another fifty years. We knew that would never happen, of course, but the important point was that this amendment gave them that power. But the Pentagon is often an incomprehensible beast. Sometimes ego and other factors go into equations about what the Pentagon will support, and often the reality of ticking political clocks do not. In any case, although it was not what they really wanted and it was not what we really wanted, we had gotten what we needed to push forward. It was all about sufficiency, and both the amendment and the White House and Pentagon statements were minimally sufficient to move ahead.

Given that news of the meeting had leaked to *Politico* before we even got there, it was no surprise that reporters started calling almost as soon as I walked the two blocks back to my office. I tried to avoid media calls and e-mails for a while, but one small-time reporter caught me picking up the phone because of an unrecognized area code (most media calls were coming from DC, New York City, and Los Angeles area codes). This reporter for a small gay publication seemed to think she had hit the jackpot by getting me on the phone, and she started barraging me with frantic questions about the meeting. When I politely told her that she would need to try someone else for information about the meeting, she chastised me for not wanting to give her what would become publicly available information later anyway. That certainly was not the way to get me to open up, and after that I would not give her anything, not even a comment on what the weather had been like on the way to and from the meeting.

But news of the meeting did make it out, and once again the conspiracy theories abounded about what secret plans had been hashed out between Gay Inc. (into which we were now ironically cast) and the White House at this meeting. The biggest and most inaccurate collective public conclusion from the whole episode was that this was the meeting where the "deal" about the amendment had been worked out and agreed upon by all parties. Clearly, that was far from the truth.

Most of the amendment language had been developed weeks prior and had already been discussed and debated within the organizational and Capitol Hill DADT coalition. It had been presented as a unanimously supported option to Senator Levin, who liked the idea and agreed to push it forward as chairman of the Senate Armed Services Committee. There was no negotiation with the White House, contrary to popular belief and popular reports. Had there been, we might have ended up with even less.

By the time we got to the Roosevelt Room, the final amendment language was a done deal. At this point, the White House and the Pentagon could either be with us or they could be against us. They chose reluctantly to be dragged along. But to hear them tell it later, they had been conducting the train the whole way.

14

★ ★ ★ ★ ★

VICTORY AND DEFEAT

With the Pentagon now reluctantly on board and the White House finally supporting moving forward with legislation that would repeal the DADT law in 2010 instead of 2011, we hoped we had the last bit of leverage behind us to go out and lock up the votes. The final push began on Monday, May 24. The House floor vote on the NDAA for fiscal year 2011 and the Senate Armed Services Committee markup of the same bill coincidentally ended up both being scheduled for Thursday of that week. This allowed us the opportunity to know immediately if we had the votes in both the full House and the key part of the Senate to pass the amendment and keep it intact. We were fairly certain we had the votes in the House of Representatives, but the SASC vote would still surely be a nail-biter.

On Tuesday, word came from Senator Mark Udall's chief of staff, Mike Sozan, that Senator Evan Bayh of Indiana would vote with us for sure. (Senator Udall—of Colorado, not his cousin Tom, a senator from New Mexico—was a progressive member of the Senate Armed Services Committee who had taken a particularly genuine interest in getting DADT repealed, and his staff had become the most helpful and active team on the issue after Senator Lieberman's.) That day also brought public confirmation that Senator Bill Nelson of Florida would vote for the amendment. Although Senator Nelson had been one of the more likely targets to vote with us, his office hadn't previously confirmed his position publicly.

The senator from Florida was one of two conservative Democrats named Nelson on SASC; the other, Senator Ben Nelson of Nebraska, was considered less friendly to our cause. But that night, I got a call from a blogger and political consultant, Adam Bink, who had close ties to the Nebraska senator's chief of staff. Adam was calling to confirm that the senator would be coming out in favor of the amendment the following morning. Senator Nelson's office had given Adam's blog, *OpenLeft*, a scoop on the fact that the senator would be confirming his vote on a conference call with Nebraska reporters and via a public statement late Wednesday morning, a story that Adam broke forty-five minutes before it was released to the public.

Although I had the info the night before from Adam, I patiently waited until the minute the story was posted the following morning to send the news out to the organizational and Senate office coalition. "The blog OpenLeft just got the scoop from Ben Nelson's office that he *will* vote for the amendment. His statements are actually extremely supportive too. . . . They've confirmed to me over the phone just now that it came directly from Tim Becker," I wrote, under the subject line "We Got *Ben* Nelson!!!" The news elicited a quick "Wooooooo Hooooo" from Senator Udall's military aide back to the entire group. The sentiment was certainly representative of everyone's feelings as history fell into place, one confirmed vote after another.

A committee vote we were sure we had in theory but which wasn't locked down was that of Senator Daniel Akaka of Hawaii. The senator was generally supportive, and no one had really been worried about him, but as we lined up final confirmations of each vote from each respective Senate office, no one had been able to pin down Senator Akaka's staff on his yes vote, either in writing or via verbal confirmation. And so late in the game with the vote so close, we didn't want to take any chances.

Senator Lieberman's office asked everyone to scramble to try to get a firm yes out of Senator Akaka's office. Finally, just after noon Senator Lieberman's legislative director e-mailed his colleagues to let them know that Senator Akaka's legislative director had just called him to say that the senator was, of course, a firm yes. Senator Lieberman's chief of staff forwarded the news to the rest of us with her reaction: "I have Goosebumps right now. . . . Thanks, Team Repeal DADT!"

Another important swing vote that we had been working on was that of the legendary Senator Robert Byrd of West Virginia. Senator Byrd was known as a stickler for process and the formal role of the Senate in the larger American political system. He was largely regarded as the chamber's greatest expert on its convoluted and archaic rules and procedures. So when it came time for Senator Byrd to make a decision on the upcoming vote, it was no surprise to those who knew him that he would require a procedural hat tip to Congress in the overall repeal process.

Senator Byrd insisted upon a sixty-day congressional review period after the repeal of DADT had been certified by the president, the secretary of defense, and the chairman of the Joint Chiefs of Staff. During this period, in theory, Congress could review for itself the Defense Department's implementation plans and have enough time to potentially reverse the repeal if things were sufficiently askew. We knew, however, that it would be nearly impossible for Congress to make such a move even if it wanted to, and we considered this sixty-day review period to be a fairly innocuous last-minute addition to the final joint amendment language. Senator Byrd's office had actually privately requested and negotiated the change several weeks prior, so it had already been incorporated into the final, merged version of the amendment. In fact, we didn't really even consider it to be another concession. Thus, Senator Byrd joined in as yet another conservative Democrat on the Senate Armed Services Committee announcing that day that he would support the amendment. Just one month later, Senator Byrd would pass away as the longest-serving member of Congress in history, and as one of the most influential—even on the final outcome of our legislation.

Thursday, May 27, 2010, proved to be D-Day for DADT. Despite everything that happened earlier or later, this was the one day of the entire fight on which the most critical sets of votes would finally be counted. We would have either done enough to squeak by or failed and lost our chance. Based on our vote counts, we were fairly optimistic.

The NDAA first came up for consideration in the Senate Armed Services Committee. The committee met for a number of hours during the middle of the day and worked its way through the many, many provisions of the enormous bill. The markup was closed, meaning that no one except senators on the committee, their military affairs staffers, and committee staff were allowed in the room during the proceedings. We were all worried, not just over whether the repeal amendment would secure enough votes to stay in the bill but also over whether it would survive unaltered. Senators on the committee could easily have voted to keep the amendment in the bill but to change it in some way, rendering it conferenceable. With the conference committee running three to one in opposition of repeal, even the smallest change would spell the end of the amendment.

Those early afternoon hours that Thursday were quite tense. As we waited, everyone involved in the DADT repeal coalition—teams from Servicemembers United, HRC, SLDN, CAP, and Third Way, in addition to the senior staff of Senators Lieberman and Udall and House Majority Leader Nancy Pelosi—exchanged a few short group e-mails on minor side topics. But mostly we all waited nervously at our respective offices for any word out of the closed-door markup session. Then, finally, word broke over that same group e-mail. "We just won on SASC, 16 to 12!" wrote one office's chief of staff. Pelosi's office quickly responded, "Any changes? Punctuation? Lower case words?" to which he quickly replied, "Nothing. No changes. Your turn to win."

And there we had it. The DADT repeal amendment we had worked so hard to craft, build support for, and secure the votes for had survived the monumental hurdle of the Senate Armed Services Committee perfectly intact. Now it would be up to the House of Representatives to pass the same amendment without any changes in wording. Senator Lieberman's chief of staff, Clarine Riddle, invited everyone to stop by their office that evening to celebrate and watch the House vote. "I have wine in Hart 706, with my candy bowl," she enticed.

The notoriety of Clarine's candy bowl among insiders is worth sharing. As Senator Lieberman's chief of staff, Clarine had become the dean or godmother of the DADT repeal coalition of organizations and congressional offices. Senator Lieberman's office hosted the DADT repeal war room on Capitol Hill throughout 2010, in which Servicemembers United, HRC, SLDN, CAP, and Third Way joined the staffs of Senators Lieberman, Udall, and Gillibrand (and once in a while Senator Roland Burris and Congressman Patrick Murphy, and once even Senate Majority Leader Harry Reid's staff) for strategizing and intelligence sharing in the days and weeks leading up to each critical vote that year. In the middle of the conference table at every meeting, Clarine always placed her famous fishbowl full of assorted candies. While the diverse group of professionals was rather reluctant to partake in the beginning, each of us soon broke down and would regularly reach for the bowl immediately upon entering the conference room and claiming a seat around the table. Occasionally, an arm would stretch out across the table during a meeting to grab a Tootsie Roll or Jolly Rancher, and Clarine could always be counted on to push the bowl on us all once more at the end of every meeting.

In a funny and odd way, the tradition of Clarine's candy bowl reminded me of the "Snap Cup" from the movie *Legally Blond 2*. Although we didn't exchange compliments with each piece of candy drawn out of the bowl, it did lighten up these often very tense meetings and forced rival parties within the coalition to interact, at least for the purpose of passing Clarine's candy bowl around with a smile. And once, at the very end of the fight, she even supplemented the candy bowl with a heaping plate of fresh-baked cookies. Clarine, who had a grandmotherly quality about her, was certainly a unique figure on Capitol Hill, and she knew how to get rival actors to come together to get things done, even if it took bribing and distracting with delicious sweets.

Alas, very few of us made it back over to the war room that night to gather around Clarine's candy bowl and watch the House vote. At the Servicemembers United office, we still had press to do, press releases to prepare (for both an expected win and a potential loss, just in case), and member e-mails to send out immediately after the vote, which dragged late into the evening.

The House vote happened to coincide with "Active Duty Thursday," a weekly gay military night in Washington, DC, that Servicemembers United had started the previous year. Attendance had picked up considerably by May 2010, and with the Senate victory already in hand and a House victory expected that night, we knew that that week's event would be quite busy with servicemembers, veterans, and lots of supporters who wanted to celebrate together. So as we continued working at the SU office late into the evening, across town the host bar for Active Duty Thursdays, which displayed the House proceedings on the flat screen TVs behind the bar, began filling up.

At roughly ten that night, the House of Representatives voted on the DADT repeal amendment, known as the Murphy Amendment in that chamber. It passed overwhelmingly, 234 in favor and 194 against, with 10 absent or not voting. Five Republicans—Representatives Ron Paul, Joseph Cao, Charles Djou, Ileana Ros-Lehtinen, and Judy Biggert—voted in favor of repeal that day.

The White House, who until that Monday had not favored legislation to repeal the DADT law in 2010, immediately issued a statement lauding the president's support of the victory: "I have long advocated that we repeal 'Don't Ask Don't Tell,' and I am pleased that both the House of Representatives and the Senate Armed Services Committee took important bipartisan steps toward repeal tonight."

And in true Washington style, you could tell who had done the most to exert real pressure to make that happen by where the leaders of the different organizations chose to be that night. HRC's senior staff, including Joe Solmonese and David Smith, sat in Speaker Pelosi's box with Winnie Stachelberg from CAP and other senior staffers. Aubrey Sarvis from SLDN was slightly more removed from the House leadership's pay-to-play suite, but he interestingly chose to seat himself in the House chamber among political staff for the vote. On the other hand, Jarrod and I, along with the rest of the Servicemembers United team, rejected invitations to experience this most critical of moments in the company of political operatives. After sending out our press release and member e-mails, we headed straight for Active Duty Thursday to join the one-hundred-plus servicemembers, veterans, and supporters who had gathered to celebrate in a much more authentic and genuine way—with those whose lives would actually change as a result of this legislation.

It was a great night, and the alcohol flowed abundantly in celebration. As someone who almost never drank, though, I struggled to find ways to dispose of the many drinks that got passed my way as thanks. And although this was truly the biggest hump we had to get over in terms of securing votes, the jubilation of that night would soon give way to the disappointment and despair of waiting on the Senate majority leader to allow a vote in the full Senate chamber to wrap it all up.

While only about two weeks passed between the time that the House Armed Services Committee marked up NDAA and the time the full House chamber voted on it, the Senate, on the other hand, usually had about a four- or six-week gap between committee action and floor action on the defense bill each year. Given this history, it looked unlikely that the bill would get its final vote—which we were now fairly confident we would win—in June.

Nonetheless, Sarvis came right out of the gate after the SASC vote, "calling on" Senate Majority Leader Harry Reid to bring NDAA up in June. As he would argue, this increased the pressure on Reid to do it sooner rather than later. But I was still of the mind that by making such blatantly unrealistic "calls" on public officials to do things within timetables we knew good and well were never going to work, he unfairly raised expectations within our own community—particularly with regard to active duty servicemembers, who depended on realistic predictions and assessments for their mental health and career decisions.

July, however, looked like a prime opportunity for Senator Reid to call up NDAA for Senate floor action. Unfortunately, we quickly found out that one's allies aren't always one's true allies 100 percent of the time, and that the majority leader was skilled at the cunning politics of leading a diverse caucus that often maintained conflicting interests.

The looming danger was the infamous August recess, the annual period when members of Congress head back home to their states and districts, where they must often face off with angry and restive constituents on a variety of "controversial" issues. If the vote were completed before the recess, this issue at least would be resolved and off the table, and senators would be free to focus on their reelection efforts during their time back home. And angry constituents would have months to forget about this and other votes that would ultimately be a part of the defense bill before the early November midterm elections. However, if the bill were still pending during the recess, it would open up senators to increased levels of lobbying from opponents of repeal, and a September or October vote would make all of those "controversial" issues fresh wounds during the elections. Everyone agreed that wouldn't be a smart thing for Senator Reid to do to his caucus.

So if the vote didn't happen in July, it was conceivable that Senator Reid wouldn't let it happen until after the midterms, meaning no September or October vote either. And as the days and weeks of July passed, it became evident that this was the plan the majority leader was embracing, even though the delay meant an increased likelihood of ultimate failure for NDAA and the DADT repeal amendment contained with in it. So we—Servicemembers United, SLDN, and the more radical and smaller actors like GetEqual and the blogs—began pressuring Senator Reid more and more to get with the program and bring up NDAA for a vote on the Senate floor.

Just as they had refused to pressure the president because of their close—some would say incestuous—ties to the Democratic Party and the administration, HRC refused to participate in any sort of pressure campaign against Senator Reid. July came and went, and Senator Reid did not allow NDAA to come to the Senate floor for a vote. All we could do in response was to continue organizing, continue pushing, continue educating, and continue lobbying, all of which the coalition groups did to varying degrees throughout the August recess.

One interesting side note during this time was the story of how we crossed paths with a big fighter jet, a big engine, a big corporate lobby, and a big battle over all of the above. As mentioned earlier, the NDAA was a large bill with a lot of diverse provisions embedded within it. It is normally one of the largest and most important pieces of legislation passed annually, and every year during the overall NDAA political war, important side skirmishes take place over the funding of many pieces of military equipment. One such skirmish was that over the alternate—or "extra," depending on which side you're talking to— engine for the F-35 Joint Strike Fighter.

General Electric (GE) and United Technologies Corporation (UTC) had been engaged in a multiyear lobbying and public relations battle over whether the Pentagon needed an alternate engine for the F-35. Even though the new fighter jet already had a perfectly good engine manufactured by UTC and the Pentagon had declared again and again that it neither needed nor wanted an "extra," GE was developing a second one. Given that the research and development costs on the alternate engine ran the taxpayers nearly half a billion dollars each year, the administration quickly sided with the Pentagon and with UTC against a powerful coalition of lawmakers supporting funding for GE's engine, which was primarily a jobs project in many congressional districts.

The administration and the Pentagon were adamant about not wasting half a billion dollars on an engine that the Pentagon didn't want, so the president threatened to veto the defense bill if it contained funding for it. Unfortunately for us, this also meant that a defense authorization bill coming from Capitol Hill with alternate engine funding would delay and possibly derail the carefully crafted and delicate repeal of DADT. To try to preempt this scenario, Servicemembers United decided to use its extra time that summer to involve itself in the military engines business.

After looking at the vote count on the DADT amendment in the House and comparing it with the vote count that same night on the alternate engine provision, we decided to reach out to UTC's military engines division to see if there was a way we could work together to promote our coincidentally mutual goal of getting the veto-inducing funding out of NDAA before it got to the president's desk. SU staffer Clint King and I met with UTC's director of government relations in UTC's posh I Street offices, just a few blocks down from SU's less posh I Street offices. Sitting in on the meeting was one of UTC's hired Washington lobbyists, whom I had never met at the time. But when I glanced at his business card, I knew the name Tony Podesta looked awfully familiar. As I later found out, he was one of Washington's top lobbyists and the brother of CAP founder John Podesta. This military engine contract was *big* business.

Both UTC's head guy in Washington and their top superlobbyist, Podesta, said that they were quite impressed by our bravado in reaching out to UTC. We looked over vote counts together, strategized for a while about which lawmakers we might be able to persuade to drop their support for the costly extra engine if it might ruin our chances at securing DADT's swift repeal, and agreed to stay in touch.

While SU did some preliminary weighing in with the White House, Pentagon, some Capitol Hill offices, and even some of our members during our grassroots efforts around the country that summer (one of SU's summer Pride handouts on what members could do to help included a talking point about asking their lawmakers to oppose wasteful funding for the extra F-35 engine), in the end we didn't have to get too involved after all. Support for the extra engine began to fade as the year went on and the issue of wasteful Washington spending began to dominate the midterm election cycle.

After Labor Day rolled around, Congress returned to Washington to begin its last DC work period before breaking early in October for the midterm elections. Those of us still working in the DADT issue's inner circle in Washington knew that we were on an ever-narrowing road to victory that fall, and that if we didn't fight like hell against attempts to further delay consideration of the defense authorization bill, we would be left high and dry after having come so far and having accomplished so much already that year.

The first thing that Servicemembers United did after Congress reconvened in September was to ramp up the public pressure on Senator Reid. We already knew we had a very good shot at a successful Senate floor vote if only Senator Reid would schedule it, and with the midterms approaching it made the most sense to get the vote over as early in September as possible. A week after Congress came back, an impatient and scathing op-ed by yours truly appeared in the prominent Capitol Hill newspaper the *Hill* warning Senator Reid and his staff that our community would not forgive him for letting NDAA slip into the lame duck session and that we fully expected him to schedule and hold a vote on the bill that month. The article, entitled "Reid My Lips: No Forgiveness If No NDAA in September" struck a chord with the majority leader's office; Reid's staff was furious at us for the unrelenting pressure campaign. I knew it would make things tough on us to come out so strong, but anyone with even the most elementary understanding of the political and legislative calendar knew that chances for success went down into the single digits if we waited until after the midterms for a vote.

And no one else was there to keep the pressure on. SLDN was doing weak, broad calls and not specifically targeting Senator Reid. HRC wasn't targeting Senator Reid publicly at all, and they were even beginning to lean on me about being so vocal with him. In one coalition meeting, HRC's political director even asked me in a whiny, complaining tone, "Are you really going to keep targeting Reid over this?" My response: "Absolutely!" What I really wondered, though, was if they ever were going to *start* targeting him. He was, after all, the one and only person who controlled whether NDAA got a final vote and whether DADT repeal got a shot at passage that year or not. There was no one else to target except Reid—until Reid manufactured another convenient target, that is.

But before that happened, SU announced another Veterans Lobby Day initiative for mid-September, which we nicknamed "The Final Assault." Although we had a much shorter time frame with this event, as well as a shorter budget (we had intentionally not partnered with HRC this time around), we threw together a remarkably successful one-day event that saw over eighty servicemembers and veterans take off work and fly into DC to once again storm the Hill, to press their senators and the Senate leadership to support moving forward on NDAA immediately.

At the same time, we also took the opportunity to organize a simultaneous unique gathering that we called the Military Partners Forum. In 2009, Servicemembers United had started reaching out to the civilian partners of LGBT servicemembers. I had been approached by several of these partners that year who asked if I knew of any other military partners they might talk to about their unique problems and challenges. It struck me that this group of people connected to the gay military community thus far had been virtually ignored. They not only suffered all of the same things as straight military husbands and wives but also lived through their own version of DADT hell in an even deeper and unsupported closet than their active duty other halves. This community desperately needed support and recognition, it seemed, and why no one had ever thought to do this before simply baffled me.

In late 2009, SU launched the Campaign for Military Partners, with the help of a few brave initial civilian partner organizers who educated us patiently on their unique needs and challenges. SU also began pushing the story of military partners out to media, and we succeeded early on in igniting interest in this previously unrecognized community. Over the next year and a half, Servicemembers United would single-handedly cultivate, advocate for, promote, recognize, and support a growing and increasingly active community of military partners, including pitching more and more media stories about their plight and the unique needs of gay military couples and families.

These efforts eventually led to the first Military Partners Forum. As servicemembers and veterans took part in Veterans Lobby Day, twelve civilian partners flew to Washington to meet for the first time and finally share with one another the experience of being an isolated and unrecognized military spouse. But, perhaps more important, I used the opportunity that day to pitch another group meeting with the Comprehensive Review Working Group at the Pentagon.

The Working Group was just as uneasy about meeting with the partners of active duty gay and lesbian servicemembers as these partners were about meeting with Pentagon officials for the first time and speaking honestly and openly about their relationships. And while the opportunity certainly existed for the partners to meet with the Working Group's leaders and staff away from federal government property, I thought it was important that this historic meeting actually take place at the Pentagon itself, both because of the message it would send and because I thought that our group of partners deserved an audience at the Pentagon.

But a big problem remained for these partners' privacy. If the meeting occurred at the Pentagon, the Pentagon would be forced to release their names to anyone who requested them under the Freedom of Information Act. Chances were slim that anyone would ask for the names and then use that list to try to figure out who their partners were and out them in retaliation, but it remained a risk nonetheless that a few of the partners were a little concerned about, as was the Pentagon.

We ended up getting around FOIA by bringing the partners into the Pentagon as guests of a contractor, not a permanent government employee, in a roundabout way that was considered exempt under the FOIA law. This, the Pentagon's top lawyer assured us, would enable the Working Group—including DOD's top lawyer himself, who was a cochair of the Working Group—to be able to meet with and hear about the experiences of the civilian partners of gay and lesbian servicemembers without leaving them fearful that the meeting could bring trouble for their active duty partners. The Working Group's cochairs and senior staff would later say that out of hundreds of meetings with tens of thousands of people in the course of their comprehensive review of the DADT issue, this was one of the most influential.

SU would continue to serve as the sole source of support and recognition for the partners and families of LGBT servicemembers, but others would come in at the last minute and try to jump onto the bandwagon as if they had been involved all along, and as if there had not been a growing and thriving community and support network since late 2009. Such jump-in-at-the-last-minute attempts to claim a piece of the pie would only increase as the DADT issue heated up and as certain personalities realized that they could grab some of the spotlight in a hot minute by creating a Facebook group or a simple website, or even simply by claiming arbitrarily to be an "organization" or a new "group." Reporters often didn't know the difference, and very few took the time to look beyond a headline or an e-mail to verify substance or depth. This would lead to a situation later in 2010 that nearly derailed our entire DADT repeal effort with just one unsubstantiated headline.

First came another derailment threat, as Senator Reid finally reluctantly announced that he would allow the defense authorization bill to come up for a vote on the floor of the Senate. Advocates only had a very brief time to celebrate before realizing that the long-awaited Senate floor vote on NDAA had been intentionally set up to fail, and that the majority leader had effectively manufactured another target for the otherwise confused and frustrated progressive community to go after instead of him.

Reid announced that he would bring up NDAA using a Senate procedure called "filling the tree" to block nearly all Republican amendments to the bill and allow only his own chosen amendments to be offered. Since the defense authorization bill is one of the biggest pieces of legislation that Congress deals with on an annual basis, placing such heavy restrictions and one-sided privileges on debate and amendments in favor of the majority guaranteed that even the most reasonable of Republicans wouldn't agree to proceed with the bill in a million years. The extremely restrictive nature of the maneuver even outraged many Democrats. We knew we didn't have every Democrat voting with us on NDAA, so we needed at least a small handful of Republicans to vote with us in order to move the bill forward. Reid's gambit was widely recognized as an attempt to kill the bill.

Instead of calling out Senator Reid for this dirty trick, however, most of the other advocacy groups either stayed silent or participated in the roasting of our lead Republican supporter, Senator Susan Collins of Maine, who had been the only direct Republican yes vote for the amendment in committee. SLDN even asked pop star Lady Gaga, who had become a vocal public advocate for repeal, to go to Maine and participate in a last-minute rally targeting Collins. This infuriated the senator and her staff, all of whom had been working hard in good faith to broker a deal between Reid and the handful of Republicans we needed to proceed. Our Democratic champions of repeal in the Senate were likewise outraged that Reid had succeeded in laying the blame squarely and unfairly on the shoulders of Senator Collins.

So with the passive support of the other groups, who would not dare stand up to the Senate majority leader, Reid held the all-important cloture vote with the ultrarestrictive rules and stood by with impunity as the bill failed. It was a great setup from Senator Reid's point of view: he didn't want the bill to come up anyway, but he could still get credit for bringing it up, because he knew that Republicans would get the blame for killing it.

"Cheap Political Stunts Should Not Hold Up Repeal of DADT" was the title of the op-ed that appeared from me in the *Hill* just before the vote, in which I pledged to work systematically to educate the progressive community on how this maneuver by Reid was actually killing NDAA intentionally. Servicemembers United, and even I personally, were always truly nonpartisan in the repeal fight, going after Democrats and Republicans alike if we thought that they were realistic pressure points and that there was potential for change by pushing on them. And when we saw this transparent partisan political game being played by the majority leader, we wasted no time in calling him out on it and demanding another vote.

Yet another battle we faced in trying to structure a passable NDAA bill related to the DREAM Act. This bill sought to provide a path to citizenship to the children of undocumented immigrants through either college or military service. Republicans and numerous conservative Democrats saw it as a form of amnesty for those residing in the country illegally, while progressives saw it as a compassionate stepping stone to plugging holes in our flawed immigration system. Regardless of one's position on the DREAM Act as public policy, the legislation simply didn't have enough votes to make it through the Senate, yet Senator Reid also sought to bundle this bill in with NDAA, again without the chance for opponents to offer an amendment to remove it on the floor.

As a matter of politics, since we were a single-issue organization, we naturally opposed inclusion of the DREAM Act or any other piece of bill-killing legislation in a restricted NDAA that year. While many who supported the repeal of DADT also supported passage of DREAM, we strongly believed in putting DADT first. If anything threatened the repeal of DADT, whether it was the veto threat over alternate F-35 engine funding or the lack of majority support for DREAM, we supported eliminating it from the equation in order to get NDAA—and the repeal of DADT—passed and done.

But other organizations and actors had different interests. At one point during a last-minute lobbying blitz before a major vote, one of our teams on Capitol Hill ran into staff from another gay organization involved in the DADT fight lobbying instead with a group of DREAM Act advocates, including wearing one of their T-shirts around to Senate offices that day. In another episode, a senior staffer with a progressive lobbying firm initiated a tense exchange with Jarrod: although we had not even been lobbying against DREAM on its merits—just arguing not to include it in the *defense bill* if it clearly didn't have the votes to pass—the staffer, whose firm I suspect had numerous immigration-related clients, accused us of opposing the DREAM Act and threatened to badmouth SU to major gay community donors and foundations as a result. And given how incestuous these communities are, many of them would likely have bought into the bull, too—hook, line, and sinker.

That episode highlighted a major flaw in the gay political and donor communities that still persists and really holds back progress and wider support for LGBT equality issues: many organizations and donors insist that in order to be pro-gay, you have to be pro many other issues as well, ones that have nothing to do with LGBT equality. Both the Human Rights Campaign and the Gay and Lesbian Victory Fund have, at times, according to their own board members, said either explicitly or implicitly that a political candidate must be pro-choice in order to secure their endorsement, yet they claim to be pure LGBT equality organizations. If they publicly branded themselves as LGBT equality and pro-choice organizations in the same breath every time, that would be more accurate.

I of course see no problem with an organization wanting to be pro-choice or pro-environment or pro-immigration or just about pro-anything. But I have come to recognize a major issue with organizations that publicly claim to represent the entire LGBT community but really only represent, for example, the Democratic gay community or the pro-choice gay community: they leave those extra stipulations out of their mission statements. Even SLDN once turned away a uniquely qualified candidate for their executive director position who had been a major in the Marine Corps primarily because, according to one of its board members, he was also personally pro-life. This pathology will continue to hold us back until organizational leaders and advocates start putting their organizations' publicly stated policy goals first and leave their personal politics at home.

Servicemembers United has been asked many times over the years to come out in favor of nearly every issue under the sun, on both the right and the left side of the political spectrum. These issues were often passionately supported by many within our membership and our constituency, but SU isn't an environmental organization, nor does it trade in economics, labor, foreign affairs, or technology policy. SU is in the business of defense and veterans issues on behalf of the LGBT defense and veteran community, and we've always put our primary issues, our policy goals, and our constituency first, despite any personal political preferences of the staff. Many other organizations simply cannot say the same.

Most of the time that I had been a prominent national-level DADT repeal advocate I was also a graduate student, working first on a master's in public administration and then later on a doctorate in political science. Although I had finished all of my required coursework for the PhD before SU opened its Washington, DC, office, I delayed taking my comprehensive exams and starting my dissertation because of how much things heated up with the DADT issue in 2009 and 2010. However, as time ticked on, I knew I needed to make some progress on finishing that degree. I had originally scheduled my comprehensive exams for the spring of 2010, but when DADT got a mention in the State of the Union and things looked early on like they were quickly accelerating to a spring or summer conclusion, I bumped them off to the fall. But when the issue dragged out through the summer and on into fall, I was stuck taking grueling comps in the middle of the DADT repeal fight. Thankfully, my department and faculty advisers had always been supportive and flexible, but I also tried to refrain from too often using work as an excuse.

As luck would have it, the first Senate floor vote on NDAA fell on the last day of my first field comprehensive exam period. That meant that after having to dedicate significant chunks of time in the few days before the vote to taking those comps, I also had to stay up all night the night before the vote in order to finish one of the requirements, and then stay up all the next day for the vote and accompanying press and meetings on the Hill. The day we lost the first Senate floor vote, I had been up for forty-eight hours when I had to appear on *Hardball with Chris Matthews* that night on MSNBC.

I was nearly dead by the time I got to the MSNBC studio near the National Cathedral in DC, where Matthews hosts the show live. Jarrod was kind enough to point out that I had huge black circles under my eyes, which the studio makeup artists had to work overtime to cover. It had been a long and frustrating day—comps due, a Senate vote loss, no sleep—and I felt ill prepared for the onslaught of Chris Matthews that night. I think I handled the segment just fine, but it's always frustrating to be a guest on *Hardball* and to have to talk about an issue that requires slightly more than two-second bursts to discuss.

15

* * * * *

WINNING THE LOTTERY

In the middle of the battle to get Senator Reid to bring up NDAA for a floor vote, an extraordinary and unexpected development occurred on the judicial front that changed the calculus for nearly everyone involved—congressmen, senators, advocates, administration officials, and servicemembers alike. On September 9, 2010, US District Court judge Virginia Phillips issued a ruling in a long-drawn-out case pending before her, *Log Cabin Republicans v. United States of America*, declaring the DADT law unconstitutional on First and Fifth Amendment grounds. She also issued a far-reaching injunction barring enforcement of the DADT law worldwide.

For the first time in recent memory, gay and lesbian servicemembers could technically be open if they so chose, and, more important, they could not be kicked out for it. The lawsuit that the "establishment" gay community had shunned when LCR originally brought it back in 2004, and that ultraliberals often ridiculed because the Log Cabin Republicans' name was on it, had become the vehicle for finally ending DADT. That victory, however, would soon be put on hold, reinstated, and put on hold again in a yo-yo pattern that both complicated and greatly helped legislative repeal efforts. But this legal victory had been a long time coming—and I was proud to have been front and center on this battle, too, for longer than even the LCR staff had been involved with it.

As Sophia from *The Golden Girls* might say: "Picture it: DC, 2006." LCR's landmark lawsuit challenging the constitutionality of the DADT law had been pending before US District Court judge George Schiavelli in Los Angeles for more than a year, awaiting a decision on the Bush administration's initial motion to dismiss the case. The question was whether LCR had standing to bring the lawsuit in the first place. The organization claimed that it had "associational standing," because at least one anonymous servicemember who was a member of LCR at the time had suffered unconstitutional harm at the hands of the DADT law. The government claimed that LCR could not bring the case on behalf of a John Doe plaintiff; it contended that LCR should have to name that person if it wanted to sue on his or her behalf. But naming that person as a gay or lesbian servicemember would, of course, result in the termination of that individual's career and livelihood. Finally, Judge Schiavelli handed down his decision on the government's motion: the case would be dismissed unless LCR, along with its ambitious attorneys at the Los Angeles office of the law firm White & Case, amended the original complaint and publicly named a member who had been unconstitutionally harmed by the DADT law.

That ruling threatened to stop the lawsuit in its tracks right then unless LCR could produce someone who was willing to join the case as a public plaintiff. Since I was newly "out there" in the public spotlight at the time, and since I had been made an "honorary member" of LCR in recognition of the public advocacy work I had been doing on the DADT issue, LCR's leadership asked me to join the case as the sole named public plaintiff and save it from dismissal.

I had never been involved in suing anyone before, much less suing the United States of America, and there was something that felt a little off about it, as if I were impugning the country's good name by joining a suit that ended in "*v. USA*." But emotional reaction aside, I also worried that joining the LCR lawsuit would align me too closely with that particular organization, and I had seen in working on the Call to Duty Tour earlier that same year that organizations were hypercompetitive, jealous entities that closely guarded their "assets" and tossed them aside like yesterday's fad when one got too close to another organization.

Joe Solmonese from HRC happened to be in the room with us at the US Chamber of Commerce building across from the White House when I was discussing the issue with LCR's leadership and attorneys, so I asked him what he thought. He indifferently replied, "I don't have a problem with it." I then called up gay DC lobbyist Robert Raben and asked his opinion too. I distinctly remember him telling me, "Well, if it succeeds, then you'll be famous for having your name attached to it. And if it doesn't, then no one will remember and it won't matter anyway." Still others suggested that it didn't matter one way or another what I decided, because the case would surely be dead soon after the new paperwork was filed.

That afternoon in 2006, on the last day that LCR had to come up with someone before the case would be automatically dismissed, their attorneys at White & Case filed a rushed amended complaint with me as the sole named plaintiff. I remember being quite proud and excited at the time about joining the case and representing the entire plight of gay, lesbian, and bisexual servicemembers and veterans. But I largely forgot about the case as the months and then years dragged on without a decision on even the new motion to dismiss by the government.

Judge Schiavelli didn't seem to want to rule on the case. He consistently exceeded customary deadlines for issuing rulings on motions, at times prompting the government and the attorneys at White & Case to file joint requests for action. More than a year after the amended complaint was filed and the government again filed its request to have the case dismissed, Judge Schiavelli scheduled a hearing on the motion, which I flew out to Los Angeles to attend in person in the summer of 2007.

The question of LCR's standing was still a side issue in the case. Now that LCR had publicly named a plaintiff, the government contended that LCR could not even sue on my behalf, because I was only an honorary member of the organization and not a "real" member. This argument, of course, was in addition to its main contentions: that DADT was constitutional, necessary, just, and fair.

The judge gave each side a fair hearing that day, I thought, challenging both LCR and the government and even admitting at one point that he didn't think such a law would make it through Congress again if proposed in this day and age. But after the hearing was over, another long wait for a ruling began. Some time after the hearing, both sets of lawyers again requested action on the case by the judge, at which point we discovered from a clerk that the case file had been accidentally destroyed in its entirety. The file had to be reassembled from duplicates of case documents and from electronic copies of available case files. After this court mishap, the judge claimed to need yet more time to consider what to do. So we waited, and we waited, and we waited some more.

Judge Schiavelli never did rule on whether the case should be dismissed as the government so desperately wanted. Instead, he stepped down from the bench, announcing his retirement in September 2008. By that point, the LCR case had been before a federal court for nearly three years awaiting a decision on the motion to dismiss, a very preliminary step in the long federal legal process.

The following year, 2009, the court randomly reassigned the case to District Court judge Virginia Phillips based in Riverside, California. Judge Phillips quickly recognized the bizarre delay that had plagued the case up to that point and decided to move with deliberate speed to review the filings, hear the arguments, and consider the still-pending motion to dismiss.

Most legal challenges to the DADT law over the years were lost on the initial motion to dismiss or on some other preliminary motion. Even the two additional DADT cases that were filed after the LCR case

(SLDN's *Cook v. Rumsfeld/Gates* and the ACLU's *Witt v. Air Force*) were shot down by the trial court on the motion to dismiss. While Witt would go on to appeal and win her case—which didn't challenge the constitutionality of the DADT law but rather the law's application in her individual case—and eventually settled with the Obama administration for her ability to retire, the Cook case's dismissal was strongly upheld by the appellate court in the First Circuit where it was filed. So while we knew we had a strong case and a highly capable legal team led by White & Case attorney Dan Woods, we also knew that the chance of having the case dismissed at the outset of its consideration by the new judge was high too.

But we were wrong. In a series of rulings through mid- and late 2009, Judge Phillips handed the government its rear end back to it on a silver platter. She outright refused to dismiss the case, which surprised all of us, especially the government—now the Obama administration. And she refused the Justice Department's repeated requests to block discovery, delay or block hearings, and even allow for an emergency appeal of her decision to the Ninth Circuit Court of Appeals. The latter request was particularly suspect, as the judge noted, because the "emergency" action came nearly four months after the decision was handed down. If it had truly been an emergency, she argued, the government would have made the request expeditiously.

As discovery commenced, the Justice Department pitched a fit about having to answer some of the interrogatories posed to the administration by LCR's attorneys. When our side's legal team asked the Justice Department to admit that the commander-in-chief claimed that DADT harmed national security, they refused. When they were asked to admit that the commander-in-chief did not support the DADT law, they refused. The judge had to compel the Justice Department to answer our attorneys' questions, and that wasn't all. The government was skittish about turning over documents. They didn't want to allow anyone to be called as a witness. And they were just generally terrified that DADT would finally get its day in court.

As 2010 rolled around, Judge Phillips announced that she was scheduling a two-week trial for us, which had to be rescheduled once. The final trial dates were to be in mid-July of that year. Yet again, the Justice Department sought to have the trial canceled or at least delayed, arguing that those very admissions by the president and senior defense leaders demonstrated that DADT was likely on its way off the books. But "likely" wasn't good enough. Judge Phillips refused the many requests by the Justice Department to kill the case at every turn—precisely because of the very real possibility in 2010 that, despite advances, DADT would not get repealed, and because of the reality that servicemembers continued to be silenced and discharged even as activity on the political front increased.

In July 2010 I flew out to Riverside, California, for four days of the two-week trial. One of the first issues to come before the court was, yet again, the issue of standing—that is, whether my honorary membership in LCR allowed the organization to sue the government on my behalf. But as the government proceeded to make the case once more for why I should not be considered a "real" member of LCR, the judge responded with a question that shut down that entire issue in her courtroom. She was reported to have informed the Justice Department's lawyers that as a judge, she was an honorary member of the California bar. She then asked whether they considered her a "real" member of the bar or not. The issue of standing ended then and there. One for us, zero for them.

Dan Woods's team had arranged for a diverse variety of "lay witnesses" to testify about the discrimination, harm, and constitutional violations caused by DADT. These included a variety of gay and lesbian veterans who had been harmed or negatively impacted by the law, and even a straight veteran—former SU staffer Steve Vossler—who had served with open gays and lesbians without issue.

This case was my first time testifying or even being deposed, but I ended up being much less nervous for both than I thought I would be. In fact, I ended up being more annoyed than anything, because the Justice Department attorney who cross-examined and deposed me tried to use the opportunity to subtly twist the record about my background and several things I had allegedly said in the past.

First, out of the hundreds of times that I had explained my assigned military occupational specialty (MOS)—human intelligence collector—in the media and also explained the fact that I spoke multiple languages going into the military but had learned Arabic after I got out while living in Egypt, he of course had to pick out one of the few random times I had been misquoted in an article—the piece in which the reporter mistakenly reported that I was an Arabic linguist—and use that to try to suggest that I went around trying to sell myself as having held the MOS of Arabic linguist, which I never did. I only ever claimed to speak Egyptian Arabic after having lived in Egypt and studied the language there on a DOD-sponsored program. It may have been confusing to many, but I do not believe it was confusing to the Justice Department's attorneys. A little bit of basic research, or the application of the slightest bit of common sense, would have led them to realize that such misquotes weren't unusual and that far more descriptions and quotations existed that stated my background correctly than incorrectly. They were clearly trying to mischaracterize a random mistake by a reporter as a deliberate misstatement on my part that impugned my credibility.

Second, the government tried to suggest that it was disingenuous for me to assert that I had been assigned to be a human intelligence collector and press the case that the army lost an asset as a result of my discharge. The crux of this argument seemed to be that I did not have a many-years-long record as a human intelligence collector when I was discharged, which of course was very true. But their key mistake there was that I never claimed to have had one, only to have been assigned to human intelligence and to having come onto active duty with my language training requirement already fulfilled.

Two points are important on that topic: (1) Nearly all human intelligence collectors at the time never actually functioned as human intelligence collectors, because we weren't engaged in a large-scale active conflict until well after September 11, 2001. Furthermore, most people discharged under DADT had been fired very early on in their careers, certainly before deploying and actually using their MOS. Even most of the linguists who were discharged and proactively highlighted in the media, especially by the Palm Center, had been discharged out of training from the Defense Language Institute. (2) The DADT repeal movement (including the Palm Center, SLDN, and others) always referred to those discharged by the MOS they had been assigned while in. That was a universally accepted principle that I did not invent. But now, when I followed the Palm Center's and SLDN's lead on how to classify myself as a DADT repeal activist, the government jumped all over me.

Finally, the Justice Department wanted badly for me to admit that I had intentionally chosen to come out to the command and terminate my own career early. This could not have been further from the truth, as had been demonstrated exhaustively in the media, in the depositions, and even there on the witness stand. But they pointed to my end-of-process "admission" statement or the paperwork I'd been advised to submit later in order to ensure an honorable discharge and avoid an intrusive investigation. Their attorneys just couldn't seem to understand—or didn't want to come across as understanding—that a formal statement to a command is often the very last step in the discharge process, required to secure a smooth finish to a long and often painful series of events. In other words, the "admission" is almost never the beginning of the process but rather the end.

I stood firm in maintaining that it was not that "admission" that had triggered my discharge but rather that the original leaking of information about my sexual orientation to others within my unit was undeniably what started the chain reaction that led to my discharge, as had been the case for thousands of others as well. I had gone out of my way to abide by the DADT law while I was in, and was quite distraught for years that I was forced to become a civilian again. But these were convenient points of contention for the Justice Department to cherry-pick and try to distort in order to try to make its case that the DADT law was fair and necessary.

Surprisingly, some alleged "allies" would similarly cherry-pick these points out of the LCR trial to try to smear me during the height of the DADT repeal fight, too. The independent success I'd achieved in the repeal movement without being beholden to one of the larger establishment organizations evoked intense envy among some, and the brutally honest public voice I had as a result of that independence threatened the interests of many others.

One such character was the ringleader of an online group called OutServe. This group sprang up at the last minute in the DADT repeal fight and didn't contribute to the legislative repeal effort in the least, except to nearly catastrophically derail it at the very last minute through sheer ignorance. The organizer of this group, a junior administrative officer in the air force named Josh Seefried, was involved early on in an effort to anonymously disseminate several of the Justice Department's distortions—along with a litany of bizarre and childish slurs and personal insults against me—to a slew of gay and progressive bloggers, reporters, and others.

I had never met Josh Seefried in my life, and he knew nothing about me personally except for the public fact that I had risen to become one of the leading voices, activists, and strategists in the DADT repeal movement over the previous five years. Yet at the very height of the battle to delicately push DADT repeal forward in September 2010, while everyone else was focused on that, Seefried and his associates decided to spend their time creating fanciful e-mails to send to reporters and bloggers from fake e-mail accounts about how I was a "big fat liar" and didn't really speak any foreign languages. (I still have a few choice words in all five of those languages for all of the cowards involved in that disgraceful and shameful conduct.)

Another individual who would attempt to peddle similar falsehoods based on the Justice Department's distortions was a pro-repeal witness at the LCR trial, Mike Almy. But the ironic thing about Almy's attempt at the same behavior is that while the LCR trial actually provided an opportunity for me to clarify anything people may have erroneously assumed, misunderstood, or misinterpreted about my own background and story, it did just the opposite for him, bringing out major potential liabilities that he hadn't previously disclosed.

When I first recommended Almy to Senator Lieberman's office to stand beside the senator and his colleagues at the press conference introducing the Senate version of the repeal bill, I'd explicitly and repeatedly asked him if anything at all in his background or story could become a potential public relations liability for the repeal movement. I specifically focused on the content, which he refused to discuss, of the e-mails that he had written on a government computer, the discovery of which had formed the basis for the suspension of his security clearance, punitive action by his command, and his early discharge. When SLDN wanted to put him on the witness panel before the Senate Armed Services Committee, I had asked both him and Aubrey Sarvis for explicit assurances that nothing in those e-mails, which had led to such a mysteriously harsh reaction from his command, could possibly be perceived to be a liability for our community and our issue. Again, I was assured that there was nothing to worry about.

But when Almy took the witness stand for the LCR trial and the government attorneys gained access to those e-mails, a major potential liability surfaced. When the Justice Department brought up the subject of those e-mails, LCR's attorneys suddenly objected to their content being publicly revealed. A few moments later, those of us watching the case closely got a hint as to why no one wanted those e-mails out. The Justice Department's attorneys seemed to suggest that Almy had been discussing and soliciting sexual relations from a subordinate and engaging in potential fraternization with an enlisted soldier via those government computers in Iraq. This was clearly a major liability, which Almy was unwilling to deny under oath on the stand. Even the judge ended up admitting, after looking at the more detailed deposition, that these salacious new details "could have been ... another basis for discharge" in and of themselves.

Needless to say, had I been aware of any of this, I never would have recommended Almy for the coveted spot beside Senator Lieberman at the Senate bill introduction press conference, and he never would have become a public figure. Lucky for us all, Elaine Donnelly never got her hands on this information, although I still consider it incredibly irresponsible of Almy to have put our issue at such grave risk by attempting to conceal something he knew would be a major potential liability.

During the trial, lead LCR attorney Dan Woods also arranged to interview a number of expert witnesses on the stand, including Dr. Aaron Belkin and Dr. Nathaniel Frank of the Palm Center; Dr. Alan Okros, a veteran officer of the Canadian military and a distinguished professor of military psychology and leadership at the Royal Military College of Canada and the Canadian Forces College; and Dr. Larry Korb, the former assistant secretary of defense for manpower, reserve affairs, installations, and logistics under President Reagan. While the Justice Department objected to nearly everything that our side's experts said or did, to the point that the continuous objecting visibly ticked off the judge, Dr. Korb's testimony provided some comic relief during a tense period of the trial.

Dr. Korb was considerably older than the other expert witnesses that Woods and his team had called, and he was far more credentialed than all of the others combined. So Korb had little patience for the most junior member of the government's legal team aggressively grilling him on the minutest and most ridiculous of points, especially the line of questioning regarding what he said or how he worded the most random of public remarks two decades earlier. The funniest part was when the judge asked if the government had any more questions and an exasperated Korb interjected, "Well, I have a question!" The judge then looked over to him on the witness stand and calmly said, "No."

After our side finished with its last witness, the government declined to call any witnesses in defense of the statute. Instead, it continued to contend that it was not appropriate for the judge even to have allowed the trial in the first place, and that she should have thrown the case out on their original motion to dismiss. Putting on a defense would give the appearance of their consent to the legitimacy of the trial, and they certainly didn't want to give on that point. I had to leave California the day before closing arguments occurred, but Dan Woods gave a rousing performance that seemed to seal the deal.

As the days and weeks passed after the end of the historic trial, we were fairly confident that the winds were blowing in our favor, but we also knew that the judge could easily find justification for ruling against us, letting the fact that she had allowed us to even put the law's rationale on trial suffice for having gone above and beyond. We fully expected a ruling within ninety days, but I think the entire system was shocked when a ruling came down much sooner, on Thursday, September 9, 2010.

I was at dinner that evening on Seventeenth Street in DC, luckily just relaxing and chatting on the outdoor patio of Floriana after having just finished eating, when several text messages started coming in saying "Congratulations on your win!" I immediately suspected the messages were in reference to the LCR case, but rather than immediately experiencing joy I actually felt panic. The decision had come earlier than expected, and we didn't have any press statements ready to go out. I also wasn't near the office, so I began a desperate scramble to find Internet access. I hastily excused myself from dinner after explaining to my companions the news that had just broken, and I bolted over to a Starbucks that had Wi-Fi. Luckily I happened to have my laptop with me at the time.

As I drafted a rushed press statement praising the decision on behalf of SU and myself as plaintiff, I noticed that I had made it in the nick of time, since Starbucks was closing down as I typed. There was only one other patron in the café, and both of us were soon ushered out. I retreated to the sidewalk patio to continue using the Wi-Fi and begin answering press inquiries about the victory.

It felt like we had just won the lottery. In fact, each victory along the way, from the win on the motion to dismiss to the win on forcing discovery to the win on the summary judgment motion to the win on the merits that night, felt like a lottery win as well. The government had usually prevailed easily on each one of those hurdles in the past, so it truly felt like we were serial legal lotto winners in 2009 and 2010.

And yet more good news was still to come. The judge didn't just rule in our favor on the merits. She also indicated that she intended to issue an injunction barring enforcement of the DADT law by the Pentagon. That meant that as of the effective date of the injunction, DADT would be dead for the time being. Almost two weeks later, another trial judge presiding over air force major Margaret Witt's case also came out with a favorable ruling. And exactly three weeks later, Judge Phillips issued the promised injunction barring the Pentagon from enforcing DADT worldwide. The winnings just kept rolling in. For eight full days, DADT was dead and new possibilities—namely, a world without this burdensome law—finally seemed within reach.

The court victories also gave us a tremendous advantage when lobbying members of Congress. "Vote with us to enact this orderly transition legislation," we argued, "or the Pentagon will have to deal with a much more radical, court-imposed, abrupt change in policy as a result of our legal wins." It totally changed the calculus for both lawmakers and the Pentagon; although the Pentagon knew that it could comply with the order, it had griped and kicked and screamed and worked itself into a tizzy about the prospect of immediate repeal, and it much preferred our moderate amendment to this judicial imposition.

Elaine Donnelly had a field day with the decisions, and she unilaterally crowned Judge Phillips the "Supreme Judicial Commander of the Military." Naturally, she also threw around phrases like "judicial activism" and "San Francisco military" to try to enhance her fearmongering efforts.

But in the end it was the reliably liberal Ninth Circuit Court of Appeals, to which the Obama administration had run after Judge Phillips refused to stay her injunction, that soon restored the status quo. The appellate court ended up issuing a temporary stay less than two weeks later, and the DADT policy was technically back in force. Still, although the military didn't fall apart during those eight days, the Pentagon began to worry that it would not be allowed to carry out the measured and orderly repeal process that it had been planning for. Many troops, commanders, and senior leaders started to just wish that the issue were over so that they didn't have to deal with the flip-flopping anymore. The fear of having to go through a court-ordered end to DADT took its toll not just on senior defense leaders but on moderate lawmakers as well. If we didn't have enough votes to pass NDAA with DADT repeal language in it before, we certainly did after Judge Phillips's rulings.

As the pre-midterm Senate work period in DC wound down, however, Senator Reid still had not scheduled another vote on NDAA. It was now far too close to the elections and things did not look good for the Democrats, especially in the House. Trying to get something passed when this Congress returned for its lame duck session was a free-for-all, but we had no alternative but to push for it anyway.

Our chances for success had dropped into the single digits, but we knew we would have at least one new advantage to bolster us: the long-awaited report of the Comprehensive Review Working Group on DADT from the Pentagon. Preliminary data and findings from the study had begun to leak out, and that gave us confidence that we had a shot at using those findings as extra political cover to push through repeal on the fourth down. But little did we know even then that it would end up being another fumble followed by a Hail Mary pass during overtime before we finally won the game.

16

★ ★ ★ ★ ★

LAME DUCKS

Although the now-critical lame duck session of Congress would not start until nearly two weeks after the midterm elections, the Senate recessed several weeks prior to them so that its members up for reelection could go back to their home states for the final stretch of their campaigns. Exactly one week before Election Day, DADT repeal advocates were summoned back to the White House for another meeting with senior administration officials. I should have suspected that something was up when I got to the Eisenhower Executive Office Building and saw that Joe Solmonese was there for the meeting.

Joe had almost never been personally involved in DADT repeal work. Only once before had he attended a full coalition meeting at the White House, back in May, and he never attended DADT coalition meetings on behalf of HRC on the Hill or even at HRC's headquarters. At first I assumed he was in attendance because things were so heated on the issue, we were down to the wire, and he was under pressure to get directly involved. But I soon realized that such thoughts were far too generous. Joe was only there that particular day because, as it turned out, we had been summoned to the White House in order to meet with President Obama himself.

The meeting started out in EEOB with several senior administration staffers, including Jim Messina, Tina Tchen, and others. Of course, Brian Bond was there along with several of the gays from the White House Counsel's office. But when senior White House adviser Valerie Jarrett arrived, she asked us to move over to the Roosevelt Room in the West Wing to continue the meeting there, just steps from the Oval Office. Phil Schiliro, the president's legislative affairs director, also joined us in the West Wing. With this lineup of senior officials, it was already one of the most high-powered meetings at the White House the DADT repeal community had ever had.

Representing our side at the meeting were Jarrod Chlapowski and I from Servicemembers United; Joe Solmonese and Allison Herwitt of HRC; Aubrey Sarvis from SLDN; Winnie Stachelberg from CAP; Clarke Cooper from LCR; Shane Larson from Stonewall Democrats; Nathaniel Frank, now of the Movement Advancement Project; and Jim Kessler from Third Way. Normally Lanae Erickson represented Third Way in coalition meetings, but she wasn't able to make this one, nor had she been able to make our big meeting back in May with Senate Armed Services Committee chairman Carl Levin. Unfortunately for Lanae, the two she had to miss were probably the biggest meetings of the year in Washington on the DADT issue. She had been at nearly every other DADT coalition meeting representing Third Way, thankfully, bringing a calm, rational voice to the tension, irrationality, and passive-aggressive hostility that often marked those meetings. But that distinct coalition of five groups—Servicemembers United, SLDN, HRC, CAP, and Third Way—that met in Washington nearly every week, and sometimes twice a week, did more than 95 percent of the DADT advocacy work on the ground during 2009 and 2010. The remaining portion was done by LCR, which was only invited to coalition meetings two or three times during that whole period, and the Palm Center, which wasn't in Washington and wasn't part of that core coalition.

Even before we left the EEOB, advocates had been having quite a tense exchange with White House staff about its role, or lack thereof, in our work to push DADT repeal through that year. To my shock, Solmonese timidly and carefully started off the meeting by telling Jim Messina that a number of people in our community had been hearing that the White House still wasn't engaged on the DADT issue on the Hill. Messina categorically denied this, but it was certainly backed up by what foes and allies alike on the Hill had been telling us at the time. Hearing Messina's denials, I let loose a barrage of questions toward him in a fit of frustration. "Well, what offices *are* you talking to, and what are you telling them?" I asked defiantly. "And why can't the Working Group's report be released earlier so that Senator Levin can schedule hearings on it in time to follow that up with legislation? And if the results of the report aren't favorable, is President Obama prepared to go against the defense leadership and push for repeal anyway?"

I blurted out so many questions in rapid succession that I could tell I had surprised Messina and the other White House staff. When I noticed this, I dialed back the aggressiveness a bit but continued to press them for more concrete answers than the generic overtures with which they had started off. But I even surprised myself a little with that outburst, and on the walk between EEOB and the West Wing, I had to quietly ask Jarrod if I had overstepped. He assured me that I hadn't and that it was good for us to be honest with them about our questions and frustrations.

When we got to the Roosevelt Room in the West Wing, the assault continued. Nathaniel Frank argued that the perception in the community was that the White House was only now starting to dial up its rhetoric and activity in response to the sustained public pressure campaigns waged against it over DADT. Valerie Jarrett got testy over that suggestion and exclaimed, "That's not true! That's just not true!" But when Frank persisted, Messina piped up and got quite hostile. To defuse the situation, Frank apologized for possibly "miscommunicating" his point. But I understood his point perfectly well and agreed with it 100 percent.

I spoke up to defend Frank, telling the White House staff in the room that this perception really did exist within our community and that it was vitally important that they understood this. When Jarrett responded by suggesting that we as representatives needed to go out and convince our community members that this wasn't the case, Jarrod quickly interjected that it wasn't our job to be the White House's PR machine, and that if the perception existed then maybe it existed for a reason. He suggested instead that the White House do more to overcome the perception instead of asking us to simply try to calm the gay community's furor. This exchange ended up being very telling for a number of reasons, not least of which was that it revealed the role the White House expected constituency groups and their leaders to play for it when things got tough.

When the president finally entered the room, I was still somewhat taken aback. I used to have a professor and adviser in my master's program at North Georgia College, Dr. Barry Friedman, who would always stress to us how rare it was for a person to even get to meet a sitting president. Dr. Friedman would express the probability as an equation that factored in the number of people in the country and the number of minutes the president had during his term, minus the time the president spent sleeping, traveling, with family, etc. The point was that there were incredible demands on any given president's schedule and time, and to be one of the limited number of people who got to spend a few seconds with him during his tenure was statistically quite rare. Although I had met the president before and had even spent a few moments speaking with him about DADT, this would be by far the longest our community's representatives got to spend with him during the DADT fight—about fifteen minutes.

After going around the table, shaking everyone's hand, and exchanging pleasantries, the president sat in his chair in the middle of the conference table and began to lecture us on our community's impatience, his role as commander-in-chief, and other assorted topics. I thought it funny that he felt the need to remind us that as commander-in-chief, he had certain responsibilities and consider-ations in policy that we civilian activists didn't necessarily under-stand. He obviously didn't catch, or no one informed him, that two of us in the room—Jarrod and I—had actually served in the military under DADT, the only two in the room again, and that we understood broader defense policy considerations quite well. If that wasn't evident in our higher-level conversations with them, it was certainly pasted all over the media as we specifically sought to educate the rest of the progressive community on why certain options were not realistic and why others were, all based on nuanced defense policy considerations. But instead of taking advantage of the opportunity to engage at a more advanced level on where we were and what still needed to get done, we got lectured on the least common denominator by the president.

President Obama also took the opportunity to bring up the LCR lawsuit. The administration had been defending the constitutional-ity of DADT in court, and it was taking a pounding from the left for doing so. It would later refuse to defend the constitutionality of the Defense of Marriage Act in court, but it continued to mount a vigor-ous defense of DADT procedurally, despite our string of wins against his administration. Two individuals involved in that case were in the meeting with the president that day—me, who continued to serve as the sole named veteran in the lawsuit, and Clarke Cooper, who was the current head of LCR. In an e-mail before the meeting, Brian Bond had strongly warned everyone who would be attending against bring-ing up or discussing anything related to the LCR lawsuit with admin-istration officials. He also warned that if the lawsuit did come up, the White House Counsel's office had instructed them to immediately end the meeting.

But one of the major points the president brought up himself during the meeting was in regard to the LCR lawsuit. Several of us looked at each other funny when he began talking about it, wondering if Bond, the lowest person on the totem poll in the room, was going to shut the meeting down as he had so strongly threatened. But no one was going to jump in and stop the president from talking about whatever he wanted to talk about, not even his lawyers in the room, so we listened for a good five minutes to the president explain that he felt an obligation to defend the statute in court. He also said that as a constitutional law scholar, he was of the opinion that a ruling in our favor by a major appellate court would be a lot stronger and more widely accepted by the Pentagon than one from a random lower district court. Most notably, he said that he would actually consider reevaluating his appeal of our win if we did not succeed in getting repeal legislation through in the lame duck session.

This nugget of news was encouraging to hear, but as a possible path to a DADT-free military, the president's hypothetical scenario came in a very distant second place in terms of our preference. We were there, in fact, precisely to press for more White House action during the upcoming lame duck session, including help with getting Senator Reid to actually allow us to have a real floor vote on NDAA.

When the president finished talking, he asked if there were any questions from us. Aubrey Sarvis quickly piped up and asked if the president could envision a scenario in which Secretary Gates would ask Congress to repeal DADT during the lame duck immediately after the Working Group's report came out. The president thought for a moment and then responded, "I could envision it." Then that was it. A quick "Thank you, everyone" from the president was followed by rounds of "Thank you, Mr. President," first from his staff and then from us still-stunned advocates. The conversation continued for about fifteen or twenty minutes more with the administration staffers who stayed behind in the room after the president moved on.

The following year, we would see that very same tactic of a "surprise" presidential drop-by into a meeting between administration officials and issue advocates when things were heating up and getting tense with other interest group communities. It is widely assumed that these gifts of time with the president, especially just before critical events like elections, are transparent attempts by the administration to mollify a restless community. In fact, news of the meeting leaked out so fast that we were convinced that the White House itself had leaked the information this time.

As had been strongly suspected since at least the summer, although for most as early as the spring, the 2010 midterm elections gave Democrats a "shellacking," as President Obama would describe it. Not only did they lose control of the House of Representatives, but a sizable portion of the newly elected Republicans had an ultracon- servative ideological bent. That surely meant that no DADT repeal legislation would be allowed to come to the floor of the House in the next Congress, but more important, it meant that we now absolutely had to get DADT legislation through during the lame duck session of the current Congress. Failure could mean that we would be waiting two years, four years, or more before another window of opportunity presented itself.

There was also now an increasing sense of urgency within the White House to try to paint the highly unusual situation that had resulted as having been their "plan" all along. If it were publicly known that the deal with the Pentagon had been to do the study in 2010 and try to move legislation in 2011, the administration would have looked either arrogant in thinking that they could have held onto both cham- bers of Congress through the midterms or reckless and cruel in tak- ing such a big risk with a major policy objective of such an important constituency. But keep in mind that in late 2009 and very early 2010, when this deal was made and this "plan" hatched, virtually no one could imagine a party switch in Congress as a result of the midterms. It wasn't until the spring that the thought of the House being in danger started to surface and spread, and it wasn't until the summer that the administration really started taking this possibility seriously.

This explains why through the first half of 2010, our allies in the administration and the Pentagon genuinely didn't think they were screwing us over by not supporting legislative action *that year*. At that point they were still confident that the study could be released in December, when it was originally scheduled to be released; press and advocates could read it and digest it over the holidays and have time to put their PR game together based on the results; and legislative language could be pursued to repeal the now-debunked law as part of the normal defense authorization process in the spring of 2011. That would have ensured smooth sailing toward repeal by summer or fall of 2011, at which point the Pentagon could have tolerated the original immediate-repeal bill that had been in play up until May 2010.

In hindsight, of course, we know that sticking to this plan would have been disastrous. But the point at which one accepted that this plan might not work because of possible seat losses, or even a leadership loss, in Congress is directly correlated to when one began to proactively support the compromise repeal amendment being pushed through in 2010. We activists never wanted to take the risk of waiting until 2011 to begin with, so we wanted 2010 all along (except for those who unrealistically wanted 2009). For the administration and our allies in the Pentagon, we only got tepid, reluctant support in May 2010 (remember their we'd-prefer-you-not-do-this-yet-but-this-amendment-will-minimally-suffice-if-you-do statement that month) when the train was leaving the station without them, thanks to Senate Armed Services Committee chairman Carl Levin.

But it wasn't until late fall, especially after the midterms, that the administration started getting serious, and seriously worried that one of their major policy goals wouldn't make it through at all. After the midterms was when the White House, especially their legislative affairs shop, finally got comprehensively engaged to the point that we advocates—those of us working with both the White House and the Hill and aware of what the White House was and wasn't doing on the Hill—were finally minimally satisfied with the president's level of commitment on pushing the DADT amendment through *that year*.

When the lame duck Congress finally reconvened on Monday, November 15, we got just a few minutes into the session before one of the biggest betrayals I've ever seen came from out of nowhere to nearly derail the entire DADT repeal effort in one swoop.

First thing that morning, headlines began appearing in mainstream media outlets that gay groups, troops, and vets had flip-flopped and now supported passage of the defense bill "whether or not the repeal of don't ask, don't tell is included." All of Washington, especially all of the gay and progressive community, was simply stunned. This was nothing sort of sheer treason against the long and hard-fought DADT repeal effort, and it was—and still is—utterly unforgivable.

Opponents of repealing DADT had long sought to remove the repeal amendment from the defense authorization bill and take NDAA up without DADT, and every attempt to kill repeal took the form of a motion to strike that amendment. Lucky for us, those attempts had thus far failed, although the votes were close and the balance was still incredibly delicate. The annual defense authorization bill was a huge piece of legislation, and it typically took about two weeks of floor time to get through, plus an additional week or so to conference the separate House and Senate versions and pass a merged bill back through both chambers again. Also, because the Senate requires unanimous consent to move on to other legislation while working on any given bill, it is virtually impossible to leave a big and often controversial bill like the annual defense bill once the Senate begins work on it.

With a few other primed bills lined up for Senate floor action in the lame duck prior to the defense bill, all of this meant that taking the DADT repeal amendment out of the defense bill at that time and tackling the defense bill first would have been absolute certain death to the cause of DADT repeal that year. The Senate would have been stuck on the defense bill for weeks and weeks, arguing over funding levels and every other minor provision still included within NDAA. Unanimous consent would *never* have been given by all Republicans to leave that debate and go pass DADT repeal, and our opposition would have made damn sure that there was no time left by the time the defense bill was wrapped up. Yet this certain-death option—take the DADT repeal amendment out of the defense bill and tackle the defense bill, then see if you can come back to DADT later—was precisely what these rogue activists were lobbying for.

So who were these seditious nut jobs, anyway, and in precisely what region of Colombia had they obtained the drugs they surely were injecting directly to their brains? These were the questions everyone involved in the DADT repeal movement was asking, and all in practically that exact same way. And furthermore, given that these were virtually unknown and uninvolved actors making these bizarre claims out of the blue, why was any media outlet worth its salt actually reporting this? If the mainstream reporters had done the least bit of homework before copying and pasting these moronic statements into their articles and columns that morning, they would have quickly seen that these were people who had not been the least bit involved in the DADT repeal movement, that they weren't involved in any type of real or respected organization in Washington, and that they didn't speak for anyone except themselves. But there *Politico* and others were, printing headlines like "Gay Troops OK Defense Bill Without Repeal."

The first character to surface on this historically ignorant and irresponsible stunt was Josh Seefried, the same guy, as it turns out, who had been involved in several other questionable and dishonest endeavors in the recent past. His online social group OutServe counted its Facebook fans as real members and called itself an "organization," but, as mentioned earlier, the group had not been involved in the DADT repeal movement in the least. No one from this Facebook group had ever participated in our meetings with senior White House officials and the president, nor on Capitol Hill in Senator Lieberman's war room, nor in Senator Levin's office as the compromise amendment was hashed out—despite their false claims at times that they had been. They simply were not involved, and they had absolutely no clue what was going on other than what they read or were told second- or third-hand.

Another responsible party surfaced who also wasn't involved in the repeal movement in the least. Brenda "Sue" Fulton had been a part of Knights Out, the small West Point LGBT alumni group that Dan Choi popularized when he came out and began his activism, but other than Dan's work, neither that group nor Sue had been involved in the repeal movement, nor did they have any firsthand knowledge of the delicate dance that was going on in Washington. Yet here Fulton and Seefried were on the first day of the lame duck session of Congress, yelling as loudly as they could for an idea that every real repeal activist knew would be disastrous.

Luckily, within hours of this absurd declaration making it into the headlines that day, a unanimous progressive community started coming out against it. The gay media blew up with incredulous reports about the proposal, and the blogs ripped these ringleaders and their respective "groups" to shreds. But it was soon revealed that Fulton and Seefried weren't the drivers behind the idea after all—it had actually originated with none other than the Palm Center's Aaron Belkin.

Belkin had a knack for trying to manufacture momentum for ideas he wanted to push forward, and about seven out of ten of his ideas were helpful. But occasionally he would get a wild idea that was just a little off, and once in a blue moon he would go out of his way to push an idea that wasn't just off but unintentionally harmful—and this idea was the king of them all. Neither Belkin nor any of the proxies he cultivated and managed were skilled in the art of Washington politics. And while that's sometimes a good thing—I'm all for fresh, outside-the-box perspectives sometimes—it's the worst thing when the neurosurgeons are elbow deep in complex brain surgery and the shaman wants to push them out of the way and start casting spells.

By early afternoon, a diversion had luckily come along to distract from the Monday morning madness. Thirteen activists from GetEqual, nearly all of them veterans, had mounted the White House fence and handcuffed themselves there yet again to demand action on DADT. This was now the fourth time the feisty direct action group had conducted this type of dramatic protest, and the numbers of those willing to spend a night in jail in order to make a point were obviously growing. At the same time, SLDN and, to a greater extent, Servicemembers United were increasing the pressure on Senate Majority Leader Reid to commit to floor time on NDAA and DADT. With yet another recess coming up, this time for the Thanksgiving holiday, we knew that the Senate needed to get started on NDAA very soon if it was going to have time to get through the bill by Christmas, before which the 111th Congress was expected to adjourn.

Two days later, on Wednesday, November 17, I got word that a secret meeting was taking place on Capitol Hill with the Senate majority leader about DADT. Servicemembers United, and I in particular, had become public enemy number one of Harry Reid and his senior staff, because of our relentless pressure on Reid to bring up NDAA and DADT. It had become clear that Reid didn't intend to bring the bill up at all—because of his opposition to other provisions within it, as well as the delicate dance he was doing with the immigration community over the DREAM Act—and someone needed to hammer him on that fact. HRC had been doing absolutely nothing to pressure Reid, and SLDN hadn't been doing much more than politely "calling" on him to do this or that, so I stepped forward to play the role of the bad cop. But in exchange for publicly calling him out and proactively educating the progressive community about his attempts to delay or derail consideration of the bill, we were treated harshly by his office in retaliation. They even suggested that Senator Lieberman's office stop working with us. (Lieberman's office obviously balked at the suggestion.)

At the secret meeting, Reid informed us that he was finally going to bow to pressure and schedule floor time for NDAA, but it would unfortunately be after the Thanksgiving recess. With so few Senate work days available in December, however, many of us were skeptical right off the bat. There didn't seem to be enough time to do NDAA, which automatically triggered thoughts of another doomed-to-fail bill structure like we had gotten in September. We would have to wait and see how Senator Reid decided to structure the debate on NDAA this time around and just hope that it would be drastically different than the last time.

Two additional days later, we had a secret meeting of our own between SU and Valerie Jarrett in her spacious West Wing office. The meeting, arranged by Brian Bond, was supposed to be a "kumbayah" meeting between us and Jarrett to make nice after we had gone after her in the media the previous month. Back in October, Jarrett had headlined a major HRC fundraising dinner while the White House was still not putting its weight behind the repeal of DADT as the clock ticked. HRC itself had been more than complicit in this effort by refusing to pressure either the White House or Senator Reid on DADT. So we saw Jarrett's appearance at the HRC dinner as clear back scratching for HRC's complicity, and we duly called her and HRC out for it publicly.

In response, HRC's new vice president of communications, Fred Sainz—who came on board after HRC's previous communications director quit out of frustration with the organization's betrayals he had witnessed firsthand—lashed out in a statement to the *Advocate*'s Andrew Harmon. It was an incredibly unprofessional and nasty personal attack against me as opposed to the merits of my message or my organization's stance on Jarrett's actions. Sainz was characteristically reckless in his vicious rants, and his demonstrated willingness to lie on behalf of HRC earned him the honorary title of "Vice President of Threats, Lies, and Propaganda." Clearly my point about Jarrett had struck a nerve with HRC and caused Sainz to lose it again, and the gay blogosphere had a field day defending me and going after Sainz and HRC.

But it wasn't just the bloggers who had my back. Twenty-seven of the nation's most prominent DADT repeal advocates, including many whom Jarrod and I had recruited to be involved with our joint work with HRC and several closely involved with SLDN, cosigned a joint

letter backing me up and tearing into Sainz and HRC. The letter concluded, "No matter the disagreement on strategy, we will not tolerate
an attack against one of our own. We are united as veterans to fight
'Don't Ask, Don't Tell,' with effectiveness, diligence, and veracity. And
we are determined to see legislative repeal this year, with or without
HRC. Our brothers and sisters still serving in silence deserve nothing
less." But the best summary of it anywhere was the story headline on
the gay gossip and politics blog *Queerty*. It simply read, "Dear HRC.
Go F—k Yourselves. Signed, Gay Veterans."

After that episode, Brian Bond wanted to get Jarrod and me
together with Valerie Jarrett to talk face to face about precisely what
we and others had seen as the problem with her headlining the HRC
dinner while the White House was slow-walking DADT repeal efforts
and HRC was giving them cover for doing so. I guess the thought that
we might take issue with that scenario surprised them. But we nevertheless readily agreed to meet with Jarrett, and we did so for a full
hour on Friday, November 19.

We started the meeting out with pleasantries, and then Bond
wanted us to share some about our backgrounds and how we got
involved in the DADT repeal movement so that Jarrett could get to
know us a little better on a personal level, which we did. But after
what I thought to be enough of making nice—she understood that
our activism may have been personal for us, but it wasn't anything
personal toward her—I bluntly asked if we could get down to business. "Brian wanted us to share some personal history with you, but
I'd really like to switch gears and talk politics now if you're OK with
that," I suddenly said. And without missing a beat, she responded,
"OK. Let's go."

Jarrett, who has a brilliant mind and is truly a very pleasant woman
whom I actually like a lot, naturally defended the White House's handling of the DADT issue and assured us that both the president and
his legislative affairs team were already putting in a noble effort on
Capitol Hill to help us push DADT repeal forward. I told her that

I believed that they were probably doing something, but what we needed was actually several times the amount of pushing they were currently doing. I was never good at math, but after wrangling back and forth with Jarrett and Chris Kang of legislative affairs over what constituted an acceptable level of effort on the White House's part, I reduced our request to a simple algebraic expression. "Let's say what you're currently doing in terms of activity on DADT is x. What we're saying we need is $4x$," I said.

After some further discussion and assurances from the White House team that they would continue to ramp up activity as things progressed, I turned to Jarrett in the end and said, "Look, you're doing x and we want $4x$, so how about we meet in the middle and you all at least give us $2x$." Without missing another beat, Jarrett smiled and said, "Deal." We all got in a good a laugh and wound up the meeting.

17

★ ★ ★ ★ ★

THE REPORT, MORE HEARINGS, AND FINAL VICTORY

On November 30, 2010, coincidentally the seventeenth anniversary of the signing of the DADT law by President Clinton, the Pentagon publicly released the final report of the Comprehensive Review Working Group on DADT, and the results were overwhelmingly positive for the DADT repeal movement. The nine-month-long study constituted one of the most exhaustive examinations of an issue that the Pentagon had ever done; it had reviewed attitudes within the force toward gays and lesbians, systematically identified issues that might come up as a result of such a policy change, and offered recommendations for smoothly managing the expected policy change. Although the report was intended to be a road map for how the Pentagon could successfully transition to open service should Congress decide to repeal the DADT law, the data uncovered in the process of building that road map provided significant political cover for finally moving forward with the repeal of DADT, especially since the legislative model still on the table for doing so granted discretion to the Pentagon's leadership as to when repeal would go into effect.

The Working Group had been set up by the secretary of defense to be a much larger commission than any of us had anticipated— much larger, in fact, than many of us felt comfortable with. We were reminded of the original Military Working Group set up in 1993, ostensibly to conduct an independent review of President Clinton's proposal to allow gays and lesbians to serve openly in the military. We knew in hindsight that the 1993 study had largely been an incompetent sham, as evidenced not only by the poor work product it put out but also by subsequent whistle-blowing by members of that very group. Although we knew it was highly unlikely that the 2010 Working Group would get that far out of control, our community was nevertheless a little nervous.

And as the new Working Group's efforts got under way in the spring of 2010, what made us even more nervous was the distance at which it kept all of the advocacy groups. In the beginning, its cochairs and senior staff held meetings with what they referred to as "stakeholder groups," including pro-repeal groups, anti-repeal groups, and supposedly neutral mainstream veterans groups. They also met en masse with groups of military sociologists and psychologists, representatives of healthcare organizations, and several other categories of experts and stakeholders. Present at the initial pro-repeal stakeholders meeting were Servicemembers United, SLDN, HRC, the Palm Center, and CAP. We primarily engaged in a back and forth with cochairs Jeh Johnson and General Carter Ham on our questions and concerns about the process as we understood it thus far, and Johnson and Ham threw questions back at us that they were curious about regarding our community. At the end of that first meeting, we were told that our primary point of contact as the stakeholder liaison for the Working Group would be Gautam Raghavan.

Gautam was a gay former Obama campaign staffer who had secured an appointment to the legislative affairs shop in the Department of Defense shortly after the new administration took office. He was very cordial and nice and strictly professional but did his duty of also keeping us at arm's length during the Working Group's nine-month life span. I found this frustrating and certainly tried in good faith to "turn" Gautam, politically speaking, hoping he could serve as a deeper source of information and intelligence. To his credit, he refused to be softened up. In fact, this more formal relationship with Gautam at the time may have allowed us to do our job in a more hard-nosed fashion, as there are things we may have been talked out of doing if we'd had a cozier relationship with the Working Group's stakeholder liaison.

Servicemembers United probably became one of the Working Group's biggest public critics on certain issues. Although we certainly couldn't hold a candle to Elaine Donnelly and her Center for Military Readiness, who painted the group's very existence as proof of a pre-determined outcome in favor of the radical homosexual agenda, we eventually found ourselves rather outraged at the nature of the Working Group's two surveys of active duty and reserve troop populations and of military spouses.

Our concerns about the surveys were threefold. First, the scope of the surveying was truly excessive. The first survey was sent out to 400,000 servicemembers, including 200,000 active duty troops and 200,000 reserve component troops. A sample size of only 1 percent of that total number would have been more than adequate for the results to be scientifically valid. Additionally, 150,000 surveys were sent out to military spouses, a population that, while highly valued, is largely irrelevant to this issue. The Defense Department wouldn't dare consider surveying military spouses on policy changes that are potentially much more relevant to marriage and family life, like certain gender integration and deployment issues.

Second, the cost to taxpayers was astronomical: $4.4 million to hire a contractor to develop, implement, and analyze the survey. The winning firm, Westat, was banking while the American taxpayer was bankrolling an unnecessarily extravagant expense. In order to raise awareness about this fiscal waste, SU created a rather successful side campaign called SurveyRefund.org, which highlighted the exorbitant cost of the survey and rhetorically demanded that the contractor refund the American taxpayer. Ironically, the $4.4 million survey went on at roughly the same time that the conservative Tea Party movement was organizing and rallying against excessive extravagance and fiscal waste within government agencies—a theme that led the Republican Party to victory in the midterm elections.

Third, this survey instrument that we paid $4.4 million to develop and deploy ended up being remarkably biased against us. As I said in the statement we put out on the morning we obtained a copy of the first round of survey questions, "Flawed aspects of the survey include unnecessary use of terms that are known to be inflammatory and bias-inducing in social science research, such as the clinical term 'homosexual'; an overwhelming focus on the potential negative aspects of repeal; and little or no inclusion of the potential positive aspects of repeal or the negative aspects of the current policy." Additionally, the survey didn't even correctly explain the existing DADT policy to survey takers. It erroneously said that gay troops would only be discharged under the current policy if they engaged in "homosexual acts," which was clearly not true, since you could also be discharged for actively or passively making a statement about being gay or lesbian, also known as "homosexual admission." These biases weren't just superficial, and surely any social scientist would agree that they could have a substantial impact on the study's results.

Despite our criticisms of the Working Group's survey, we knew it would be hard for us to put a dent in its credibility by way of a preemptive assault against future results that we knew would be biased against us. But one way we tried to call out the ridiculousness of the whole thing was through humor. Dylan Knapp, a straight veteran who worked for Servicemembers United, was an unusually skilled writer and a natural comedian. We asked Dylan to come up with a mock survey that we could "leak" to blogs and at least get a laugh out of a lot of people and perhaps pick up some organizational coolness points along the way. Dylan immediately got to work, and the resulting "2010 DOD Review of the Gays and All That" was quite the hit:

Answer all questions as honestly as your level of insecurity/ religious fanaticism allows. This survey will be used to measure the general disposition of Average Military Servicepeople towards the presence of Known Gays and the activities of Known Gays. With the repeal of the "Don't Ask, Don't Tell" policy on the horizon, it is important for the Department of Defense to know what impact the sudden onslaught of Known Gay Troops and their Known Gay Activities will have on our red-blooded, sin-free 'Merrican forces. Rock, Flag and Eagle.

1. If you discovered that there was a homo-sexual in your unit, what might you do to them/their personal belongings?

    A. I would welcome him with open arms because I am a homo-sexual.

    B. I would cross my arms and pout endlessly because I am sexually confused, insecure, and filled with rage and self-loathing.

    C. I would lead my friends in a re-enactment of the Bob Fosse–choreographed opening scene of "West Side Story" so he/she would know that I and my straight, masculine comrades are not to be trifled with.

    D. I would probably not care. A given person's sexual identity has nothing to do with their on-the-job performance.

    For the full survey, see www.fightingtoserve.com

Another major concern expressed by SLDN, but with which SU did not agree, was the question of whether gay servicemembers could safely take part in the survey without risking discharge under DADT. SLDN advised gay, lesbian, and bisexual troops not to take the survey, because although the surveys were confidential, some small amount of personally identifying information could inadvertently be made available to the Working Group. But even if the Working Group could identify a particular gay or lesbian servicemember, it would then have to take the politically dicey step of initiating separation proceedings against someone who inadvertently outed himself or herself through the course of completing their own survey, a step which the cochairs repeatedly assured us stakeholders and servicemembers that they had absolutely no interest in doing. In fact, so many layers of protection and distance were built into the process that we saw inadvertent self-outing and subsequent discharge as about as likely as Elaine Donnelly joining the military, taking the survey, coming out as a lesbian, and then being discharged.

The study was originally intended to collect data for the purpose of preparing a repeal implementation plan, with the plan being the primary objective of the Working Group and the data collection being simply a means to achieve that objective. However, the data collected ended up being the star of the show, and the actual plan to ensure a smooth transition was relegated to a supporting role. Politicians, of course, were primarily interested in the data as political cover. Although the survey didn't ask if troops thought that DADT should be repealed (to the chagrin of Senator McCain), it nevertheless contained questions that could serve as proxies for that fundamental question that many politicians wanted to know.

The primary proxy was a question about servicemembers' comfort level around gays and lesbians. Although the results were not officially released until November 30 (a date that was moved up by several days as a result of political pressure), in early November word was leaked to *Washington Post* reporter Ed O'Keefe that "more than 70 percent of respondents to a survey sent to active-duty and reserve troops over the summer said the effect of repealing the 'Don't Ask, Don't Tell' policy would be positive, mixed, or nonexistent." This finding formed the basis of a bombshell story in the *Post* on November 11.

When news of the leak broke, Secretary Gates furiously ordered an investigation by the Office of the Inspector General (IG) of everyone within the Defense Department who had been granted early access to the Working Group's results for evaluation and comment. As the highest-ranking openly gay person in the Pentagon, assistant secretary of defense for public affairs Doug Wilson came under intense suspicion by Gates, although the IG's report cleared him and every other Pentagon employee of leaking the early positive data point. The report concluded that the leak likely came from one of a small handful of White House officials who had seen or been briefed on the report two days before, since the DOD's IG was not authorized to investigate those officials.

We were lucky that despite the documented bias against us in the survey, the overall results were favorable to our cause. There were, however, pockets of negative results, such as the fact that nearly half of army combat arms troops and more than half of Marine Corps combat arms troops predicted negative outcomes if the policy were to change, and our opposition tried desperately to seize on those points. But the problem with these pockets of negative data was that there was always a qualifier: when those same categories of troops were asked if they had actually ever served with gays and lesbians, and when they were subsequently asked if there were actual problems, the same overall positive trend reappeared. In all, most active duty and reserve component troops said they would be OK serving and working beside known gays and lesbians, and those who already had worked with them said there were few if any problems with the arrangement.

While our organizational opponents complained the entire year that the favorable data outcomes had been predetermined, it was more the favorable *planning* outcomes, if anything, that had been predetermined. In the end, it was a surprise to no one that the Working Group was able to identify a path forward and create a plan for a smooth transition to a post-DADT military should the law be changed. It wasn't because of any preexisting agenda but simply due to the fact that *of course* the Pentagon was capable of coming up with a contingency plan to maintain good order, discipline, and readiness. There was never a real question that this could be done. The Working Group was more about just taking the initiative to do it—and, of course, about creating political cover for the politicians who would have to take the vote.

In order to firmly establish that political cover in the public record, Secretary Gates, Admiral Mullen, and Working Group cochairs Jeh Johnson and General Ham came back up to Capitol Hill on December 2 to testify before the Senate Armed Services Committee about the findings and recommendations of the comprehensive review. The support that this report provided to the political and advocacy effort to push repeal forward was undeniable. Although we already had the votes to pass a repeal-inclusive NDAA under normal Senate procedural conditions, the Working Group report pushed us even further over that line. It also pushed senior defense leaders, including both Gates and Mullen, out further in favor of repeal. Most notably, Admiral Mullen testified that as a result of the report and its findings, what had previously been his personal opinion—that the military and American servicemembers could handle repeal of the DADT law— had now become his professional opinion.

However, opponents led by the committee's ranking member, Senator McCain, were still dissatisfied with the defense leaders' testimony, the report's findings and recommendations, and most of all with the comprehensive review itself. McCain continued to complain that servicemembers were not directly asked if they wanted this policy changed and pressed Gates and Mullen hard for why this still shouldn't be done. Mullen, always the gentleman, aptly countered, "Because I fundamentally, sir, think it's an incredibly bad precedent to ask them . . . to essentially vote on a policy." Gates subsequently added, "I can't think of a single precedent in American history of doing a referendum of the American armed forces on a policy issue. Are you going to ask them if they want fifteen-month tours? Are you going to ask them if they want to be part of the surge in Iraq?" The point could not have been clearer.

But Senator McCain did get a little more of what he wanted to hear the following day, when the service chiefs testified, along with the vice chairman of the Joint Chiefs of Staff and the commandant of the Coast Guard (who was not officially a part of the Joint Chiefs of Staff). Each one of the chiefs expressed reservations about lifting the ban, with General James Amos, the Marine Corps commandant, leading the charge on the Hill as he had all year in the press. But strangely, the other marine at the witness table, Joint Chiefs vice chairman General James "Hoss" Cartwright, seemed to come across as the most support-ive of repeal DADT. Clearly there were politics at play.

I decided not to attend the service chiefs hearing in person that day and instead stayed home to work on our press statements while watching the hearing live on C-SPAN. As I watched the hear-ing unfold with the six men seated side by side at the witness table, I couldn't help but recall the similar iconic scene from the 1993 hear-ings, when the Joint Chiefs sat side by side before the same committee and went down the line saying that homosexuality was incompatible, incompatible, incompatible, incompatible with military service, and of course with Colin Powell giving his caveat that *open* homosexual-ity was incompatible with military service. I said aloud to Jarrod that I wished that moment could be re-created at this hearing, given the visual and historical parallels, but obviously with the opposite senti-ment now expressed in light of everything that had happened.

About that time I noticed several familiar faces sitting behind the row of senators at the hearing, including Senator Lieberman's military legislative assistant, Chris Griffin, and Senator Udall's military legisla-tive assistant, Jennifer Barrett. I began typing Chris an e-mail rather energetically with the subject line "Creating a Classic Moment." How-ever, before I could finish the e-mail, Senator Lieberman finished up with his round of questioning and the next Republican in line started in. But Senator Udall was next up, so I redirected the e-mail to his defense aide instead.

"Jennifer, if you could get your boss to ask something along this line, it could create an historic media moment in this hearing: 'I'd like to go down the line quickly and get a simple yes or no answer from each of you on this. In the end, if we change this policy, can your branch and the US military make this work?'" I wrote hastily, hoping she was checking her Blackberry. "I will try," she immediately responded, as she quietly slipped Senator Udall a short note. Then, almost as I had imagined, came the bombshell historic moment from that hearing. In nearly the same language as I had suggested, Senator Udall asked each of the witnesses to briefly tell him if they believed the military could make repeal work if Congress decided to do it. As predicted, each admitted one after another that if ordered to carry out this change in policy, they could make it work.

"That was beautiful!!!" I shot back to Jennifer, with my character-istically annoying multiple exclamation points. "So glad that worked out!!" We immediately began pushing the clip out to blogs and cable producers as the money shot from the hearing and pointing out the obvious parallel of this moment to that iconic moment in the 1993 hearings. Not only did the clip start making the rounds on the blogs and online media immediately, but we also succeeded in making it into yet another iconic Senate hearing moment as it made the cable news show rounds that evening alongside its sister clip from 1993. Oh, how far we had come.

That same day, another big development came out in the form of a statement from the nation's fastest-growing veterans organization, Iraq and Afghanistan Veterans of America (IAVA). I had become friends with IAVA's executive director, Paul Rieckhoff, over the pre-ceding year, and Servicemembers United had established a friendly relationship with IAVA's staff in both New York and Washington. We kept them in the loop on internal developments on the DADT issue over the course of the year and frequently pressured them to take a favorable stand on the issue. While the organization's forward-looking leadership and staff were clearly on our side, their general membership was still more divided on the issue.

IAVA had already weighed in heavily on the overall defense bill, which contained many provisions that were an integral part of their legislative agenda and also needed a vote. They knew, of course, that a fair vote on the defense bill would mean a positive outcome for DADT repeal, but up until this point they had shied away from weighing in specifically on the repeal amendment. In the end, though, IAVA decided to come out boldly on the right side of history. "IAVA shares Secretary Gates' and Admiral Mullen's opinion that upholding the integrity of the military as an institution is critical. All men and women who have committed their lives to service and sacrifice in our military should be treated equally," said IAVA in a statement from Rieckhoff. "We urge the Senate to move quickly to pass the NDAA, including the DADT provision."

Despite the fact that 110 percent of the pieces were in place for a repeal-inclusive NDAA to pass if it were brought up for debate under normal Senate procedure, we still had to convince Senate Majority Leader Reid to bring the bill back up for a second vote without filling the amendment tree again, which felt increasingly impossible. There was also more talk at this time of extracting several controversial provisions from the defense bill and just making NDAA the last hurrah without giving those provisions a vote, especially given the dwindling number of days in the calendar before the Senate would have to recess for the winter holidays. Senators were ready to wrap up and go home after the first week of December, and we fought to get Senator Reid to extend the legislative session even further into the month.

Had DADT repeal been extracted from NDAA and the defense bill debated and voted on first, that would have absolutely, 100 percent been the last thing that got done that legislative session. The repeal of DADT and anything else taken out of the bill would be brushed aside and NDAA would have taken up every remaining moment of the dwindling session, after which the chamber would have adjourned. So it was critical to keep repeal in NDAA—or at least to keep it out *in front of* NDAA.

After we racked up a few more small victories—rounding up a few more votes following the last set of hearings, including more Republican votes, and pressuring the Senate to stay in session past the first week of December—Senator Reid reluctantly announced that he would bring the defense bill back up, possibly on the night of Wednesday, December 8, but again under severely restricted conditions. He also threatened to consider the bill before a crucial tax cuts vote, which the Republicans had made clear must come first—a totally workable demand. Our Republican allies who were willing to vote for repeal were of course at the height of their frustration, but so too were our Independent and Democratic allies and champions like Senators Lieberman, Udall, and Levin, and others.

Wednesday night on the Senate floor, our Republican champion Senator Collins continued to negotiate with Senator Reid over these obstacles on behalf of the delicate coalition of moderate Republicans she and Senator Lieberman had assembled. We could see her growing increasingly frustrated. Sensing that something was afoot, I shot Senator Udall's chief of staff, Mike Sozan, an e-mail to see if he had the scoop. "Noticed your boss in a huddle on the floor with Reid, Collins, and Lieberman, then Levin joined in. . . . Any news? Her body language looks like she's frustrated." A response came several minutes later. "Things are moving in the right direction," Sozan replied. "Udall is trying to find the consensus on this."

Time ran out for the night soon thereafter, and all pending Senate business and accompanying negotiations carried over to the next day. But when Thursday came, what Senator Reid did next caught everyone utterly by surprise—Republicans, Democrats, Independents, journalists, and advocates alike. The majority leader unexpectedly brought the defense bill up on the Senate floor earlier than anyone had expected: at about three thirty that afternoon. He wasn't even trying to hide it anymore that he was intent on ensuring that NDAA would be dead on arrival.

The advocacy group coalition representatives were all at our respective offices patiently awaiting any word on when Reid might announce a vote to move forward on NDAA. Senators Lieberman and Udall were still busy working on helping Senator Collins secure a wider bill-structuring deal that would guarantee needed Republican support. And Senator Collins was in an important private meeting that she had scheduled for that time slot in the absence of any announced votes. Even Senator Blanche Lincoln, a very conservative Democrat from Arkansas who had finally agreed to support a repeal-inclusive NDAA and whose vote we were counting on, was away from the Hill at a dentist appointment, again because no floor votes had been scheduled for that time. But suddenly, Senator Reid moved to bring up a restricted version of the defense bill without prior notice and called for an immediate cloture vote.

Word spread quickly across the Hill that Senator Reid had just brought up the defense bill for a quick-kill vote. Advocates in their offices immediately turned on C-SPAN and Senate staffers scrambled to get word to their bosses about what was going on. Shortly thereafter, in one of the most dramatic moments of an otherwise mundane set of Senate floor proceedings, an out-of-breath Senator Collins burst into the Senate chamber and made her way down to the first floor microphone she could find. In a state of shock and disbelief, she interrupted the Senate majority leader on the floor in order to ask him what he was doing. A surprised Senator Reid immediately tried to stop Senator Collins from speaking, pointing out to the presiding chair that debate was not to be allowed.

But an exasperated Senator Collins was not to be toyed with. "I am perplexed and frustrated that this particular bill is going to become a victim of politics," Collins pleaded. "Senator Lieberman and I have been bargaining in good faith with the majority leader. I think this is so unfortunate." And with that, an unmoved Senator Reid called the vote without a deal in place and completely on his ideal terms. However, not even all Democrats voted with the majority leader. Senator Collins herself refused to vote until the very end, at which point she threw her hands up and voted "Aye" anyway. Without a deal in place, however, the vote still failed.

Virtually no one who watched what went on that afternoon and even slightly understood it supported what Senator Reid had done. Allies, opponents, the White House, and objective observers all readily admitted that this cloture vote had been a quick-kill maneuver, one custom designed to try to screw over Senator Collins in the process. A defensive Senator Lincoln of Arkansas quickly issued a statement saying that she would have been there to vote for cloture had she known about the vote. But defiant Senators Lieberman and Collins angrily left the Senate chamber with spontaneous plans of their own.

Minutes later, an e-mail showed up in my inbox from Senator Lieberman's chief counsel, Bret Hester, and his legislative director, Todd Stein. "We are holding an impromptu PC [press conference] right now with Sen. Collins announcing a stand alone bill. More details to come." I quickly shot back, "Your boss is awesome! And so is his staff!!" to which Bret immediately responded, "Help us keep hope alive! We need the help."

With NDAA again sidelined, we began a full-court press in support of passing the new stand-alone repeal bill *before* considering the defense authorization bill. "This was a major failure on the part of the Senate to simply do its job and pass an annual defense authorization bill. Politics prevailed over responsibility today, and now more than one million American servicemembers, including tens of thousands of gay and lesbian troops, are worse off as a result," I said in a statement that was reprinted over and over again in mainstream media. "Since the votes are there in isolation, the Senate should still consider a stand-alone bill to repeal the 'Don't Ask, Don't Tell' law before adjourning for the winter holidays."

While Aubrey Sarvis at SLDN issued a broader call on Congress and the administration "to find another path for repeal to get done in the lame-duck," HRC seemed to dismiss the thought of an immediate, pre-NDAA, stand-alone bill altogether. Clearly revealing their internal thinking that DADT repeal was dead, HRC issued an odd statement asking the president to issue an executive order to halt DADT discharges, saying that it was now the only way for the president to keep his promise from his State of the Union speech. HRC's quick shift away from the Hill exposed just how disarrayed its senior staff was at the time on DADT.

Having come that far, however, there was no way in hell we were giving up. We knew we finally had the upper hand politically, and there was no way Senator Reid, who had boxed himself into a corner, could let the Senate adjourn without letting Senator Lieberman and Senator Collins's stand-alone bill get an up or down vote, and he had to do it before even thinking about touching a stripped-down defense bill if DADT repeal still had any chance of passing. The following day, the wider DADT repeal coalition—meaning SU, SLDN, HRC, CAP, Third Way, LCR, and Stonewall Democrats—banded together and issued an extremely rare joint statement staking out our demand: "Despite the unfortunate result of the Senate's cloture vote on the defense authorization bill, there are other viable legislative options to repeal 'Don't Ask, Don't Tell' before Congress adjourns, and a solid 60-vote Senate majority is still in favor of repeal. With commitments on record from the Senate Majority Leader and the Speaker of the House to move this new bill, as well as Secretary Gates's urgent and renewed request that repeal happen in this Congress, we are confident repeal can still happen this year."

Senator Reid tepidly committed to giving the Lieberman-Collins bill a vote, but he was already starting to talk about pushing that vote off until after Christmas. In a private Democratic caucus meeting, the majority leader suggested that they might be able to extend the calendar by coming back to Washington after the holidays but before the new Congress was sworn in, and in a press gaggle immediately following that caucus meeting he floated the idea of using that time to tackle DADT. Given that we already needed every vote we could get in case one or two senators decided to leave early, we certainly couldn't bank on all those senators taking the rare step of flying back to Washington between Christmas and New Year's or in the week or two after New Year's just for this vote. We were finally at the end of our rope. The following week was the only week left in the year before the week of Christmas, and if it didn't get done that week, it just wasn't going to happen.

With the stakes this high and time running out, we were not willing to take one single vote for granted. In our next war room meeting in Senator Lieberman's conference room, his staff asked the coalition if the groups could turn out any sort of last-minute lobbying blitz to both shore up our swing votes and, more important, lobby even our majority of allies to ask that they support staying in Washington until DADT repeal got a vote, with or without NDAA. If just a handful of supportive senators decided to leave early, we could easily be screwed. Not only was Christmas Day just two weeks away but many of our committed votes were also from the Pacific region, including one of our postelection Republican pickups (Alaska's Senator Lisa Murkowski) and the two senators from Hawaii, so it was unlikely that they would wait until the last day to go home. And at the last minute, news also broke that pro-repeal Democratic senator Ron Wyden had been diagnosed with prostate cancer and needed to return home to Oregon for surgery.

While there was no way we could in good conscience ask Senator Wyden to delay treatment for cancer, we could certainly ask every other ally and potential ally to support staying in session until the job was done. In response to the request from Senator Lieberman's staff to blitz the Hill, Servicemembers United's staff scrambled to round up as many local members and supporters as possible who could take one or more days off work and join us in this last-minute effort to push.

The result was a surprisingly well-organized third DADT lobby day of the year by Servicemembers United, which we termed Operation Renewed Engagement.

Over the three days of this effort—Wednesday, December 15, through Friday, December 17—a hard-core group of just fifteen locals systematically visited seventy-one Senate offices daily in order to keep the pressure on and raise visibility for the DADT vote throughout the Senate office buildings. Many of them were wearing SU's popular "You don't have to be straight to shoot straight" T-shirts, designed by former marine and SU staffer Jon Martinez. As these citizen lobbyists went from office to office, we encouraged them to announce their visits in advance via their social media pages and platforms, complete with pleas for friends and followers to support them via telephone. As many of them entered these Senate offices and met with policy staff there, front office staffers were suddenly inundated with calls on the DADT issue to coincide with the visits.

At the same time, the House of Representatives needed to move quickly to pass an identical stand-alone bill. The offices of Speaker Pelosi and House Majority Leader Steny Hoyer immediately jumped into action and began working overtime to put a rushed floor vote together. On Monday, December 13, Leader Hoyer had spoken with us on a conference call, briefing us on his efforts to introduce the bill and push it through as a "privileged resolution" so that it could be called up immediately by the Senate and bypass at least one of the time-consuming procedural hurdles of that chamber. The following day, Congressmen Murphy and Hoyer introduced the stand-alone House bill, and on Wednesday it was scheduled for a quick vote. Unlike the more drama-laden upper chamber, however, the House bill once again sailed through. The final tally: 250–175, with a total of fifteen Republicans voting for repeal, ten more than the previous House floor vote back in May. This second solid House victory was a testament to an ultrasupportive leadership cadre and to the bill's tenacious quarterback—Congressman Murphy.

Wednesday evening, representatives from SU, SLDN, CAP, HRC, and Third Way joined Speaker Pelosi, Leader Hoyer, Congressman Murphy, and other House leaders for a victory press conference at the Capitol. I stood beside Speaker Pelosi for most of the event, during which she would humorously turn toward me at random moments and mumble responses to what was being said at the podium, such as "Yes, it is," "Yes, he does," and "Oh, that's wonderful." When Pelosi began her remarks, she started off by squinting to read aloud what was written on the shirts of several SU members standing on the side wall of the press conference room who had just finished up day one of Operation Renewed Engagement. "You don't have to . . . let's see . . . you don't have to be straight to shoot straight. That's right," Pelosi remarked with a big smile. That day, the now-iconic Servicemembers United T-shirt appeared as the primary worldwide homepage graphic of the *Huffington Post*, one of several times this happened over the next few weeks.

That same week, as DADT proved to be the issue that just would not die, opponents tried one last-ditch dirty trick to stir up hysteria and thwart repeal. In a press call with selected Pentagon reporters, including one from *Stars and Stripes*, Marine Corps commandant General James Amos made the despicable suggestion that the repeal of DADT could mean that marines might lose lives and limbs in combat due to the policy change. "I don't want to lose any marines to the distraction," Amos grumbled. "I don't want to have any marines that I'm visiting at Bethesda with no legs be the result of any type of distraction." General Amos's comments that day represented a low point in his misguided opposition that I feel certain he now regrets.

The last-minute attempts to thwart our hard-charging effort failed to peel away even one vote in favor of repeal. Following the second House vote, Senator Reid finally filed for cloture on the new Lieberman-Collins bill. After everything our community had been through with the Senate majority leader, it was all I could do to muster together a half-hearted statement of gratitude for the press. It was absolutely ridiculous that we had been dragged along to this point. We likely had sixty Senate votes for repeal back in May immediately following the committee vote. We felt confident that we had them in July. We definitely had them in September. We had even more after the midterms. And we had more than a comfortable margin after the Working Group report hearings in early December. This could have been done long ago and everyone could have been saved many headaches and many new gray hairs. But there we were, and there would surely be no more chances after this.

Senator Reid held the Senate in session through the weekend for the all-important cloture vote on Saturday morning, exactly one week before Christmas Day. According to Senate procedure, if the vote succeeded, our opposition could only obstruct for thirty hours more before we were entitled to a final passage vote. When the cloture vote finally went down, the ayes were comfortably beyond the sixty-vote threshold required to prevail. Surprisingly, instead of wasting any more precious legislative time on what was by now clearly a failed attempt to hold back the inevitable, Senate Republicans gave unanimous consent to skip the normal thirty-hour waiting period, and a final vote was taken that same afternoon.

In all, eight Republicans—Susan Collins, Scott Brown, George Voinovich, Olympia Snowe, Mark Kirk, Lisa Murkowski, John Ensign, and Richard Burr—voted with us, for a remarkable final tally of 65–31. That last name, Senator Richard Burr of North Carolina, was such an unexpected surprise that I still to this day hold his vote up as a testament that anything is possible. Senator Burr later said that he would have preferred not to have to take that particular vote at that time, but since it was happening anyway he didn't want to be on the wrong side of history.

The only Democrat not voting, the new Senator Joe Manchin of West Virginia, originally planned to vote no, according to his staff, but he decided to abstain instead at the last minute in response to intense and uncomfortable pressure on him over the issue. In the days before the vote, Jarrod had several conversations with Senator Manchin's senior staff, including his chief of staff, and with Senator Manchin himself. The new senator's staff was rather frustrated that Manchin was willing to betray the deal regarding the sixty-day provision that the legendary senator he was still technically replacing, Senator Robert Byrd, had worked out in exchange for his vote.

In a brilliant move designed to rattle the senator in advance of the vote, Jarrod spread the word among Senator Manchin's staff that a no vote on DADT would undoubtedly become the new senator's "Strom Thurmond moment," a reference to the late senator from South Carolina's shameful and infamous opposition to landmark civil rights legislation. Jarrod also posted the phrase on Facebook and asked people to call Senator Manchin's office and use the same phrase to make the senator's staff nervous. As he left his private conversation with the senator the day before the vote, a sudden influx of calls began coming into the West Virginian's offices coincidentally also talking about the senator's upcoming "Strom Thurmond moment" if he voted no on DADT repeal.

On the other hand, a surprising yes vote—for quite different reasons—was that of strong pro-repeal advocate Senator Ron Wyden of Oregon. Despite a recent diagnosis of prostate cancer and a recommendation by his doctors that he fly back home for immediate surgery and treatment, Senator Wyden stayed in Washington, DC, long enough to cast his vote to end DADT. This remarkable decision stands out as a testament to the sheer resolve of our allies in the Senate and elsewhere to see this discriminatory and archaic law finally done away with. Likewise, our leader in the Senate, Joe Lieberman, temporarily set aside his Orthodox Jewish tradition of not working on the Sabbath to come into the Senate that day and help lead us to a remarkable victory. After the final passage vote was over, Senator Lieberman said to me with a big grin on his face, "I told you I had a few more votes than you all knew about. There you go."

And there we were. Nearly eighteen years after DADT had become the law of the land with overwhelming congressional support, on Saturday, December 18, 2010, the Senate voted overwhelmingly to repeal it, just days after the House of Representatives did the same. As I made the print, radio, and cable media rounds in the days following the victory, I was careful to note the long path still ahead, but I began to zoom out a little in my commentary and look at the big picture that was at last coming into focus. "Those who defend our freedom while living in fear for their careers will finally breathe a sigh of relief tonight," I remarked that Saturday afternoon, continuing on a more personal note, "and those who have fallen victim to this policy in years past will finally begin to see true closure and redemption on the horizon."

The next few days went by incredibly fast, and nearly everyone who had been intimately involved in the core process—and had the scars to prove it—experienced a shared combination of perpetual exhaustion and joyous relief. Speaker Pelosi hosted an unusual but memorable bill enrollment ceremony the following Tuesday in a large auditorium in the Capitol Visitors Center, leading the crowd in a spontaneous rendition of "God Bless America" at its conclusion. Meanwhile, the White House scrambled to plan a presidential bill signing ceremony befitting the historic nature of the victory we had just won and the truly epic battle it took to get us there.

It was decided that the ceremony would be held on Wednesday, December 22, at the Department of the Interior building, primarily because it had one of the only auditoriums available that was large enough to hold all of the people the White House wanted to invite. Servicemembers United, along with the other core pro-repeal organizations, coordinated quickly with the White House to draw up lists of recommended attendees. SU ultimately submitted a list of over fifty servicemembers and veterans for the event, a number of whom really should have been invited by organizations like SLDN or HRC. But those organizations prioritized the placement of their staff, boards, donors, and other loyalists, and as the signing day approached I had to adjust SU's list to add in quite a few deserving longtime veteran advocates who were more closely associated with other groups but whom those groups had surprisingly snubbed.

The day before the signing ceremony, Brian Bond informed me that Jarrod and I would be placed together in reserved seating in the front row of the auditorium, directly in front of the president, and that our "VIP" status enabled us to skip the frigid early morning lineup outside of the Interior Department. The next morning, we took advantage of the ability to get some extra sleep and arrive a little closer to the actual start time, but when we got there we were heartened to learn that the very first person in line that morning had been the head of SU's military partners program, David Durette of Minneapolis. In fact, he was there so early that Bond had to come outside to see who he was, because his unusually early arrival made the Secret Service nervous.

I was especially proud to have been able to use some of SU's seat slots to have several partners of active duty military there that day too, along with many of our other active duty and veteran members. Together, we all joined nearly five hundred other advocates, supporters, members of Congress, senior administration officials, and senior Defense Department officials to watch the president sign into law the DADT Repeal Act of 2010.

And there I was, sitting directly in front of the president, scarred and exhausted, as he penned his signature to our bill and uttered those iconic, and ironic, words, "This is done." If only the journey had been as simple as he made it sound, and if only the challenges still to come were as nonexistent as that capstone phrase implied. But as incomplete as the moment was for me, it was a necessary and likely a fitting end to the fight for nearly everyone else. And that's what all of this had actually always been about—everyone else—right? Because it is unlikely that two of the most active leaders in the DADT repeal movement, Jarrod and myself, will ever directly benefit from this new liberty that we fought so long and hard to secure. But both the journey and the victory have been more than worth the personal investment and sacrifice, the full extent of which will never be fully known.

18

★ ★ ★ ★ ★

CERTIFICATION AND THE COUNTDOWN TO REPEAL

As soon as the presidential bill signing event wrapped up, Jarrod and I decided to get as far away from Washington as possible, and as far from the "gays in the military" issue as we could possibly run. We took off to the Middle East for a few weeks in late December and early January and spent that time blissfully roaming around Israel, Jordan, Egypt, and the Emirates. It was good to be back there, and it was good to be able to speak colloquial Arabic again. As challenging as it was to learn, I still love that language and I still savor every opportunity I get to use it and improve it.

Even while on this much-needed vacation, I still got calls and requests to do major media on DADT-related segments, but I finally felt justified in turning them down. When a friend of mine who was a producer for CNN called to ask if I could come into the studio and comment on the impropriety of a sexually suggestive video that had been broadcast on a navy ship by a rogue commander, my response was simply, "Sure, but does CNN still have an Amman bureau?"

For the first time in years, hard-core DADT repeal activists finally had a chance to take a real vacation. Up until the bill was signed, summers were always for Pride season, Congress's typical August recess was always dedicated to in-state and in-district organizing around target members, and the rest of the year was consumed by lobbying, media outreach, administrative minutiae, fundraising, events, and so on. But in January 2011, our community finally had a brief chance to relax, decompress, and attempt to regain the sanity we had lost over years of fighting our opposition, the Pentagon, Congress, the administration, public opinion, and one another.

But as much as I would have loved for that to be the end of the story, my inability to sit back and truly enjoy the high points of December was due to the fact that the work was still far from over. When I returned from the Middle East, I managed to squeeze in one more quick trip to Aspen in January before settling back into Washington and into the Servicemembers United office.

In 2011, our mission became markedly different: we aimed our sights westward across the Potomac toward the Pentagon and out to our constituency across the rest of the country. The Working Group had virtually disbanded, and a smaller Repeal Implementation Team (RIT) took over the task of implementing preparations for an eventual certification of repeal by the Joint Chiefs chairman, the secretary of defense, and the president when the Pentagon decided it was ready to pull the trigger.

One of the primary tasks of the RIT was to see to it that nearly two million servicemembers received a relatively uniform and thorough briefing on the repeal of DADT. While the Defense Department often disseminates routine briefing materials down the chain of command to ensure that troops are aware or are reminded of various policies and regulations, the training on DADT took on a life of its own. After these repeal training sessions got under way in early 2011, media, especially print reporters, began clamoring to find out what the briefings contained, what went on during the sessions, and how troops were reacting to them.

In reality, most of these DADT repeal briefings were rather uneventful—about as exciting as a finance briefing, as Jarrod often described them. There were essentially three tiers of training: the top tier for senior commanders, chaplains, judge advocates, and others in professional fields; the middle tier for trainers, often unit commanders or senior staff NCOs; and the third tier for the overwhelming majority of rank and file servicemembers. Some DOD civilian employees were also required to undergo training, especially if they had active duty troops under their supervision on the job.

Just as neither the DADT "compromise" policy in 1993 nor the "compromise" repeal amendment language of 2010 satisfied those on the far right or the far left, so too did the DADT repeal training ruffle feathers in both camps. Many on the left, particularly in the gay and wider progressive communities, thought that such an extensive training regimen over many months was unnecessary, obviously a means to delay certification and the effective date of repeal. Many on the right, however, saw the training as an indoctrination plot designed to use the convenient opportunity of this upcoming policy change to spread political messages about the liberal and gay "agendas." In truth, however, it was always known and accepted that the military would require some sort of interim "adjustment" period in order to at least brief commanders, legal advisers, and others on the policy and regulatory changes that would need to accompany a change in law. The question was just how long that period of time would be.

Of course, one could convincingly argue that the Pentagon should have had this stuff figured out already and that it should have been prepared long ago for any potential personnel policy changes, especially ones that it had argued all along would be "major." But the reality was that DOD never did that; as an institution it didn't even begin accepting that repeal was inevitable until late 2009. One could also argue that if there had been a change in policy overnight, the rank and file troops could have easily handled it and there would have been nary a hiccup—as had been the case in the United Kingdom, which lifted its ban on open service with a one-page memo following an order from the European Court of Human Rights. That's also very likely true, but no one in the Pentagon's senior leadership would publicly support doing anything that quickly, and getting their buy-in was crucial to securing the votes for passing any repeal legislation in Congress.

Servicemembers United had publicly indicated that six months was an acceptable amount of time for the Pentagon to prepare for repeal, with the expectation that certification should come no later than midsummer. After that point, we warned, we would start to get nervous and would once again go on the offense. But throughout the spring, we patiently monitored the repeal training effort across the force.

As head of Servicemembers United, I was invited by both the army and the Marine Corps to sit in on repeal training sessions to judge for myself how they were conducted. These observation visits included both sessions in which media and other official observers were present and ones in which no other outsiders were in the room except for two SU staff members. There was a significant distinction between these two types of observations: in the former case, the troops being trained were notified ahead of time that outside observers would be present, whereas in the latter sessions, only the commanders knew that we were present. The result was that when media were present there was little or no interaction, questions, or concerns raised by the troops being trained, whereas the training sessions we sat in on without media were much more real, raw, and lively.

SU members and supporters also took the initiative to send us surreptitious recordings of training sessions and a variety of written reports of how their own trainings were going. These recordings and reports very closely matched what we saw in person at the "real" trainings (i.e., the ones without media). While we would hear once in a while about a rogue instructor or a less-than-enthusiastic group dynamic at one of these briefings, the overwhelming majority of what we heard about and saw with our own eyes and ears was strictly professional. While professionalism is, of course, a hallmark of American NCOs and officers (those who were giving the DADT repeal briefings), it is also possible, while maintaining a professional demeanor, to subtly send the message through voice intonation or excessive formality that one disapproves of a briefing topic, and subordinates always pick up on such indicators of command and leadership climate pretty quickly. But we were fortunate to see very little of that during the entire DADT repeal training process throughout the force.

Some in the wider gay community took issue during these sessions with the antigay or perceived antigay questions that would come up in them many times over. At the end of the briefing, servicemembers would often bring up opposition talking points in the form of questions such as "Why should I have to share a barracks room with someone who is gay or lesbian if that violates my religion?" or "What do I do if somebody who's gay starts hitting on me and I don't want to get accused of harassing them just because they're gay?" The premises behind these questions—that one person's religion should be allowed to dictate public policy for everyone or that gays are naturally predatory—and other questions like them were certainly offensive, not to mention ignorant. But other than a very small minority of true bigots, most of those who asked these types of questions did so out of honest curiosity. Many of them had never been exposed to the rational counterpoints to these questions that naturally came to their minds, but when an instructor provided that counterpoint or referred to existing regulations that would take care of a potential issue, like same-sex sexual harassment, that was almost always the end of it.

The overall effect of this drawn-out process, I would argue, had enormous benefits both for those asking these questions and for those about whom these questions were being asked—that is, gay and lesbian servicemembers. First, these training sessions provided a needed safe space in which those who actually had honest questions or concerns could pose them and get answers. Had this information not been disseminated in a structured and orderly fashion and had NCOs and officers—including often JAGs and chaplains—not been on hand to provide professional responses in a formal training session, much of it would have become fodder for so-called barracks lawyers, and inappropriate assumptions or inaccurate facts could have easily been reinforced elsewhere.

Second, the hour-long briefing on this policy change was the first time many servicemembers had ever had any exposure to the idea that gays and lesbians are also patriotic, fit, capable, relationship-oriented, and normal, as opposed to whatever stereotypes they may have previously held or whatever propaganda may be touted elsewhere. Despite large majorities already knowing this, significant minorities still maintained false stereotypes of the gay community, and DADT certainly didn't help dispel those stereotypes over the years. What struck me most while sitting in on these trainings was the fact that within a six-month period, two million of America's most conservative people were being shown that gay men and women are normal, they are often in committed long-term relationships, they have families, they raise healthy and happy children, and they can be skilled and effective leaders at every level. This reality check will have far-reaching intermediate- and long-term benefits for the LGBT equality movement nationwide.

As DADT repeal trainings proceeded smoothly and without incident throughout the spring, I often told reporters that the big story about the repeal training was the non-story that it had really become. But this wasn't what some journalists wanted to hear. Early on, one reporter for AOL News spread the word among several pro-repeal groups that she was on the lookout for any repeal training sessions that went badly. Specifically she wanted examples of antigay comments made during the Q&A and even examples of fights breaking out during the briefings. As the trainings progressed, I shared with her on

CERTIFICATION AND THE COUNTDOWN TO REPEAL   255

several occasions the fact that these sessions were going remarkably well and that no such examples could be found. I agreed to go on the record with her about how the sessions went that I had observed, and even shared with her one surreptitious recording of a Marine Corps training session that had been sent to us by an SU member, since she was particularly interested in the Marine Corps.

She also joined other members of the media in sitting in on a repeal training session at Camp Lejeune but said she was quite disappointed that it had turned out to be a snooze. The horror stories that she was trolling for simply weren't materializing. But when her article on the repeal training came out soon thereafter, I was quite shocked to see it come across as basically an unjustified hit job on the Marine Corps. She had taken a snippet of the recording I had given her and excerpted the worst parts, largely out of context. She tried hard to find the most mundane complaints and spin them for negative effect. And she omitted or played down the reports she received of the positives that came out of the trainings, including the extreme professionalism of virtually all instructors.

I quickly realized that all along she had only been looking to write a sensationalist piece, and when she couldn't find any drama she tried to manufacture it. In communicating with her both before and after the story, the unusual severity of her agenda for that particular piece really made me stop and think about what else I was reading from otherwise trusted and credible mainstream news sources. How many stories on other issues had been similarly agenda-driven but had gotten by me because I didn't have the inside view to recognize the manipulation?

It was the hyped-up fear of this very scenario—straight troops reacting negatively, even violently, to the upcoming repeal—that prompted several right-wing members of the House of Representatives to take advantage of their new Republican majority in 2011 and make a rather pathetic attempt to thwart the certification of repeal. Even under the previous Democratic-controlled Congress, the House Armed Services Committee had been no friend to the gays, and then-chairman Ike Skelton of Missouri would not even let our repeal bill onto the agenda in his committee. That's why, instead of going through the normal process of committee-first-then-floor as we did in the Senate, repeal legislation in the House was originally offered only as an amendment to the larger defense bill once that bill got to the floor. After the viciously antigay Buck McKeon took the reins of the House Armed Services Committee, several pieces of legislation designed to kill, delay, or water down repeal quickly surfaced in committee. But as bad as they looked, these bills and amendments never realistically threatened repeal. Even if these provisions passed the full House of Representatives, with a Democratic-controlled Senate and a pro-repeal president, there was a 0 percent chance that they would ever make it into law that year. Other organizations certainly used them to stir up fear and—shocker!—raise money, but I refused to paint these efforts as anything more than an unnecessary distraction. Since gay and lesbian servicemembers were still making major life and career decisions, such as whether to stay in or get out, based on the likelihood of repeal actually happening anytime soon, I for one firmly believed in being honest with our community about the seriousness, or lack thereof, of these developments.

The rabidly antigay Republicans on the House Armed Services Committee did try their best, however. Most notably, Congressman Duncan Hunter Jr., son of the longtime anti-gays-in-the-military champion Duncan Hunter Sr., advanced an amendment to the following year's defense authorization bill that would expand the certification requirement out to the other members of the Joint Chiefs beyond the chairman, in hopes of at least one of them refusing to sign off on it. This just goes to show exactly how low Congressman Hunter was willing to sink to thwart repeal. A marine himself, Hunter was proposing a piece of legislation that would actually give veto power over the most senior US servicemember—the chairman of the Joint Chiefs of Staff—to several of his subordinates. This precedent flew in the face of long-standing military tradition of lawful obedience to superiors and the function of rank and command authority. It was not only ridiculous showboating but also fundamentally bad policy. Anyone who had even spent one day in uniform, and many who had not, could immediately recognize this flaw straight out of the gate. Yet Congressman Hunter was shamefully willing to weaken the authority structure of the armed forces simply because of his own personal prejudice against gays and lesbians.

When the Hunter amendment passed out of committee and sailed onto the House floor, the now–minority leader's office called the major pro-repeal organizations—SU, SLDN, CAP, and HRC—up to the Hill to ask us about whether we wanted the Democrats to take a stand against this and a few other amendments on the floor. While there was some desire from HRC to try to fight these hostile amendments, Aubrey Sarvis either couldn't make up his mind or wasn't communicating a strong desire one way or another. I expressed reservations on behalf of SU about waging a battle that we were sure to lose on the floor of the Republican-controlled House. They had the votes; we didn't. Publicly fighting against these hostile amendments and losing would weaken our position while things were otherwise progressing well. Eventually, the other groups saw the light and agreed to not expend any effort fighting the House version of the defense bill, which we all knew would be shot down in the Democratic-controlled Senate anyway, and it was.

As the summer of 2011 came, anticipation continued to build about when certification would happen, and many in our community started growing understandably anxious. When Secretary Gates retired at the end of June without finishing the job on DADT, it put people even more on edge. Everyone had a prediction about when certification would come, and each person's predictions were always allegedly based on "inside information" from a "well-placed source." Aaron Belkin was supposedly predicting early July based on his "well-placed source," according to one of the Palm Center's board members, but I ventured to bet that board member a beer that his information wasn't as good as he thought. That was only a few days after the new defense secretary, Leon Panetta, took over the job, and I predicted that there was no way he would certify that soon. He would surely at least spend a good two or three weeks talking to the RIT, the Joint Chiefs, the service secretaries, and possibly even the combatant commanders before acting on DADT.

In truth, I really shouldn't have made that beer bet, because I knew I had better cross-referenced political intelligence within the Pentagon than the others did. All the stars seemed to be lining up for certification to come sometime in late July, and the source I actually trusted the most at that point told me to look out for something "by July 23." Thus, while we still diligently ratcheted up the public pressure on the administration and defense leadership a little in late June and early July, just in case, I was personally comfortable that we were on the right track for certification soon.

In the meantime, Servicemembers United embarked on its biggest summer LGBT Pride season ever. The summer Pride festival circuit is always a prime opportunity to expose SU to more people in the LGBT community, sign up new members and supporters, disseminate updated information, and meet and interact with both our members and the wider community. While we always tried to have a presence at the major Pride festivals around the country, that summer SU went out of its way to have an outsized presence to reflect the increased prominence of our constituency within the LGBT community and the outsized role that SU had played in the DADT repeal fight over the preceding years. Throughout the summer, the gay military community was energized everywhere we went, and the civilian LGBT community was noticeably more supportive of our presence than in years past. But nowhere was there a bigger celebration of DADT's impending doom than in San Diego, California.

San Diego's Pride festival had always been one of SU's biggest, primarily due to the large concentration of navy and Marine Corps installations in the area and the generally more accepting and laid-back nature of southern California. But it was an enterprising young sailor who had just left active duty and settled down in the area who helped give that Pride celebration the biggest boost that year. Sean Sala had the idea to organize a contingent of LGBT servicemembers and veterans to march openly in that year's San Diego Pride Parade, accompanied by several straight allies. While many in the area's gay military community quickly jumped on board with the march as an opportunity to help mark a turning point and give one final "screw you" to DADT, others didn't welcome the idea.

Several SLDN board members viciously derided Sala for daring to organize such an event, and the organization itself advised him that he could be putting active duty members at risk by inviting them to participate. But Sala soon found out that SLDN had recently sent one of its own assets to be the grand marshal of the Pride parade in Denver and had similarly invited other servicemembers and veterans to march with him. According to Sala, soon after he pointed out this announcement and the accompanying hypocrisy, the announcement disappeared and the organization went silent. While SU wasn't sure if this first significant contemporary Pride march contingent would actually take off, we nevertheless refrained from criticizing or discouraging the effort and instead voiced our support to Sala for the organic effort he was organizing, which remained completely unaffiliated with any organization or group.

When the parade actually took place on Saturday, July 16, 2011, more than two hundred defiant active duty servicemembers and veterans, including scores of SU members and even SU staff from DC, turned out. They once again helped make history as they led the annual LGBT Pride celebration in one of the largest military cities in the country. The effort made national and international mainstream news, and many of those marching described having emotional moments as they received thunderous ovation from the crowds throughout the parade route.

But as proud as he was of having organized and pulled off such a momentous event in the face of such sharp criticism and derision,

Sala was also exhausted and exasperated with the unexpected politics of the experience. I recognized what he was going through as nearly the exact same crap I had gone through when I decided to launch an independent initiative back in 2006—the Call to Duty Tour. I, too, had been criticized by the SLDN crowd (mostly its staff, as several of their board members had actually been very supportive of our efforts) as they seethed at me not simply falling in line and becoming one of the marionettes. Jarrod and I met Sala for coffee two days after the San Diego Pride Parade, and we listened as he unloaded about the frustrations and challenges of dealing with the naysayers. He also spoke about the immense pride that he and others felt in pushing through it all anyway, moving forward despite the nasty politics. What I admired most about the organic San Diego effort was that its organizers had succeeded by maintaining their integrity and refusing to resort to backstabbing, dishonesty, or other unethical methods as other upstart groups had been so quick to do.

As the DADT issue had heated up over the previous year, several new groups and initiatives began popping up at the last minute and making broad and unsubstantiated claims about having contributed to the repeal movement and its momentum. But no one can change the record of who was actually in the room when the DADT issue was being worked on and who was actually out in the field organizing those actually impacted by the issue to speak out, lobby, and get directly involved in influencing the debate.

I'll readily admit that Servicemembers United, HRC, SLDN, CAP, and Third Way were all "in the room" on the DADT issue as it was negotiated and pushed forward against the odds on Capitol Hill, in the White House, and at the Pentagon. And it was by all accounts Servicemembers United at the helm of the intense grassroots organizing effort across the country for years leading up to 2010 that ensured we had a solid foundation of affected constituents to be visible and make noise on Capitol Hill and in the media when the time came.

Outside of that inner coalition in Washington, an outer ring of organizations, namely the Palm Center and the Log Cabin Republicans, was also crucial. Belkin and Frank of the Palm Center focused on gathering data and on creating pressure by offering a more immediate administrative alternative to legislation (i.e., the executive order option). LCR pushed the train forward faster via its groundbreaking lawsuit, for which I was proud to have served as the sole named plaintiff.

And I would be remiss if I didn't also acknowledge the activism of GetEqual, which was a latecomer to the game but actually did make a substantial impact on the debate and help push repeal forward. So did independent activists such as Dan Choi; Dan refused to be co-opted into yet another marionette and instead became the single most important active duty voice in the fight. Both he and GetEqual faced unprecedented criticism for their aggressive and controversial tactics, and I fully respect the uneasiness (sometimes outright disdain) that many gay and lesbian servicemembers had for Dan's choice to conduct his activism in uniform. But it is undeniable that he greatly increased the level of attention paid to the DADT issue in the media and in the wider progressive community.

Similarly, enough cannot be said about the LGBT and progressive print media and blogs, which delicately balanced arm's-length reporting with a unique form of activism that helped educate and inform the masses within our widespread and diverse community, keeping them up to speed on the often hard-to-understand twists and turns of the issue throughout 2010, from the limits of executive authority and legislative policy transmittals to cloture motions and privileged resolutions. This was no easy task, and the material they had to work with was not always sexy, but I firmly believe that they too played a historic role in this fight.

In particular, the DC-based reporting of Chris Johnson and Lou Chibarro of the *Washington Blade*, Kerry Eleveld and Andrew Harmon of the *Advocate*, and Chris Geidner and Yusef Najafi of *Metro Weekly* provided increasingly important sources of comprehensive information on what was going on inside Washington, often behind opaque windows and closed doors. These enterprising journalists always impressed me with their professionalism and zeal, and their consistent presence in places like the White House and Pentagon press briefing rooms helped keep the DADT issue front and center, not only for the LGBT community but also for the administration officials whom they publicly pressed with difficult questions on a regular basis and for the other mainstream media outlets in the room covering Washington politics.

The hybrid medium of the LGBT and progressive blogosphere also proved to be uniquely critical in the fight to keep the public informed of convoluted developments, dwindling options, concealed threats to progress, and urgent calls to action. John Aravosis and Joe Sudbay at *AMERICAblog* were especially aggressive and enterprising, and they were never afraid to go after the administration or the establishment advocacy organizations when progress was stalled. Likewise, the blogmistress and head barista at *Pam's House Blend*, Pam Spaulding, played an important role in the fight to repeal DADT without even having the advantage of being located at the center of the action in Washington.

Other sociopolitical blogs that effectively collaborated with organizations such as Servicemembers United and SLDN and consistently covered the repeal saga included *Joe.My.God.*, *Bilerico*, *Blabbeando*, *OpenLeft*, and many other worthy and enterprising web-based operations. And the blogs that covered a full assortment of topics—gossip, sex, film, television, fashion, and culture as well as politics—proved to be unexpectedly influential too, because of the general tendency of most Americans to be more interested in everything else except politics and wonky intrigue. People all over the country would frequently cite these popular outlets, especially *Towleroad* and *Queerty*, as their primary sources of information on the repeal fight.

A medium of communication that didn't get a lot of attention but should have was radio. Its live interview and commentary formats, and the depth of coverage and analysis it was occasionally able to give to the DADT issue, helped drive coverage and accountability during the fight. The satellite radio company Sirius hosts an all-gay channel called OutQ, and two four-hour-long weekday shows on that channel deserve special mention: *The Michaelangelo Signorile Show* and, believe it or not, the *Derek and Romaine* show. Signorile, a tough and hard-charging political talk radio personality, played a role on the airwaves similar to what the political blogs did on the web, and Derek Hartley and Romaine Patterson served up the daily dish of gossip and entertainment with the occasional side of helpful political updates for their loyal band of listeners.

True to his unsung hero status within the Pentagon, the source who had suggested that certification would come "by July 23" turned out to be dead on. On July 21, mainstream news outlets began reporting that defense secretary Panetta and Joint Chiefs chairman Mullen would transmit the long-awaited certification to the White House the following day, and additional sources inside the Pentagon were quick to confirm the news. The following day, in the early afternoon of Friday, July 22, Secretary Panetta and Admiral Mullen met with President Obama in the Oval Office to formally put the final nail in the coffin of DADT. The president was the last to put his signature on the simple, one-page certification document during a private moment with the White House staff who had worked on the issue, the vice president, and the two defense leaders.

Shortly after the certification document was signed, I got a call on my cell phone from Valerie Jarrett at the White House. I was out of DC and over in Annapolis that afternoon, but I had obviously been following the developments that day, hour by hour. Jarrett said that she was calling to tell me personally that the president had just sent the signed certification document over to the Hill, and we chatted for a good five to ten minutes on the phone. Recognizing that she had borne the brunt of our community's frustration, I wrapped up the call by saying to her, "Valerie, I know we've had a love-hate relationship over the past year, but I do hope you understand that we were just doing our jobs and that we really are grateful for everything you've done for us on this," to which Jarrett warmly replied, "Well, I do understand, but today it's just all love." We both had a good laugh again before wishing one another a good weekend, and that was that.

At midnight, Senator Byrd's sixty-day clock began ticking; per the repeal amendment, the end of DADT would become effective sixty days after the day on which certification was signed and transmitted. That technically put the first moment of open service at one second past midnight on Tuesday, September 20. While all other groups and organizations planned to celebrate repeal on the evening of that day, Servicemembers United planned a series of "Countdown to Repeal" parties across the country on the night of Monday, September 19. That allowed us to do a New Year's Eve–style countdown at midnight to the exact moment when DADT became history.

Over the next sixty days, with the end of DADT finally in sight, several right-wing lawmakers in Congress griped and complained to the president, the secretary of defense, Admiral Mullen, and virtually anyone who would listen, but their complaints fell completely flat. No one, even the Republican leadership, had any appetite for revisiting the issue, and the utter lack of attention on these attempts by the mainstream media further underscored their lack of seriousness.

Everyone knew by that point that the first day of open service would be a nonevent, but, amusingly, many journalists weren't too interested in the expected reality. Instead, we fielded countless calls in the weeks leading up to repeal's effective date, as I'm sure SLDN did too, from reporters and media outlets wanting help in putting together dramatic stories about hordes of discharged gay and lesbian veterans going back to recruiting stations to reenlist. We politely explained each time that few if any would likely go back on the very first day, and even fewer would want to make a big media event out of it. Some reporters even went so far as to ask us if we could find someone who would be willing to stage such an event, but we again refused to participate in blatantly manufactured stories.

When Monday, September 19, arrived, it had been relatively smooth sailing through the final waiting period. That night, we had our biggest crowds for our Countdown to Repeal parties in the biggest military and veteran cities, including over 200 revelers in Washington, DC, 250 in Seattle, and more than 250 in San Diego. The mood that night was nothing short of euphoric, and as the clock struck midnight at our flagship party in DC, I made sure the DJ played Lady Gaga's uplifting anthem "Edge of Glory"—a personal favorite. Two hundred and thirty three (and one-half) years after the first incident of an American servicemember being expelled from our military for homosexuality, the ultimate end to that practice and its accompanying policies had finally arrived.

Other groups and organizations had scheduled similar celebratory gatherings around the country for Tuesday, later that week, or over the following weekend. But after our countdown celebrations, Jarrod and I were both ready to relax and enjoy "Repeal Day" without any major responsibilities other than issuing prepared statements via SU's press release. We had originally organized a small news conference at the National Press Club with Senators Lieberman and Udall, two active duty officers (a Marine Corps major and an air force lieutenant colonel), a military partner, and a discharged veteran, but soon other senators got word and wanted to join in as well. We moved the event over to Capitol Hill in order to better accommodate the senators' schedules, but Senator Lieberman's press secretary quickly maneuvered to make the servicemembers and veterans actually impacted by the issue the background ornaments for a press event dominated by members of Congress. In response to their jockeying for the microphone on that day, we unilaterally pulled out of the event and decided to simply take the day off to enjoy. Just as we had come into the DADT repeal movement by refusing to be hood ornaments and marionettes, so too we finished up the job on September 20 by maintaining that standard.

We also turned down multiple offers to do the mainstream cable news and talk show rounds and instead just turned the television off that day, both at home and in the SU office. The only semiofficial thing we did do on September 20 was attend a private celebration in the Pentagon office of Doug Wilson, assistant secretary of defense for public affairs, immediately following that day's more muted press conference by Secretary Panetta and Chairman Mullen. But what happened immediately following that small gathering really capped off the day—and the entire DADT repeal fight—for Jarrod and me in a big way, and I think for Admiral Mullen as well.

One of Mullen's aides over the previous two years had been a close friend of ours and a member and strong supporter of Servicemembers United. After the festivities in Doug's office wound down, Jarrod and I met up with the aide, and we walked together over to the part of the Pentagon in which the Joint Chiefs chairman's offices are situated. There, late in the afternoon on Repeal Day, the first day of open service on September 20, Jarrod and I shook Admiral Mullen's hand again and thanked him for helping make that day possible. He then handed each of us a Chairman of the Joint Chiefs of Staff coin—ensuring that we will win virtually any military coin challenge for the rest of our lives—and gave us a brief photo op with him.

Realizing that the two of us had come in the room with one of his aides, the chairman casually asked him how he knew Jarrod and me. Proudly, the aide replied, "Well, because I'm gay too, sir." (Amusingly enough, "knowing Alex and Jarrod" had sort of become the modern-day equivalent of "friend of Dorothy" in some circles; we heard on more than a few occasions that gay and lesbian servicemembers and civilian DOD staff would sometimes cautiously ask one another if they "know Alex and Jarrod" to see if the other might be family.) The experience could not have been more perfect for any of us that day, and I could not have imagined a better way to round off a momentous victory. To be the only two DADT repeal advocates who got to meet with Admiral Mullen on Repeal Day, to be given one of his coins just before his retirement, and to be there when one of his aides personally came out to him on the first day when he legally could, was all more than a little surreal.

19

★ ★ ★ ★ ★

BEYOND REPEAL

In the days and weeks following the official end of the DADT policy, gay, lesbian, and bisexual American servicemembers all over the world began slowly coming out to their peers, superiors, and subordinates. Despite our opponents' dire predictions about the doom and gloom that would surely follow, the US military remains cohesive and strong. As predicted, the change in policy turned out to be a non-event for everyone—except for gay and lesbian servicemembers, that is. To them, the change meant that the cloud of fear hanging over their heads had finally been lifted; they no longer needed to worry that they could be fired at any time if the wrong person happened to find out their secret. The deeply flawed and arbitrarily enforced DADT policy was no more, and an entire community of American heroes experienced a collective sigh of relief.

It remains to be seen whether I will ever personally benefit from this historic policy change, but my work on and devotion to this issue was never about me. It was much bigger than me, much bigger than Servicemembers United, much bigger than the coalition of organizations and activists that brought about repeal. It was really about the current and future generations of gay, lesbian, and bisexual servicemembers who will never again have to go through what we went through, and about pushing forward the goal that the discriminatory treatment of our nation's transgender servicemembers soon ends as well.

Many gays and lesbians currently on active duty are already unaware of the full extent of the enormous war that was waged on their behalf in the auditoriums, local television stations, and editorial pages of Lincoln, Charlotte, Waterville, Little Rock, Vermillion, Morgantown, Kearney, St. Louis, Kendall, Evansville, and so many other unlikely battleground sites; in the meeting rooms, balconies, and hallways of Dirksen, Hart, Russell, Rayburn, Longworth, and Cannon; in the West Wing's Roosevelt Room and in EEOB's old Secretary of War suite; in the secretary of defense's conference room at the Pentagon and in the studios of 400 North Capitol; in the courthouses of Los Angeles and Riverside; in the Hawk N' Dove, Monocle, and Union Pub on Capitol Hill and at the Pennsylvania Avenue Caribou; in the offices of 1725 I Street, 1612 K Street, and 1640 Rhode Island; and in so many other places and ways over so many years.

One of my biggest fears is that future generations of LGBT servicemembers will forget—or never know—who really fought for them, where the real battles took place, and how the war to repeal DADT was really won. Another fear is that they, the rest of the LGBT community, and even the public at large will fall victim to the historical rewrites that began surfacing before the ink was even dry on the bill. There is already no shortage of false claims of which groups and individuals were substantively involved in the process and in what ways, and an intense desire for undue credit, legacy advancement, and career preservation will surely continue to drive this pathology.

But the truth needed to be told and the history preserved. This book joins with the work of Randy Shilts in *Conduct Unbecoming* and Nathaniel Frank in *Unfriendly Fire* to complete the story of DADT and further illuminate the experience of the gay military, veteran, and defense community in the United States.

As the post-repeal months turn into years, gays and lesbians in the military will surely continue to slowly come out, but they will also likely base the decision about whether to be open or not within a given unit on the command climate, the attitudes of colleagues, and an independent judgment grounded in their personal circumstances. The military is still a very conservative workplace and always will be, but open gays and lesbians will find more and more that they will indeed be able to successfully integrate their military life with their family and personal lives without affecting their unit's cohesion or readiness, without alienating themselves within the unit, and without negatively impacting their careers.

There was no Internet when the US military went through racial desegregation, nor was there anything resembling today's Internet when women were admitted to the service academies and given access to significantly expanded job opportunities within the force. We will never know most of the opponents of those policy changes who predicted similar doom and gloom only to see their "professional" judgment proven wildly inaccurate. However, in the modern world, writings, postings, video, and other forms of remarks are preserved in perpetuity. Predictions of apocalypse, violence, and degraded cohesion and readiness were similarly made in advance of this policy change, and while there may be some isolated hiccups along the way, these dire scenarios will surely not come to pass. And in this day and age, those who made such unfounded predictions can and should be held to account.

Our civilian leaders need *true* professional military judgment to independently inform the political process. These lessons should not be forgotten by Washington, nor should the lessons of the uniquely successful DADT repeal movement be forgotten by the wider LGBT and progressive communities. Without a fundamental realignment in the way these communities operate politically, the overall equality movement will continue to progress at a slower rate than it needs to. Remember, DADT was supposed to be the "low-hanging fruit." It was supposed to be an easy fight, but it was not. In reality, it was far from easy and far from assured, and our final victory almost did not happen at all.

But in the end, we won, and as I proudly said publicly on the first day of the post-DADT era, "Justice has prevailed and 'Don't Ask, Don't Tell' is dead. God bless America."

INDEX